DIRECTORS CLOSE UP

DIRECTORS
CLOSE UP

Interviews with directors nominated for
Outstanding Directorial Achievement in a
Feature Film by the Directors Guild of America

Moderated and edited
by Jeremy Kagan

**Focal
Press**

Boston • Oxford • Auckland • Johannesburg • Melbourne • New Delhi

Library of Congress Cataloging-in-Publication Data

Directors close up : interviews with directors nominated for Best Film by the Directors Guild of America / moderated and edited by Jeremy Kagan.
p.   cm.
ISBN 0-240-80406-6 (pbk. : alk. paper)
1. Motion pictures--Production and direction. 2. Motion picture producers and directors--United States--Interviews.   I. Kagan, Jeremy Paul.

PN1995.9.P7 D543 2000
791.43'0233'092273--dc21   99-057057

British Library Cataloguing-in-Publication Data
A catalogue record for this book is available from the British Library.

The publisher offers special discounts on bulk orders of this book.
For information, please contact:
Manager of Special Sales
Butterworth–Heinemann
225 Wildwood Avenue
Woburn, MA 01801-2041
Tel: 781-904-2500
Fax: 781-904-2620

For information on all Focal Press publications available, contact our World Wide Web home page at: http://www.focalpress.com

10 9 8 7 6 5 4 3 2 1

Printed in the United States of America

Table of Contents

Introduction

This book is for all who are interested in what a director does and how the best of them do it. You can read it from beginning to end or dip in almost anywhere to taste the personalities and practices of outstanding contemporary directors.

Those who study the art of film are essentially examining the works of the great directors. Though moviemaking is certainly a collaborative medium, the visions of the master film directors are what have expanded the form and content of movies. Unforgettable images come to mind by just hearing the names of some of these innovators, such as D.W. Griffith, Sergei Eisenstein, John Ford, Frank Capra, Alfred Hitchcock, Orson Welles, Luis Buñuel, David Lean, Francois Truffaut, Federico Fellini, Akira Kurosawa, and Woody Allen.

Yet the question is often asked: What exactly does a director do? It might be better phrased: What doesn't a director do? As you will discover in this collection, the responsibility of the director extends over every aspect of filmmaking.

What follows are edited selections from in-depth interviews begun in 1992 when the Directors Guild of America started a series of yearly seminars with the nominees for outstanding feature film directing.

The structure of each of these discussions explored the various stages of the director's process. Facetiously, it has been observed that the process starts with inspiration and enthusiasm, followed by entanglements and panic, leading to a search for the guilty ones and punishment of the innocents, and ending up in rewards to the non-participants! Though there is some truth to the above, these symposia concentrate more on creative and pragmatic issues.

The making of a movie is evolutionary. Along the path, the film
goes through four primary metamorphoses, each guided by the
vision of the director. The first stage usually begins with overseeing
the development of the script. The second phase concerns all the elements of pre-production which change the work from a story on
paper to a three dimensional, ever transforming entity that encompasses casting the actors, assembling the crew and its key personnel,
among whom are the cinematographer, the production designer, the
assistant director, the wardrobe designer, the editor, the composer,
and many other artists and technicians. During this time period,
working closely with these other craftspeople, the director develops
the design of the picture: where and how it will be staged and photographed. This means scouting locations, the construction of sets,
costumes and props, the preparation of special effects and stunts,
and the myriad choices that must be made before the first day of
photography. Along the way there is often a rehearsal period where
the director works with the actors to explore the script and the characters. The production or "shoot" is the third phase, and here many
adjustments arise, both practical and creative, that bring the movie
to another level, as the director daily leads the often hundreds of
people to deliver their best under the pressures of time and money.
The fourth stage is post-production. Now the director is guiding the
editing team and supervising the assembling of sound and visual
effects. Music enters this realm of work as well. And finally, the
director oversees all these elements of sight and sound as they are
mixed together to make the final look and feel of the film.
Throughout all these stages, the work of the director is aesthetically,
emotionally, psychologically, and physically challenging.

In this book you will be reading how individual masters of the
medium explain their particular approaches to all these aspects of
directing.

As to the language in these selections, we have tried to retain the
style of speech of each of these directors, so you can hear how they
speak as well as what they say. Consequently, sometimes the grammar and the vocabulary aren't quite "proper."

We have also included an appendix, a lecture given by Elia Kazan,
entitled "On What Makes a Director," which was delivered in 1973

at Wesleyan University. Though it reflects the pronoun gender predilections of its time, this still is one of the most elegant statements as to what characterizes all directors.

We are indebted to many people for making this book possible. Our thanks to Robert Wise and all the members of the Special Projects Committee of the Directors Guild and to former Guild Presidents Arthur Hiller, who initiated these seminars, and Gene Reynolds, and current President Jack Shea; to Jay Roth, National Executive Director of the Guild, who pressed to make this book happen; to the National Executive in Charge of Special Projects, Zack Reed; and to the staff that did the labor, especially Pamela Kile, who was invaluable in organizing all the transcriptions.

We all hope you enjoy and learn.

Jeremy Kagan
Moderator and Editor
Los Angeles, 2000

— 1 —

"How I Got Here"

Robert Zemeckis

Forrest Gump

I grew up watching a lot of television and going to the movies when I was a kid to see horror movies and fantasy movies and action movies and war movies. I was entertained by movies and tried to figure out how they did things because it was an awesome power. The idea that millions of strangers are moved by your work. I found out there was a college that had a course in filmmaking and I was lucky enough to be accepted at that school. It was USC Film School and I've been doing movies ever since.

By the time I got to film school, I understood it was a director's medium. I'm actually not sure that filmmaking can be taught—I don't think it can. They give you the tools, but they can't make you a filmmaker, there's no way. You have to have that fire inside. They can teach what to do—what not to do.

When I was in film school it was a very exciting time because Lucas and Coppola were just about to crack in the industry. We had a sense that something was going to happen because all we did was think about movies all the time. And, the first year in film school *The Godfather* came out and the second year I was in film school *American Graffiti* came out and it was this big explosion. I mean George Lucas was our hero 'cause he made it happen. And, we were all in that kind of campaign to have film students be able to get into mainstream moviemaking at the time.

1

I think the same exact problems that I had when I was making my little student films are the exact same problems that I have making features, and everything just gets bigger and more expensive.

I have a long list of directors who have had a tremendous influence on me, but I think if I really broke it down, the director who had the most influence on me probably more than any was Jules White. Jules White directed almost every episode of *The Three Stooges*. Seriously, I think that I have memorized every one of those episodes.

Quentin Tarantino

Pulp Fiction

I don't ever remember a time in my life where, like, movies weren't my favorite thing. I didn't have a ton of varied interests as far as like what I wanted to do in my free time. I wasn't into sports, wasn't into building models, and wasn't into all that other boy stuff. I was into movies. I mean, it was, like, it's my birthday or something and if an uncle said to me, "OK, Quentin, you could go to Disneyland, Knott's Berry Farm, or to any movie you want to see," I'd always pick a movie. When I was a little kid, you'd look at movies and television and go "I want to do that. I wanna be a part of that." And who you see are the actors. That's who you identify with. So, all through my childhood, I wanted to be an actor. I quit ninth grade, I quit junior high, to become an actor.

I studied for years as an actor and that's when I really started kind of understanding how the film medium works, I realized that I just loved movies too much to appear in them, I wanted them to be *my* movies.

I wanted to be this student of film. This film historian of my own mind, you know, nobody was hiring me to do it—I just did it. I believe that Jules White is the first director credit that I ever remember seeing, 'cause I watched *The Three Stooges* every single solitary day, alright? "Directed by Jules White" at the end . . . I thought it was Jules Verne!

When I was a little kid, my favorite kinds of movies in the world were horror films and comedies. I remember I saw *Abbott and Costello Meet Frankenstein*, then I saw *Abbott and Costello Meet the Mummy* and

I remember thinking these are the greatest movies ever made because the funny stuff is really funny and the scary stuff is really scary! Two movies for the price of one!

When I was a teenager I really had a love and a passion for exploitation films because they were naughty.

In Los Angeles they used to have Filmex, where they would have these 52-hour marathons. They would pick a genre and just show them. I was there all 52 hours. Man, it was really kind of cool, because you'd just fall asleep and you'd wake up in the middle of *My Fair Lady* or a comedy marathon and it was there the very first time I saw *His Girl Friday* and I just thought, I had never laughed so hard. In a life of laughing I had never laughed so hard consecutively in a movie in my life. I always knew who Howard Hawks was, but it was like, gosh, I've got to see everything he's done! And after a year, I did. And it was really interesting because, he taught me storytelling. He taught me how to be entertaining or try to make it an entertaining experience for an audience. When I see *Rio Bravo*, which is one of my favorite three movies of all time, the script is just a masterpiece of storytelling, alright, and it's all tight and confined and there's really wonderful stories going on. But as you're watching the movie little by little, the characters become such great company. You know, you just really like hanging out with them. And at one point in the middle of this tense situation, four, five, six scenes happen where the bad guys are around and they're kinda laughing and joking. And you forget about, like, the drama and you just get into hanging out with these guys. You just want to hang out with your friends and there's this one moment in it when John Wayne is visiting Angie Dickinson and the bad guys are there and they don't know and they're going to lay this rope down the stairs and they're going to trip him and get him. You know, it's like they're your friends, you want the bad guys to go away. You just want to see these people just having a good time for the rest of the movie and that got me.

Then I discovered Godard and he taught me experimentation. He taught me how to try to make the medium bend in on itself, entertain the audience, but challenge them. You know, give them an uncomfortable experience.

In the movie *The Misfits*, there's a line that Clark Gable has where Marilyn Monroe is complaining about their sorry state of life and he goes, "Hey! That's the way it goes, but, it goes the other way, too." And I've been told by, seems like everyone on the planet, about what a ridiculously lucky guy I am, OK? The thing is though, I went through my entire twenties with the worst luck in the world! For 10 years everything that could go wrong, went wrong, alright? Now, it's funny, but at the same time when you've donated your twenties, which are your "topsoil years," you know you don't piss your twenties away! If you're going to have a harvest, then you'd better start planting!

I had nothing to show for my twenties except hopes, dreams, and my own aspirations. I had even tried to make a movie, at 23 just paying for it myself, getting the equipment on the weekends, shooting in 16mm film and I worked on it for four years and it ended up becoming guitar picks. The single number one thing of my whole life that I am the proudest of that I've done is, that I didn't give up then.

Rob Reiner
A Few Good Men

I think basically for me, I'm better at giving orders than taking them! While I was acting, and particularly in shows that were done in front of a live audience, I did the worst possible thing you could do as an actor. I was aware constantly of what the audience was doing every second. I was aware of every camera. I was always more aware of the overall than I was of my part. So I think that was my natural instinct, to go in that direction. And I always said that a director was somebody who's the worst at any job on the set. He stinks at everything, basically. He's not as good an actor as the actors, he can't light like the cameraman, he's not a good prop guy, he can't do a stunt like a stunt man, he can't do anything basically, but he kind of knows a little bit about everything. And so I figured I know a little bit about music, I know a little bit about putting furniture in the right place, I know a little bit about acting, I know a little bit . . . and this is a job where I can put all those little bits of knowledge into something and the sum total hopefully would be better than just those little things.

I spent most of my youth hanging around the *Dick Van Dyke Show*, watching how my father [Carl Reiner] worked. And I saw how each week a play got created from nothing. And then I had firsthand experience when I did *All in the Family*. I got to see what an audience responded to every single week for 200 shows.

Elia Kazan was always somebody I looked towards as a great storyteller and also somebody whose pictures had a lot of humanity in them. They were character driven pieces.

John Madden
Shakespeare in Love

I kind of backed into it. I started out as an actor. I was a mimic as a kid and a lot of people mistake that for acting. And I found myself on stage in quite a lot of Shakespeare and thinking not ever about what I was doing in the scene. I wasn't playing very interesting parts, I have to admit, but always thinking about everybody else on the stage. And it kind of dawned on me rather late that perhaps I was in the wrong position, that I should be outside looking in. But even then, I took awhile to get to it. I was sort of a director in my social life, I suppose. In the sense that I had a kind of fascistic tendency to want to make people see the world the way I saw it. And I thought that was probably unhealthy. You can ask my wife about that. But then I decided that maybe there was a way that I could channel this professionally. But it all happened kind of accidentally.

Barry Levinson
Bugsy

I'm not sure how you learn what we do. And I'm not exactly sure how we really do what we do. There just doesn't seem to be this one book that explains it all. I think probably it goes back to watching movies and being in awe of what you see on the screen.

I've always been impressed with John Ford's movies. I find it extraordinary how he made it work. There's a great simplicity to the way he did it. Obviously Orson Welles' *Citizen Kane, Magnificent*

Ambersons, Touch of Evil, and *Chimes at Midnight,* you look at some of his movies and you see an incredibly brilliant mind at work. Although he never had a large body of work and many of his films got butchered along the way, I think you're looking at true genius.

I had not intended to be a director. But I'll never forget when I went onto the set of the film that I co-wrote, and there was a barroom, interior barroom, I looked at it, and as soon as I saw the set, I knew it was a totally different movie. It was a square room, and the people at the table were very close to the bar. And in my head I thought it was a very long room and sort of dark, and the people sat very far away from the bar. What it does is it changes the relationship of those people as outcasts in terms of the position to the bar. It makes them more friendly or more disenfranchised by their position to the bar. Making it long to me made it more of a lonelier situation. I think that was the first time I began to think about—well maybe, how would I do it?

Then I wrote *Diner,* really by accident, and I thought I ought to direct this because I know these people and I've lived this life and I don't know who would do it in the way that I see it. And all of sudden you say, here's the script and I want to direct it. And if we can't make the script with me directing it, then let's not make the movie.

Oliver Stone

JFK

My dad didn't like to go to movies that much and it was a big thing on a Saturday afternoon if he'd take me to a movie. And I just remember being struck by Kubrick because he liked him. And then Lean, my dad liked and respected David. That made a real impression on me. And a little later—I remember when *La Dolce Vita* came: this was something very intimate and about life, urban life, contemporary life.

Then in film school I was nuts about Godard. That was again a breakthrough, because everything was disassociated. There was no narrative line.

Of course, the big breakthrough was when Scorsese did *Taxi Driver*, which we thought was like the world's end. It was like the first American film. It was the first one that really hit me between the eyes and said, "We can do what the Europeans have been doing." Marty had a lot of passion. He loved movies. That's all he talked about. There was no video in those days so he'd stay up till four in the morning, five in the morning, to watch a Von Sternberg picture. He had these bags under his eyes, his hair down to here. Believe me, it was hard before VCRs to see pictures. It was a hotbed, a ferment of new ideas. A very radical time. People were stealing cameras, taking over universities, or trying to make films into collectives. That didn't work. You can't make a collective movie.

I learned a lot from DePalma, too. He goes out there and he just says: Well, nothing is going to stop me, no matter how insane the idea is.

When I got out of film school I thought I was as good as Godard. Nobody else agreed with me. It took me fifteen years to convince anybody.

I did two horror films that flopped and that was a really tough experience. On *Salvador*, I bit the bullet: this is the line no one is going to cross. I'm going to make this movie. We mortgage the house, my wife agreed. We went down to Salvador and tried to con them into giving us all their helicopters. We said we want to portray the government as the good guys. We gave them a dummy script and we almost pulled it off. We came within *that* close of doing it, and our adviser got killed. Unfortunately he got shot by the communists on a tennis court, so that ended that escapade.

I went up to Mexico and shot the film there, and we ran out of money, they closed us down and threw us out of Mexico on the forty-second day. But I hadn't shot the beginning or the end, which was a brilliant move on my part. I just shot the middle and I told John Daly at Hemdale, I said, "Look, you can't release this film. You can't release just the middle of the picture, you need a beginning and an end." He gave me nine more days and another million dollars, I think, to finish it in Las Vegas. That's how the first one got made.

Peter Weir
The Truman Show

Well from my background, from Australia, and making short films and acting in reviews and so on in the 60s, there was no film industry. I was drawn to the life of the theatre, of show business. It was something that was distant from me. So I got into university reviews and began to make film clips. Australia was in great upheaval, we were, of course, in the war too, the Vietnam War and it was the year of you know, do your own thing. And there was a feeling that you could as it were, do anything. You could break from the life that your parents hoped for you, university and so on, and that was my own case. A lot of heartache with my family because I was going into something that they had no idea, you know, "What's this acting?" and so on. And slowly by making the film clips I began to think I was far better at doing this than the acting, and I continued writing. So again, it was something that happened to me. It was a case of finding which part to play in this wonderful theatrical life. I never planned it. One day somebody said, "You are a director, not a producer," because on a little short film I had put down that I was the producer. They said, "No no," and I said, "Well, what does it matter?" The screen was your teacher as you went along. And sometimes I craved those elders that you knew existed in Europe and America. But on the other hand we were free. Inasmuch as you didn't get advice, you were free to do anything. You were blazing trails—it was terribly exciting just to get an image up on the screen.

Clint Eastwood
Unforgiven

Well, I'd been an actor for quite a few years—I was figuring one day it might not be a thing I'd like to do, or else I'd look up there and say, "That's the end of that, kid, you'd better get lost." I started getting interested in directing in the 1960s, especially working with European directors. And then in 1970 I found a little script I liked [Play Misty for Me], which I could do for a very modest price, and so I decided to dive in. They said, you're welcome to direct the film, no problem, as long as you're in it. So, I had that little bit of leverage to get me started.

The thing that kills you about directing is the amount of questions that are asked per day and how can you possibly come up with the answers. And you have to get to a point in your psyche where you say, I'm gonna answer this even if it's wrong—I've got to come up with something. But then after a while, after you've been with it quite a few years, I think you build a routine and some of the questions you can answer.

I grew up on John Ford movies, and Howard Hawks I like very much. *His Girl Friday* still knocks me out. I like Preston Sturges a lot. Later I became a fan of Kurosawa. On the *Rawhide* days I got to work with a lot of directors and you see ideas that they do, you see the way they operate and you get opinions, and even directors you don't care for sometimes, you say, "Well that's great but, this isn't the way I would do it." Of course, Sergio Leoni in the 1960s was a very big influence on me and the whole different approach of European filmmakers at that particular time. Don Siegel, I'd say, was on the top of the list for me because he was a close friend and he was a terribly efficient filmmaker, very underrated because he came up through the ranks.

Andrew Davis

The Fugitive

I was always interested in reality. My degree is in journalism, and I was drawn to films that had a certain kind of honesty. I was not one of those filmmakers who studied Hitchcock, for example. I was more interested in films by the Italian realists, Fellini, Bertolucci, Stanley Kubrick, Sidney Lumet, Bill Friedkin's early work—these were all filmmakers that did things that inspired me.

My parents had a big role in my getting involved. My father and mother were friends with a man named Haskell Wexler, a great filmmaker and cinematographer, and a role model for me. And I actually was very lucky, because when I was 21, I got to shoot a commercial and I became a cameraman. And then I came to California and I couldn't get in the union because they had these restrictive policies. I said, "You know, it's easier to be a director." I was fortunate to have worked with young directors, and we struggled together and I said, "Well, I'll do a film about my kid brother." And I made a movie called *Stony Island*, which was very autobiographical. So I did that film, and it led to another film, but eventually, through very strange circumstances, and sort of falling out of windows and landing on my feet, I was offered a film called *Code of Silence*, which I desperately needed because I thought I'd never work again. And the film was fairly successful, so I became an action director.

Mike Newell
Four Weddings and a Funeral

The first film that I remember seeing was a film called *Bad Day at Black Rock*. Which was a Spencer Tracy movie and it was on my tenth birthday and my mother gave us all half a crown and sent us all off to the local cinema. And then we came back and played the film out in the field afterwards. I remember *Grand Illusion*, a Renoir film about the First World War. There was an extraordinary sequence with a German aristocrat and a French aristocrat. The German being the commander of the prison camp in which the Frenchman is talking about their common aristocracy rather than they're being on opposite sides. And I . . . I found that a lot of my expectations were overturned by that. It's sort of humanist stuff that was the stuff that got me.

The films which made me laugh were obvious. There is a wonderful film called *Kind Hearts and Coronets,* which is a blinding piece of storytelling apart from anything else. But then there's Billy Wilder and you used to go and see everything that Billy Wilder ever made.

I wanted to become an actor, because clearly they had fun and I thought I was very beautiful. But then as a student, I did an audition in front of another student and looked up after doing my piece of *Hamlet*, and he said, "Thank you." And so I stopped being an actor and became a stage hand. And then I went into television because I couldn't get a job in the theatre, and they showed me the instruments of torture and I was hooked and that's where I stayed.

When I started there weren't film schools in England. You started out working. If there were mentors, they tended to be people who worked along side you. And there were wonderful television directors. I started in television because that's where you started work.

Steven Spielberg
Saving Private Ryan

I was always looking for a way to act out, and I found that the best way to act out was to get a movie camera and let that do it for you. I also got in less trouble because they'd blame the film, not the filmmaker.

When I first started out making movies, it was just simply a matter of taking a camera and trying to make ends meet, if you know what I mean. The best advice, not the best advice, but I remember the advice Fellini gave me. I met Fellini when I brought *Duel* over to Europe for the first time in 1971 or '72. And I met the master. I was waiting for some sage advice from him. I kept asking him, "Help me be a better director. What can I do?" and he said "When you talk to the press, lie," he said, "because you'll bore yourself. You'll tell the same story which is the truth over and over again. You'll have forty interviews today, right?" I said, "Yeah." He says, "Lie to each one, tell each one a different story."

Roberto Benigni
Life Is Beautiful

I think that making movies is — and we know I'm saying now a very idiotic thing — that it is the most wonderful way to tell a story. Nothing is more beautiful. Directors they are dreaming for us, they are the benefactors. So I would like to thank every director. And the advice I had, for example, Fellini told me, "Robertino, remember, always tell the truth." Now I understand, he was lying to me. Wonderful advice!

Frank Darabont
The Shawshank Redemption

For me, seeing George Lucas' *THX 1138* when I was 12, I remember thinking that if I could stick my head into the screen, through the screen, and, like, look off to the side of the camera frame, I'd see whoever the hell it was telling me the story. I always wanted to be a storyteller.

These were my gods: David Lean, John Ford, Kubrick, Buster Keaton, *The General*, one of the greatest movies ever. Carol Reed's *The Third Man*. It really comes down to every movie that kind of rocked you back in your seat. When you're sitting in the theatre and in the back of your mind there's a little voice saying, "Holy shit!" There's something about a film when it grabs you on some sort of visceral emotional level and just pulls you into that world. That's irreplaceable. The filmmakers I've admired the most are the most versatile ones. Robert Wise was sort of amazing; *The Day the Earth Stood Still* and *The Sound of Music, West Side Story* . . .

The delightful thing I've discovered in working in this business is that, if you put out the effort, if you really care about what you do, you will find people along the way who lend you a helping hand, and that's lovely. It's just a kindness I think that is motivated by shared enthusiasm for what you love—in this case, movies.

Sometimes bad luck comes along and I think that the people who are able to weather that or think their way through it, rather than be consumed by it, are the people to admire.

I've been writing professionally 10 years now, I'm stunned to realize it's been going on that long and I've been given the opportunity to now direct as well. I feel damn fortunate. But, I also think that you make your own luck by expending the effort. There's a persistence I think that one needs in order to get lucky. And I think one needs to apply the elbow grease of determination and have faith in oneself in order to get lucky. I think you manufacture your opportunities as you go along. Knowing lessens the luck of it, it just heightens your chances of seizing that luck. Somebody once pointed out to me that it took Thomas Edison a thousand attempts using various methods and materials before the damn light bulb turned on. So, what I always keep planted in my head is, "What if he'd gotten really discouraged after 999 times?"

Mel Gibson

Braveheart

One of my most favorite things to do is tell a story and have it work, just in a room. That, to me, is one of the greatest sources of pleasure you can give other people, and you feel pretty good doing it your-self. And, it just seemed the natural progression from where I was. And I was frightened and terrified to do it. But I worked with a director who shall remain nameless, and I thought, "If he can do it, anybody can." It sort of creeps into your dreams a little bit.

I was a TV junkie in the 60s, and they put everything on television then. So I had a lot of things to watch and analyze and reenact. But, surely the people that I worked with were the strongest influence, directors like George Miller and Peter Weir.

Michael Radford

Il Postino

I fell in love with the cinema when I was 16. When I was a kid, I went to an English public school where the cinema wasn't considered to be a cultural activity. But, when I was 16, I was allowed to go to the Bedford Cinemagraphical Society to watch movies with subtitles, which somehow were considered to be superior in some kind of way. You could smoke quietly in the back of the cinema and nobody would notice. And I remember the first movie that I saw was Truffaut's *Shoot the Piano Player*, and it was amazing. I was just kind of knocked out by it. And as I sat entranced every Sunday afternoon, I thought to myself, "Gee whiz . . . I'd like to do that."

I went to film school and made a little film—I don't say that everybody has to go to film school to become a director, but for me it was very good because I found myself able just to concentrate on my own heart's desire without any economic pressures. I was able to just soak up the cinema and soak up the great directors. In my early formation it was in European cinema, it was Godard and Antonioni and we all tried to make films like Godard and we all failed miserably, because he was always one jump ahead of you. And then I started to study Hollywood cinema, American cinema, and I began to see the fabulous techniques that directors could use with sometimes incredibly shoddy material. I saw these movies which were theoretically run-of-the-mill movies made by guys like Nicholas Ray and Raoul Walsh and other great moviemakers in Hollywood and I was amazed how this voice would come through.

But the thing about directing, finally, is that you have to do it yourself. I mean, there's no substitute.

Cameron Crowe
Jerry Maguire

I started out as a music journalist. I began to write for *Rolling Stone* magazine, and at a certain point I decided I wanted to write a book about a kid working in a fast food job than some of the fat and happy rock stars that I'd begun to interview so often. And so I wrote the book *Fast Times at Ridgemont High*. And because I was the least expensive guy they could find, they gave me a shot to write the screenplay. My first dream to be a rock critic was a wonderful thing to kind of experience and realize. Now my heroes are guys like Billy Wilder and Truffaut. And I'm just having fun seeing where this takes me.

Neil Jordan
The Crying Game

I was in Ireland and there had never been any directors in Ireland as far as I knew, and I was very interested in films and I thought movies were made from creatures from the United States or from Italy. Irish people, what they did was write books, or they got very black and dark and said they were writing a book. But I started writing scripts. I was very interested in movies since I was a kid, and the books I was writing were so overlaid with visual description for some reason, probably because my mother was a painter. After a certain stage it became redundant for me to write them as books any more, so I began to write screenplays. And I would have been perfectly happy writing scripts forever if I could have found someone who would do exactly what I wanted them to do as a director. Honestly, because I had no idea what directing entailed. So, if I said, "Exterior day, rather dark, but not too dark," or something like that; and, "The guy comes through the door and he coughs," if somebody would have done exactly that, I would have been perfectly happy to be a writer for the rest of my life —

but that person was not around, of course. So I decided to do it myself. I got a friend of mine, John Boorman [director of *Deliverance* and *The Emerald Forest*], who I'd written a screenplay with, and I'd written part of the screenplay for *Excalibur*, and he agreed to produce for me. So that was the first film I did [*Danny Boy*]. But I really didn't know anything. I just knew about the pictures that I wanted to see in my mind, really.

I'd made two kinds of Hollywood films, and I was kind of exhausted because there they didn't do very well, neither of them — they were a bit both wearying experiences and they didn't perform at the box office. And you get exhausted, you get depressed, you feel rejected.

Mike Leigh
Secrets & Lies

I grew up in the 40s and 50s in Manchester. It was a period where there were movie houses on every street corner and I spent a huge amount of time going to the "pictures," as we all called it. So I kind of had an early passion for the movies. I think that I wanted to be a film director from quite an early age because it was very exciting really. I got to London in the 60s and started to discover the international cinema of every kind. And it really took off from there. I trained as an actor and went to art school and did a film course and really moved in the direction of filmmaking.

Barbra Streisand
The Prince of Tides

I think directing comes from the instinct. I did have the great fortune and privilege to have my first director be William Wyler, whom I adored. He is one of the greatest directors of all time — a great storyteller. It was interesting, because he wasn't a man of many words. In fact sometimes he couldn't tell you what he really wanted, but he knew when it was right. And you knew that he knew. So he was the best audience that you could have — the best director I could have learned from. He gave me a silver megaphone at the end of shooting and encouraged me to direct.

Scott Hicks
Shine

I heard somebody say in Australia that everybody who can't play the piano wants to become a director. Which has sort of taken on a whole new resonance for me because I wanted to play the piano but I never did. I didn't grow up as a child of film. I grew up in Kenya. There was no cinema. There was no television. And, I didn't discover film until quite later when I was at a university. And I set about acquiring an education in film, which really for me was looking at the great masters of European cinema of the 60s. There was Bergman and Fellini, and Orson Welles was an enormous sort of pal to me, as a teenager, when I was on this discovery voyage.

People often ask me how your career sort of develops, and I remind them that if you look up the word *career* in the Oxford English dictionary, it's defined as something like an uncontrolled lurch downhill. You know it is a series of accidents in a way and it depends on how you seize certain moments.

Anthony Minghella
The English Patient

Well, I am a pianist and that's what I wanted. I wanted to be a musician. I remember driving my father's ice cream van on the Isle of Wight thinking, I promise myself, I'll never have anything to do with selling anything. I'll be a writer, or a musician, or a director. And then I find myself here a few years ago with my ice cream trying to sell it to somebody.

You know, I'm a wop, so all of the Italian cinema appeals to me: Fellini, Visconti, Taviani brothers, Olmi. I mean those are the films that I cherished when I was growing up.

I think that the gift you have as a director is that if your interest is in music and in painting, as mine was as a student, then it's the one activity that you can do which calls into play all of your passions and enthusiasm.

— 2 —

The Script

Oliver Stone

JFK

I do not worship the script as a sacred thing at all. I sometimes just get rid of it and say let's go without it. I like to keep that improvisatory nature on the set. It has to be spontaneous, it has to be felt. If it's not working, rip it up and change it right then and there. The writing process is — like writing. You sit there. Ass plus seat equals writing.

It takes a long time. I'd read all the books I could that are credible and I hired a very brainy young researcher. She read everything: 300 of the credible books and every article. We joined the network of research buffs. We got a lot of information, the usual witnesses that came into the office and said they were there, that they killed so-and-so. And we got all the theories. We listened to everybody. It was the longest research job I've ever been involved with.

We refined the script, Zack Sklar and I, over a period of a year. There were six drafts. The first of which, of course, was notoriously stolen from the Warner Xerox room.

There were approximately 2,000 facts that we wanted to have in the original draft. I think we dropped it down — there are 1,200 facts in this movie at this stage. We simplified. We had to. We had to condense characters. We had to redistribute events to a certain degree because the Kennedy killing is so mosaic, the fragments have come out over eighteen or twenty years and they're all in different places.

It's a 180 page script, 2,000 camera set ups at least, and probably 2,500 cuts in the movie.

The hardest part of the writing was refining the facts to where somebody could understand them. How can you say it in a simpler way? Two sentences instead of three. You're down to counting words. Literally, with a stopwatch, because you want to move the thing along.

Themes change. This was a tricky one because it started out as a microcosm of Jim Garrison investigating a small police report that leads to the macrocosmic, global crime of the murder of a president. I didn't see all the themes that were coming. I never saw the linkage of Kennedy's murder to the differences in policy in Vietnam. It was not just about some ancient history. It's about whether we have a democracy in this country, whether the state is keeping the secrets. Who owns reality. That's certainly a philosophical theme of the movie. It comes up again and again in the style of the movie, because it's fractured. It's disassociated, like Godard. You can never get into a conventional linear pattern, because there's no conventional linear pattern to the history of that period. The media owns reality. The government owns reality. It's so fractured, and the camera and the style really tries to reflect the *Rashomon* truth to that story.

Salvador was about a small theme. At the beginning it was a journalist I knew who was a rascal who got hooked by a woman and a boy, and a family. And all of the sudden he's a less selfish individual at the end of the movie. I thought that was a nice transcendent theme.

Mike Newell
Four Weddings and a Funeral

The script, and it isn't always, should be questionable. You should have the right to work on the script and change things. Sometimes that can be very harmonious and sometimes that can be very distressing. An unharmonious relationship with a writer will never produce anything. And I suppose one of the lessons that I also learned was to make harmony no matter what. Then I guess what you do is follow your nose — you tend not to follow logic.

When I started work in television in the middle to late 60s, you'd do shows with a six-week turnaround. So you could do eight, ten, twelve shows a year. And you'd get to learn the writing process from the ground up and a lot of the time I remember spending in preparation for the television shows with scripts spread out on the floor of an office and actually cutting and pasting. With the producer who would say "No, no put that there, put that there" . . . what you were learning was structure and editing. And it was a very simple unmysterious process. You could actually take scene 3 and put it next to scene 18 and then put that next to scene 25. And fiddle about and watch it be different and that was tremendous. A pair of scissors and a pot of glue.

Four Weddings was a very good script and it was very funny, but it was too funny, there wasn't anything lying through it. It was simply a succession of very well-honed jokes. But also it didn't work—there wasn't an arc in the character properly. We did a dozen drafts. We would just play a theme: commitment or the lack of commitment.

I don't like writing during shooting, and I try to have it all done. Of course, it's going to happen, little bits and pieces are going to happen. I have also found myself in the situation where things are much looser than that because people have asked for them to be looser or you've lost control of it or whatever and it's always a nightmare.

You'd better use it—the script process—for finding out what it's about. I mean, it's a long three-month, four-month process of understanding what's on the page. So to start to visualize is irrelevant to me. That has its own time.

And part of the director's job is to say in a very large overall way, "I won't have it like that, I will have it like this."

James Cameron

Titanic

Well, as a director I was constantly cursing that son of a bitch the writer every day for getting me into this mess! There was the evolution of the script, certainly, from a pretty nebulous first idea, which was, "Wouldn't it be cool to make a movie about the *Titanic*?!" So how do you deal with that subject? How do you treat it respectfully? How do you do something new, carve out your own territory? And I pretty quickly hit on the idea of doing a love story.

I wanted to do something with great passion so that the interior power of the story was as strong as the exterior. And I couldn't find any true story that had actually transpired from history that had that kind of passionate energy to it, so I thought it was better to do it with fictitious characters.

I start with images because I started as an illustrator and production designer and so for me it always becomes a number of visual set pieces. I sort of collect a few and then I'll start at the very beginning, and build the character and really start to tell the story from the character standpoint, with those set pieces in the back of my mind.

I had written an early version of the script which I euphemistically call a "scriptment." Because if I can't think of the exact dialogue for a scene, I don't bog down, I just write: "And then they have an argument and the argument is about this." It drops into a novelistic default kind of form and then it goes back into script form when I can actually think of what the people might be saying, so it oscillates back and forth. It's kind of a bastard document but it's a great starting point. And we went and dove the ship and coming back from that experience, it colored the directing process after that quite a bit. I had wanted suspense thriller elements in the story to kind of energize it and keep it moving and I found those becoming increasingly less necessary as I went along.

Anthony Minghella
The English Patient

I can't imagine wanting to write a film and not direct because they're such an organic activity and I think that the pen continues to work all the way through filmmaking and in a sense that I think that you begin with ink, and you write on paper, and then you swap that instrument for a camera and that continues to write. And I'm incredibly alert to the fact that you're writing all the way through the filmmaking process. And then you get to the cutting room and again you become another kind of writer. And I felt that I was directing on the very first day that I was writing. And writing literally about a week before I finished the film. Literally writing new material. I have the advantage in the sense that there was a novel that provided the source for this film. In many ways that became as much a curse as a blessing, because it's an incredible novel, but it's got nothing to do with the movie.

I remember somebody calling me and saying: "I like it. Where's the third act?" And I said, "Where's the second act of this screenplay?" I mean one thing about Hollywood is that it's become more Aristotelian than Aristotle about this notion about what a screenplay has to be like. I didn't share that belief, but I do very much think that our job is to tell stories. The two years that I was working on the screenplay were very much about how to transport the audience in the way that I had been transported as a reader. I felt in a way that I couldn't adapt the book. I could only respond to it. I felt as if I were the only person allowed to read this novel and then my job was to try and find a way to communicate it to an audience who knew nothing about it.

I think you need architecture in films. Architecture in the sense that I think there needs to be a guiding idea. There needs to be a sense that there's a phrasing. The shape of the journey is stated very early so that the audience feels in safe hands.

I had this image that I brought out from Japan where they were telling us how the samurai sword is made. They bang out a piece of metal until it's very sharp and then they shove it in the furnace and fold it over and bang it out again until it's really sharp. And when it's as sharp as it can be then they put it back in the furnace. With my screenplay, I'd bring it out, bang it very hard, and lots of my favorite bits would drop off. That process was an incredible time for me, meticulous and rigorous. I think that the film finds itself. I don't think that I woke up on the first day of this project and knew what this film was going to be.

When I'm writing I like to work by myself for long periods of time. And so I enjoy the process of imagining what a film would be like and imaging how it might play.

Barbra Streisand
The Prince of Tides

I read the book many times. And every time I kind of pared it down to what jumped out at me, what was the essence of the story for me, what was the story I wanted to tell. I took it on a trip to Greece, because I wanted to visit the ancient site of myths, because I believe in the archetypal nature of stories—and then all of a sudden it was there for me.

We worked on the script for two years—the original script had no flashbacks, had no rape. It was very important to me to show [the hero's] background and what affected his present-day nature, what gave him the problems he had.

I constantly worked with the novel. I said there has to be a way to put in narration to remind people this is a novel and to respect this form. I couldn't quite figure it out at the beginning but I had Nick Nolte read passages from the book into a tape recorder, and I ended up using them in the film. I had a wonderful time with Pat Conroy listening to the stories of his childhood.

I had Becky Johnston move into my house with me for three weeks and we just worked morning till night. I had to put down first, the structure I saw in my head. And then we would flesh out the dialogue. She would go away and write for a couple of hours, or I would write for a couple of hours, then come together, talk it out, and read it. That was the process. The script had to serve the story that I wanted to tell, the story I felt was relevant to today, the theme of this man's journey, this man's growth, this theme of transformation through love.

I guess I'm a little obsessed with the notion that people should be all that they can be. The theme in *Yentl* is that women should be able to live the full range of their capacity. I guess it's striving towards wholeness that we can accept the masculine and feminine within us.

The Prince of Tides has a lot of themes. It's about forgiveness, about acceptance, about consciousness, how fear and oppression come in the way of being the most loving human being you can be.

John Madden
Shakespeare in Love

There were two writers on the script, Mark Norman and Tom Stoppard. It was Mark Norman's idea originally, it was his concept, he wrote a script, which had very much the kind of basic concrete of the movie that you now see. Tom came in to work on it fairly early on. The movie was going to be made at that point with Julia Roberts and nobody definitely playing Will. And I think that's the reason it floundered in its first incarnation, they had gotten a fair way into pre-production and they had started building sets and certainly had done some casting. But it ground to a halt because they couldn't cast Will and then the project went belly up and remained in a kind of dormant state for about the next five years. During that time, Harvey Weinstein became aware of the script and fell in love with it. I'd just done a movie for Harvey and I was the lap that was in the way when the script was dropped, as it were. And as a matter of fact, when I read the script, I remember distinctly not being in any way sure that I was being offered it. Which I suspect means that I wasn't. So I read it actually, without that kind of normal fear that one has when one reads a script, thinking, "Is this going to be as good as I think it's going to be?" Or, "Will I be up to it?" I just read it as a script, which was a pretty astonishing experience. I mean, I've never read a script that so astonished. Literally halfway through the first page I thought there's such an amazing mind at work here. It was the most astounding script. And I remember waking up the night after I'd said I'd do it, rather the way Viola does in the movie, a couple of times sitting bolt upright thinking "What the fuck have I done?" Because there's a girl playing a boy in this movie and you will never get away with it. That was just the first kind of assault on my consciousness. That I thought there were just so many things in this script that don't seem doable. It was just stupid, of course. You should trust your first instincts when you read it.

I'm dealing with story and character and emotional tone, emotional texture. And I have to get those kind of shifts and weights right before going to the next step. I mean, the trouble is, it doesn't really fall into stages like that. You find your way towards telling the story that you think needs to be told. And images pop up at certain moments and certain ideas come fully formed into your head that then find their way onto the screen, and certain others don't. It felt to me like it was a movie that I absolutely had to have nailed down as far as possible at script level before we would go into it. Because it was so complex and working at so many levels and dealing with so many kinds of kaleidoscopic tonal shifts all the time.

I love making movies where you make it and then you discover it's a different kind of film in the editing room. But, I didn't think this movie was going to be that. And when you're working with a mind like that, frankly, and somebody who writes with extraordinary economy and yet with total freedom, you know, can pluck an idea from anywhere. And, of course, you don't, you think twice about saying "Uh, Tom, I don't think this line works terribly well," given the man you're working with. But he is an extraordinary gentleman and totally open. He's directed himself, as you know, and he understands that it has to be the director's film. And so he went wherever I wanted him to go. The main work on the script was in the last third. It had to do with the resolution of the Will and Viola relationship in terms of the play and how the barriers eventually break down completely between the play and their life so there's no distinction between one or the other. That process went right the way through the filming as well. We rewrote and reshot the ending during the filming.

Michael Radford

Il Postino

A Burning Patience was a Chilean novel, about a 17-year-old boy and the death of Pablo Neruda, and it was a beautiful book. When I first looked at it I thought, "Well, why would you want to change this in any kind of way? You could just shoot it straight as it is and make a Chilean movie." But, I couldn't make a Chilean movie because I had an Italian star, so, although I speak Italian, I didn't feel confident to write the movie myself, so we handed it over to one of the great Italian writers, and he came back about three months later with the biggest piece of garbage I'd ever read in my life

And one day, I said to Massimo [Troisi, the star of *Il Postino*], "You and your co-writer have written five screenplays together—I've written four. Why don't we just write it ourselves?" Unfortunately, in Italy, you get a credit even if you brush past somebody who's tapping away at a typewriter. There's a vast number of people credited for this movie who never actually wrote a word of it.

I normally work very closely and often I write a draft myself. Obviously I can't write in Italian, so what happened was, Massimo and I came to Los Angeles. He used to like to come to Los Angeles because nobody knew who he was. So, he could walk around—it was often we would go to an Italian restaurant just to remind him he was a star. Generally speaking we sat in a hotel room and I wrote in English and then he spoke in Italian and I kind of copied it down. So we had this screenplay which was kind of, half in English and half in Italian. And then we just structured a screenplay—literally, in about two weeks.

The theme of the book was the theme of revolution and how two people got caught up in a revolution and started to need each other. I knew that I couldn't make that film. So I had to change the theme of the book. And it's very interesting, about ten years ago I made a film called *Another Time, Another Place* which was the story of three Italians in the north of Scotland. One actor I picked up, literally, off the street, and it turned out that he was a gangster. I took him to Scotland and years later we met again in Rome and he confessed to me that I had completely changed his life. As he talked to me, I saw the theme of this screenplay. I remembered all those times when you've been on holiday and you've met somebody and you've wanted to communicate with them and you didn't. And it was there that the true line of this piece was born.

Curtis Hanson

L.A. Confidential

I can't separate from myself the process of writing and directing—it's all part of the same thing, it's all part of the storytelling.

With *L.A. Confidential*, I read James Ellroy's wonderful book and just became captivated by the characters, and my reaction to them, much more than the plot. Ellroy's novel is in fact very interior. Much of it takes place in the people's heads—in our script, we tried to keep description to a minimum, and to try to make it as visual as possible.

I think the first shot that I actually sort of conceptualized during the writing process summed up the theme of the movie, which is the difference between image and reality and how things and people appear and how they really are, and it was a shot where . . . Kim Basinger's character, Lynn Bracken, who looks like Veronica Lake and she sells that resemblance to her customers, she's created a scene where she is projecting on the wall of her home, a clip from a picture called *This Gun for Hire*, and we are seeing the real Veronica Lake and Alan Ladd, and then with a camera move, Kim's head comes in and literally moves into the old movie and blocks it, and the audience is allowed to see she does look like Veronica Lake. Thematically and stylistically, we're saying, classic film noir, with it's black and white lighting, is artificial, and she knows it's artificial, her customer knows it's artificial. And that's the game. He's paying to make love with this icon from the screen. But here in the foreground is our character, Kim, who is leading her own existence. I'm trying to say, I do not want this movie to be an homage to film noir, I wanted it to have it's own life.

During the writing process, I think about the shooting of the scenes, I see the scenes, as they are being written—I'm not somebody who does sketches and storyboards and so forth, but I very much visualize it, and try to actually indicate that on the page with the choice of language, to give the script a directorial point of view.

Peter Weir

The Truman Show

I was looking for something different. I was kind of wanting to explore an area I'd never done before. The material I was getting was sometimes good, but it was more conventional, a lot of biographies, a lot of true stories and things. I felt like something different. So here it was, *The Truman Show*. It was a startling read. Very different in tone to what the film became, which you might expect. In other words, it has become my sensibility.

I don't think I'd have got working on this without a lead actor. This was such a dangerous material, it could just destroy you. It was never going to be halfway right. It was never going to be a good try, because it was too expensive. It was all so expensive, so you could never in all conscience take it on without saying, I've got a pretty good idea I can get people along to this show. And that's how Jim Carrey got involved. He read it, too, and he was looking for a change. Jim and I got on, and Andrew Nichols (the writer) and I the same thing, so we worked on the draft. Jim wasn't available, I didn't realize this, for a year. But it turned out to be very very fortunate because we then had a year to take what was already a good read, and . . . the odd thing was, I'd never had a situation where there was something working that you *then* took apart. Like a beautiful mechanism, we took it all to pieces, just so I could see how Andrew had thought, in a way, his thought processes. He could get to know me and we could rebuild it through my sensibility. And he was very willing to do that. He wasn't defensive of his material. And he had boundless energy, he wasn't written out. So for a year, sometimes I'd come over, sometimes we'd just exchange the material through the mail, but we went through an excessive number of drafts. Like an excessive number of cuts, I've never had a film where we'd done so many passes at both stages. Fourteen drafts, often minute changes.

I do say to a writer, as a kind of a joke, that I have to eat this script. It has to become organic, it has to become part of me. I mean in order to follow the analogy to its full. It in a way has to be as if I did write it. It's not always to the same extent, I mean that wasn't quite the case with *Witness*, in which I came on much more as a hired gun. I mean, I did a couple of passes on that, strong, strong changes to the extent where the writers objected strongly to those changes!

I'll record the script usually myself and then play it in the car. I think it's great, particularly driving along in traffic and hear your own screenplay coming back and you do the voices. You learn a lot about the characters by speaking their lines.

Mike Leigh

Secrets & Lies

With all of my films, and *Secrets & Lies* is my sixteenth, the job has been to discover what the film is by making it. There's always a feeling, a notion, a conception on the go, that varies in its vagueness. For me, one of the first ingredients is to get the backing for the film without the backers having any idea what the film is going to be. Because it is about embarking on a journey through which the film, characters, the whole thing comes into existence. And so with some notions on the go, we always agree to make the film on budget, in time, and not beyond a certain length. Beyond that there is *carte blanche*. Now that then leaves me free to explore possibilities and to discover things and for things to happen which I didn't necessarily or I certainly didn't know were going to happen.

The only actual piece of writing that I do is a document which is usually no longer than three or four pages long which I write at the end of the rehearsal period just before we shoot which literally says: Scene One—Cemetery—Day—Funeral; Scene Two—House; Scene Three—Maurice and Monica—House. That's all it says. To me my job as writer-director of a potential film is to push and pull and bully and cajole and massage and generally direct the whole thing into existence.

The thing that concerns everybody is how is it that what you see on the screen in my films, with the tiniest of exceptions, is very highly structured, very written, very thoroughly disciplined in the style of the storytelling and the shooting. That's really a matter of taking those one line scenes scene by scene and going to the location for each one of them. And starting with improvising and building up the thing. And writing through rehearsal and structuring through rehearsal. And finally it's a question of "you say that" and "you say this, and you move there," and it winds up being finished.

And in the case of all my films, and *Secrets & Lies* being no exception, there's a very long period of what is not very accurately described as rehearsal. Which is that period of a lot of discussion of inventing characters, doing a lot of research, and a huge amount of improvisation work through which the characters come into existence and the whole world of the film is really created in a tangible three-dimensional way. Out of which I'm then about to distill and structure a film. So what we do in the preliminary, the preparatory period, is to create, if you like, the premise for the film, but not the film itself. The truth is, I could talk about his for a month and never mention the word "script."

There's a scene towards the end of *Secrets & Lies* where they all come around to the house where Monica shows two of the other women around the house. And she puts down the toilet lid in each of a number of different toilets. I mean you can't sit home and think of that.

When I get together with a cast of people who always agree, each of them always agrees, to be in a film without having any idea what the character is going to be, any idea what the film's going to be about, or whether the character will or won't be a central character. In other words, an ensemble of actors. And it takes actors of a certain caliber to agree to embark on that risk.

Gus Van Sant
Good Will Hunting

When I read a screenplay, I'm looking for a number of things: character and setting, dialogue, and a good first act, second act, third act, and then an ending. And all these things are really crucial when I'm reading a screenplay, and they don't have to just be there, they have to be good ones!! It's very easy to find a screenplay that has great character and setting. And you get through the first act and you find out that there's not really a second act or there's not really a third act or not really a great ending. Dialogue is important as well. This screenplay, as I was reading, this often happens, you read along, you say, well this is a great setting and great characters and great dialogue, but I bet there's not gonna be a great second act. And lo and behold, there's a second act! And you go, "Oh, this is great, second act, but I'll bet there's not like development third act" and you read along and you go, "Oh my God there's actually this, ya know, all these elements" and you go, "But there can't be an ending." And there's actually an ending! And so, when I read *Good Will Hunting* all these things were there in place. My reaction was to just call the writers [Ben Affleck and Matt Damon] immediately and just say, this is fantastic and I'd be on board, because you just don't find that a lot all in one screenplay.

There was a problem in *Good Will Hunting* that the script had early on. Will was in his apartment, and he was reading very fast from a book, inhumanly fast. And you got the idea that this guy could absorb information and he could retain it. You understood in the script stage that this guy was a very brilliant character but somehow the film needed to spend more time with him absorbing information, how his mind worked. It came down to him writing equations on the wall. And working on the problems that the professor had put up on the board in the hallway. When you are describing somebody like that, who you are saying is a genius character, you sort of need some visual representation of that.

Quentin Tarantino
Pulp Fiction

There's the "writing process" and then, in a way, when I'm making the movie, I'm writing it with actors. You know they're like a collaborator, and then when I'm editing it, that's writing too.

But, the script is your safety net. I actually feel better about the fact that I can take more risks and walk the tightwire, because I know at the end of the day I have a script to catch me. If I just have to shoot it like bad television, I've still got a scene.

One of the first things that always goes after I do my first draft, that only I see, is I write down every shot, but then I always have a tremendous problem with page length.

In the case of *Reservoir Dogs*, where I had never done anything before, I went to a Sundance workshop and I drafted a couple of the scenes there. I had a meeting with a bunch of the resource directors that were there and they started asking me certain questions and they were saying, "Did you do your subtext work?" And, what do you mean? And they go, "Ah. . . . See, you think you know everything because you wrote it. But you've just done the writer's work, you haven't done the director's work." You gotta do the subtext work. And, that's interesting. So, I took a scene, one of the first scenes—when Mr. White brings Mr. Orange shot into the warehouse and he's trying to calm him down, and what I did was, my approach as an actor. Okay, I'm Mr. White, alright, what do I want from this more than anything else? I'm Mr. Orange—what does Mr. Orange want from this scene more than anyone else? And fifteen things start popping out and everything, it was growing. And then I wrote as a director—what do I want the audience to take away from this scene more than anything else?

Frank Darabont
The Shawshank Redemption

I'm a big believer in walking onto a set with a script that I feel is pretty much the movie you're gonna make. I know there are some folks in the world, Woody Allen and Robert Altman, who kind of get in and want to discover this as they're shooting. I can't think of anything more terrifying than not knowing at the end of the day, worst comes to worst, I have a scene that works, that I can put on film and it's cut together and it'll be a component of telling the story. Within the contents of that, certainly, any given day of shooting an actor will, maybe, modify dialogue a little bit here and there. I mean, you do have to be flexible. The writer does somewhat come off and the director goes and you say, "Well, OK, let's see if we can improve on what the writer did."

I always write for the director, at least in my screenplays. I find I have a projector running in my head. I feel that my job is to visualize the movie on paper as closely as possible, so that when the reader goes to the script, they see the movie the same way I do. So, I really try to replicate it in that sense. Often times things get lost in the translation. I discovered as writer that there was in the making of *Shawshank* a real advantage in having the director working towards the same goal.

This came from a Stephen King novella, and it just goes to show what you can do with a good source material. The technique of telling most of the story in flashback and then clicking into sort of real time in the last, say, ten — fifteen minutes of the movie, was a direct lift from King's structure. There was a certain amount of invention on my part as the screenwriter, but even when I was inventing or changing something, I always tried very hard to bear in mind what King's intent was. Because he just told such a good story that I didn't want to mess with too much. But it was such a sort of amicable, rambling kind of first-person narrative, that there was a certain level of mechanical screen structure that I had to bring to it.

Roberto Benigni
Life Is Beautiful

During the screenwriting. Oh, this is my favorite moment. I can say I am directing the movie twice. Now you may say, "Twice?" Because when we are writing, this is really my favorite moment. The world is in your hand now. You can do what you want. What a wonderful moment. This really is imagination, the body is exploding in the brain. And during the writing, I am directing. I like to improvise, but not to leave an open door because this isn't very healthy. I like to prepare the improvisation. It takes me as much as a week to prepare a good improvisation. Because your improvisation you can fly very very high. But sometimes it's very dangerous, you are possessed by an angel who is improvising, they can improvise something very bad. So during the script, I am playing all the characters and trying to do everything. I remember, it was René Clair who said, "There are three important things to make a good movie. The script, the script, the script."

James L. Brooks
As Good as It Gets

I had a funny journey because this was a wonderful script by Mark Andrus that I took on first as a producer. And as such, I really just was bringing it along, and then at some point I got involved where I knew I was going to direct it and then I just wanted to work with the script. Then a year later I was still working with the script and we formed some alchemy. We didn't know each other well, and we're very different men, but somehow each of us got very personally invested and we were this writing team that came out with something where we each feel very together on it. So I think that gave me a less secure footing than I've had in the past, because I was trying to represent some very deep feelings that weren't from me, and the tone changed. Tone was up for grabs—it was never an absolute tone that I started the movie with from the script that I knew that I would follow.

Andrew Davis
The Fugitive

The Fugitive had been in development for many years. There were lots of permutations of different drafts. The question was, "How could you say no to working with Harrison Ford?" Because you knew it would open these doors, and all of the sudden you would become acceptable as a director in every area. But there were certain key things that were critical, to me, to change to make the script work.

The basic story is great drama, the unjustly accused man on the run. It's a great story line, it's got great empathy and simpatico, so there was a great spine to work with. I never saw the television show, Harrison never saw the television show during the 60s, we just were not watching *The Fugitive.*

In the original story I think that the marriage wasn't so healthy, and there were problems between him and his wife. I felt that you had to be invested in the life of this doctor, and to see his loss, his fall from grace. So we tried to create a prologue, which is the beginning of the movie, in the flashbacks. You really got to believe that they had a wonderful life together, and there was a great sense of loss. I also felt that the reason that Mrs. Kimble was killed could not be about a bungled burglary. It had to be about something more substantial than that. So that the movie had a soul, and a content.

There were at least five other writers working on it before I got involved. And every time we'd talk about a scene, it's, "Oh yeah, in draft three we did that."

But the process of working on the script—and anything I say is not to demean the work of the writers who worked very hard, but this is a film that had a release date before the script was done. There was enough there for Harrison to commit to in terms of character. But, I would say sixty to seventy percent of the dialogue was written on the set. I would say that forty percent of the movie was hardly scripted at all. There were ideas for scenes that at the end of the day we would say, "Quickly, let's see, can we grab this? Can we put this scene in? Can we improvise this?" What I've learned is I'm scared to put myself in a situation where I won't experiment. I think that, especially working with actors. You can sit in a room and you can conceive a scene, and you can say, "This is a gem. We shouldn't touch a word." But then when you get there, and you see how the light is, and you see what the clothes are like, and somebody had garlic the night before and they're burping, and you take all these elements and you put it together and you say, "Let's think of it in a different way."

I would love to have a great script that I could shoot with my eyes closed. At the same time, I think the magic of moviemaking is making it happen while you're shooting the picture.

Clint Eastwood

Unforgiven

I had read it and liked it immediately, and thought it was one of the better scripts. I liked the fact that you never quite could guess where it was taking you. And then I sat on it. I bought it in 1984 and I thought, it needs to be done down the line. I felt that maybe I could even age into it a little more. It had certain things in the story, certain moralities that I thought would be a nice wrap up for me in the genre.

You kind of read it as an entertainment piece, and then afterward you start digesting the various aspects of it and it just kind of takes you over and eventually you say I'd like to present this, and see if I could successfully transfer this onto the screen.

It's a constantly evolving process for me. You get a first impression, then you get a second impression, and many impressions along the way, and I think as you get into it, it starts taking on a life of its own.

Sometimes you get committees at studios who will have input and they decide the input is important because they have a little idea that they want to inject into it, and maybe the idea is a good one, and maybe it's so far out in left field, it has nothing to do with this particular story. The big thing you have to do is either forcefully, or diplomatically, or however you chose to do so, is to try to make sure you carry on the line and be true to the story. I change things quite often, because I feel actors must be comfortable, a lot of times the lines won't fit. I'm not afraid to change the dialogue, as long as the intent is good. Sometimes you find that the actor will come up with a suggestion that might even improve some of it. That's not to say that he or she is changing the direction of the story line or main points you are trying to make, you always must be flexible.

I made few suggestions, and the more I would fool with these suggestions, the more I realized I was unraveling some of the key points to the script. And so I had to go back to my own adage of: "Lets not kill this with improvements."

One of the things that can make any film uninteresting is if you kind of assume what's gonna happen most the way.

Sometimes a writer will dry up or for some reason—maybe they just plain run out of steam. By and large I've been lucky, though. In fact, I did one picture where I shot the first draft of it, and the writer was incensed. He said, "I can do another draft, I can do another draft, I've never had a picture shot with the first draft." And I said, "Well, I like this draft." It was the film about Charlie Parker [*Bird*].

Rob Reiner

A Few Good Men

Aside from good writing and well developed characters and a good story and a theme that has something to say, I try to look to the main character and see if it's somebody I can identify with that's either experiencing something that I've gone through, or that I am going through, so that I can connect up with the main character and put myself in that character. Even though I'm not playing the part, I'll know how to tell that story.

A Few Good Men with Tom's character — this one is close to me, in that he is the son of an accomplished father who was in the same business; and he's living in the shadow of a famous father, and he's frightened to test himself. And eventually has to find *his* way, as opposed to his father's. I went through that when I was making *Stand by Me.* I realized, that's a film that my father [Carl Reiner] never would have made. It was very close to my personality, and as I was making it, I was very conscious of the fact that, if the audience was accepting this, then the audience was accepting who I was and my sensibility, separate and apart from my father's, because I'd always thought of myself as an adjunct to my father.

I had seen the play [*A Few Good Men*], and I was very bowled over by it. It was a very emotional play, and it had an enormous amount of holes, plot holes, which you can get away with on stage a lot of the times, because you get wrapped up in the emotion of seeing live theatre and you don't notice that, "Hey, wait a minute, that doesn't make any sense." When you put it on film, those things become much more apparent.

So I worked pretty closely in restructuring it, and filling in those plot holes. It wasn't — we weren't making a bad play into something good — I mean it was already a good play, but the screenplay was way better than the play, and the national touring company, *A Few*

Good Men, reflected the work we did on the screenplay, which to my knowledge, I don't think has ever been done with a successful Broadway play, that the writer has completely rewritten the play for the national touring company.

I'm very respectful of writers, I mean, if you've got a good solid screenplay, you're eighty percent home. If you've got a good solid story and good characters—Hitchcock used to say that once he's finished the script, the film was done.

You collaborate with a writer—I act out the parts, we change the lines, I open the hood and get in there. Hopefully the writers are not too upset because they see that it's not a director trying to make it into his film and ruin their material, but it's really trying to shore up what they already have. I worked with Bill Goldman on *Misery*, and it even got to the point where the last couple of drafts, I wrote without Bill. To where he would say, "Go ahead, you know what you are doing here." And it doesn't take anything from him, his name's there, and everybody knows, he worked on it, and Stephen King wrote the novel, and it's his story, it's not mine. But if everybody understands the process is collaborative and there is no ownership on it, then you get in there and do whatever it takes. Once I have the script then obviously there are problems with locations that don't work and because you can't get things there, you alter things slightly to fit what's there. A particular actor may have a problem with a certain kind of emotion so you alter it to help him, but always never to destroy what your main plan is to begin with.

Barry Levinson

Bugsy

I read the 260-page screenplay, and I was intrigued by it. I basically said to Warren [Beatty] that I was interested in making a movie if we go into pre-production now and simultaneously fix the script, just to accelerate the process.

We kept whittling the script down and changing things radically as we went along, and kept evolving it throughout the pre-production period and during the shooting period, finding new things and

exploring other aspects of it rather than sitting with a writer and working and then going into pre-production.

So everything was happening at once, which I think was probably a good way to do it. Jimmy [Toback, the screenwriter] was writing the script for six years before that, and I think that if we
would've continued that way it might've been another five or six.
Since we had a set date to start production, it forced everything to
come alive.

I think what you want to do is improve character and relationships. Ultimately we had to condense the story. We threw out some
characters. We telescoped it somewhat. At the same time we were
able to heighten the characters and the relationships. Because as you
work with structure it'll affect character, and you don't want to give
up character for structure, because then you're just going A, B, C, D,
and you're not depicting life and all the idiosyncrasies that can come
with character. I'm always fascinated by character behavior. And I
don't want to give that up just to propel the story along to some kind
of conclusion. I think *Bugsy* has a very strong storyline and at the
same time the characters have their own kind of idiosyncrasies and
certain strange and peculiar behavior that's functioning throughout
the piece.

Ideas create other ideas. Rather than looking at the problem and
just staring at it, sometimes you just start trying things and it's just
like a chain reaction. Things kick off other ideas and all of a sudden
it opens up new doors. So rather than be afraid to explore, you chase
it and see where it'll take you.

It still ended up a very long screenplay. I think we shot about 165
pages plus. And we only lost one scene, so what it is — is people are
talking much faster than they normally would.

I think *Diner* was only able to happen when I began to realize
that everything I had talked about was about male–female relationships. So even if these guys hanging out, what it was all based
on was the problems with women. When I understood that, then I
could write it.

When I read *Bugsy* it was fascinating. We always say Hollywood
is infatuated with gangsters, but here was a gangster who was infatuated with Hollywood. He basically invented Las Vegas by saying,

"Well, I'll take all the entertainment and I'll put it in the desert and I'll use all of the things that I know about gambling and invent some crazy city." That kind of lunatic sensibility and that kind of collision of a gangster in Hollywood was an idea that was real intriguing.

I think every time you do a movie, there's a strong theme and an idea that motivates you.

Neil Jordan
The Crying Game

I wrote the basic situation of the kidnapping of a black soldier by an IRA activist who basically was troubled about what he's doing, because terrorism is a very troubling and horrible thing.

I just wrote out the brief story, about three pages, and I didn't proceed with it. Over the years I'd been thinking about it and saying maybe if I did this, maybe if I did that. I came back to it last year, and I said, "OK, I'll write the script now," and it became very exciting. But I don't know why I could finish the script last year as opposed to eight years ago—it's hard to explain. Maybe because what it says about the world we live in now is somehow more relevant than it was then. It's kind of a bit mysterious. When it happens at it's best, you're a participant rather than a manipulator.

I like stories about characters who exist in situations of moral unease—who feel the need to make a moral choice, but the moral choice they're presented with is unclear. In other words, where they're kind of in a world where there should be marks between good and evil and there actually are none. And I like stories about fallen characters, probably because I'm from a Catholic background!

I think there's nothing like the pleasure of a well-constructed story. It's like a piece of music, or a piece of architecture. The pleasure of putting the shape on a script is a wonderful pleasure, whether you are the director doing it with the writer, or the writer doing it yourself.

I have to get the story solved, before I start the film, otherwise I would get into trouble with directing it. And I've been in one situation where the script has been a movable feast, which was pretty horrible, because basically if you take a script, and you get 15 different voices saying we could do this, or we could do that, I mean the choices are endless, and there should be one choice really. If there are 20 solutions there's something wrong. Maybe one writer cannot find it. I just finished doing a screenplay for this book, *Interview with the Vampire*, which is an interesting, very tangled book. And there have been a whole series of scripts written and I realized that nobody had actually told a story from beginning to end. And when you do that, it's absolutely fascinating. If you just tell the story pure and simple. It sometimes puzzles me, the way that people who are neither directors nor writers have input into screenplays—that confuses me, I don't understand.

Robert Zemeckis

Forrest Gump

I've never found a screenplay yet that didn't need massive amounts of what we call rewriting. For me the writing never stops, whether we admit it or not, film directors are writing and they're writing with film. Maybe the more appropriate word is storytellers, and I think what we are doing with the writer is both telling the same story and it's separated by our guilds [Directors Guild of America; Writers Guild of America]. But in what I do, the writer has got to be there with me all the time. The first thing I do is just lock myself in a room with the writer on the first day. It's not in the "ugly director making the writer rewrite the script" sense. It's just, we gotta hone this movie into something. As every department starts to warm up, all that has to be fed back into the screenplay. And I think the final writing that I do is color timing the negative and the final sound mix.

I believe that in the classic dramatic sense that your character arc is what proves the ultimate premise for the movie, and you have to try to see if that fits into that classic dramatic structure in Western entertainment.

The major structural thing that changed when I got on board was the idea that the movie would start off being narrated in a flashback and then we would catch up to real time. You were able to invest the audience for three-fourths of the movie in the character. Then all of the sudden, nobody knew—even Forrest—didn't know what was going to happen. It took me a while to figure out that the love story between Forrest and Jenny in actuality is the suspense that holds the film together.

Mel Gibson
Braveheart

There was a theme—it was the idea of freedom as something you can't buy, and it's something to be prized above things, and that we take it for granted and that there are people who have given everything, their last drop of blood, for something that we all possibly take for granted.

The script from sparse history, legend, and imagination was not bad. I shied away from it for a year—it was kind of unwieldy and larger than what we ended up with. There were twice as many castles and ten times as many battles. I didn't change writers because I thought that he really caught the essence of something that stirred me up, and kept me building these images in my head before I'd go to sleep at night. Gradually we married scenes together—we [he and screenwriter, Randall Wallace] would sort of sit down and wander in and out of character, just us talking, so you had to be there, you had to be in our mindsets, otherwise you were just looking at two lunatics in a room.

We were writing some of these scenes as we were shooting, too, they were last minute things. If you come across a problem, you find every means at your disposal to fix it. And sometimes a lot changes the whole tone of a scene.

Some things you really can't write: The relationship between Wallace and the Robert the Bruce character, the Bruce's journey through the story was like, the worst bastard you've ever seen on a page. But you had to be with him somehow.

Scott Hicks
Shine

I learned a very powerful lesson on the first feature film that I directed. Which, for reasons best known to himself, the producer decided since he had a first-time director and a first-time writer that we would not meet and discuss in case we sort of ran amuck. Which is really what you want people to do in a sense, is run amuck. So I vowed never again — I've been involved as a writer on all of the documentary projects which I've made. The second feature film that I made, I wrote, directed, and produced. With *Shine* it started out as an idea which I researched and developed for about four years while I was making other projects. I'd written a number of treatments and I wrote a first draft of the screenplay which was called *Flight of the Bumble Bee*. I always had in my mind the structure of how I wanted to tell the story, where I wanted to begin and how.

I saw a little story in the newspaper. I went to see a concert. I was fascinated. And from that moment I knew I wanted to make a film. And really the first year or so we [Scott Hicks and David Helfgott, the subject of the film] spent getting to form a friendship so that I could actually understand and come to the details of the story. Because nobody sits down and reveals their most intimate details of their past on first meeting.

After four or five years of working on arriving at this point, I had the structure, I had the characters, and I had made a large amount of David's dialogue because it was drawn from David's mouth. Then I wanted to bring in a new sensibility and someone who I could collaborate with as writer and director because I sensed that this was a film that was going to take every bit of my concentration as a director to execute. And Jan Sardi had worked with me as a script editor on the previous feature film that I had written. We had a very good relationship, and so I said to him: "Let's do this." And he took it on and began to make it his own. We kept the structural architecture of the piece and Jan took it into some new direction, some of which I liked, some of which I didn't. It was a very collaborative process, but with Jan as writer and me as director. And I enjoy the process of collaboration. I don't have a love of sitting down to write. I write in order to direct.

My draft was sort of a vast sprawling, embracing everything that I knew about David and his life and family. There were many, many stories that were bubbling out in it. So what we set about doing was essentially finding key turning points in David's life, which started to dictate the selection of material. In a way it was like starting with a vast and sprawling novel. If you are adapting a novel, you have to pick which story you're telling out of those hundreds of pages.

Cameron Crowe

Jerry Maguire

I originally wanted to do a movie that was about how you would arrive at your greatest success through incredible failure. Success being an emotional success, really. And it sort of began with a picture in the newspaper, of a sports agent or sports manager and his client. They were two guys of very different sizes and loud shirts. But they were clearly two guys against the world. And from there the whole story of *Jerry Maguire* over a number of years of research became a very personal story from me. The journey of a man to complete himself. And basically what I ended up with was a movie much more emotional than any of us thought when we entered into it.

I worked on the script for a long time, about three and a half years, and I felt like I directed it a number of times while I was writing it. A couple of different movies were directed along the way.

Originally the movie was written with Tom Hanks in mind. And it was Miles Davis music that I heard. Particularly this one live version of the song called "So What" which had many different changes to it. But it was a really "adrenalized," hyped-up live version of that song from a concert in Stockholm. But as I kept working, another song kept coming to mind which was a track called "Magic Bus," from The Who's album *Live at Leeds* and it was a younger man's story. I think the idea of writing for a star probably added more time to the process.

Steven Spielberg

Amistad

I feel that I'm really not a writer, I'm an illustrator trying to find ways to illustrate the story, with just a brevity of dialogue when necessary.

My involvement with this screenplay was minimal compared to my involvement with other screenplays of films I've directed. I had a wonderful script. My only real contribution, I think, to the screenplay was to try and find visual metaphors to take the place of dialogue. It was necessarily a wordy film because it was a courtroom drama. So my first idea was that I wanted all the Africans to speak in their native dialects and not speak English, which I thought would contemporize the film too much and make it very much like a Hollywood picture about a period.

Saving Private Ryan

Well, let me start by saying that it's one of the only times in my entire film career where someone actually, at an agency, gave me a script that I committed to direct. Even though the screenplay wasn't the intense experience that the film became, the screenplay was much more a morality play. About the kind of trading of lives for another life. So the screenplay really grappled with those issues of, do you really sacrifice eight people to save one, and it was really much more focused on that. But I had experienced a lot with my father who fought in Burma in WWII. I discovered post-*Saving Private Ryan* that so many of the actual veterans didn't speak about their experiences, if they in fact saw intense action—not unlike the Holocaust survivors who never speak of the actions taken against them because they're afraid they're going to taint the lives of their children and the grandchildren. But my father spoke openly about it and got me very interested in it. There were a couple of moments at home when I was growing up in Arizona that my Dad used to have reunions with his bomber squadron, every three, four years, they'd come over to the house and they'd have a reunion. It always perplexed me why they would start out laughing and then start drinking and then end up crying. Because when you're a kid and you hear eight or nine guys in a room, adults, your father's age, crying—it's kind of a disconcerting moment. And in putting all that together, and having learned a lot from *Schindler's List* about docudrama, about creating a reality that is conducive for the screen but not so much that you wouldn't really allow yourself to even watch it, that kind of fine line between what's tolerable and what's intolerable. I really wanted to bring to *Private Ryan* an experience that would be the experience of a soldier, not the experience of a filmmaker. And to that end I talked to a lot of soldiers who saw a lot of combat. And that informed me to inform

Robert Rodat (the screenwriter) and to begin the rewrite process. Which was to essentially create an experience that would be very first-person.

I began directing the movie before I began directing the movie. I began directing the movie on paper. Although I didn't storyboard and I didn't really know how to help tell that story except to sort of say to Robert Rodat (the screenwriter) and to a few of the others who helped me with the screenplay, "Let's get to location and see what happens." So here was one situation where I really went to location with a screenplay that all of us thought was going to change, but we didn't quite know how it was going to change. And the experience I allowed myself to have on this—which I'm really happy I did because it transformed what the film would have been had I not done this.

I knew that a lot of who these characters were going to be was going to happen on location, not really in rehearsal or in the casting process. For instance, the character that Jeremy Davies plays, who some people think is a coward, at the very end of the story, that entire story, was manufactured on location. None of that was in the screenplay. His trying to defend Mellish on the staircase and losing his nerve and dropping to the steps, not going through with saving his comrade's life, none of that was in the script. And that was just the evolution of being able to sit with these people and dealing with them like they were real people. And talking to them—what would you do in a situation like this? Who would you come through for, who would you fail for? And a lot of that was done just talking to the actors from day to day.

— 3 —

Pre-production

Clint Eastwood

Unforgiven

A director is like a platoon leader. You kind of get everybody encouraged to charge the hill with some enthusiasm.

Anthony Minghella

The English Patient

Whatever you think you're gonna do never quite happens the way that you imagine it's going to. I think that everything that you do before the day of filming pays off, even if it seems to be abandoned in every day of filming.

The extraordinary gift of filmmaking is that you're all trying to make this painting and you've got 150 or 200 people also holding the brush with you and guiding the brush. And somehow, out of that, something coherent emerges. And that comes from talking and planning. We were in different countries, with different languages. I dread to think how many languages were spoken on our set, but certainly into double figures at certain points. All the time trying to pursue your vision like a madman and like a bull, just get to where you want to go. At the same time, you need all these people to be coming with you and pushing you and pulling you and supporting you—and how that quite works I don't know.

You call in favors wherever you can when you are making a film.

Saul [Zaentz, the producer] has a mantra which sounds in public, like many of his things, a loud and ludicrous statement but in fact, in life, is a wonderful mantra, which is, "No me, no you, just the movie."

Mike Newell
Four Weddings and a Funeral

We were a little movie and we were a junk movie and a throw-away which got incredibly lucky. And so we were going to make it a year before it was finally made. And we couldn't make it that year because it was going to cost about 400–500,000 dollars more than it eventually cost. And we had to fight the budget down.

The thing has to have a life beyond what you've planned, and beyond what is on the page, beyond what anybody expects of it, it's got to have a kind of an eternal life. Somewhere along the line you have to legislate for independence and unexpectedness, changeability and unquantifiableness.

Mike Leigh
Secrets & Lies

We'll sit down at a planning meeting before the shoot. And they'll say, "OK, Scene 29, Johnny in office meets night security guard. Now is that a long scene or a short scene?" And I'll say that I think that's a long scene, I feel there's some length. Because don't forget the scene doesn't exist. So I've got to say instinctively that we'll need some time in there to rehearse and it will take us a while to shoot. There's other scenes and it's the same one line down there, and I'll say that's an instant thing or that's just a narrative scene that I know will be quick. We can knock it out. We don't need to rehearse it. I can rehearse it on the day. We can invent it on the spot, write it as we go, whatever. And it's a balancing act.

Cameron Crowe
Jerry Maguire

It was an L.A. movie and the challenge was to make it not look like the L.A. you see in movies everywhere, all the time. I have big scrapbooks and I'm always pulling stuff from magazines. There's also a great device that Sony made that allows you to take still photos from movies and videotapes and stills from commercials. There were two stills that I took from *Woman of the Year* that I had in the front page of my script and it was Spencer Tracy looking at Katharine Hepburn and then Katharine Hepburn returning that look, and I kept those two photos with me all the time. I would always flip open this first page and Tom would be like, "OK, I got it, I got it, I got it." It was amazing how much those little blasts of inspiration help when you're tired, when it's late, you can open up one of your scrapbooks and see what the soul of the scene should be.

Neil Jordan
The Crying Game

It's extraordinary, but you see how this kind of big, rather vulgar and noisy machine can be accessible, or can be molded by the spirit of one person, and that fascinated me.

The Cast
Mike Newell
Four Weddings and a Funeral

When you cast there's all sorts of practical things to take into account, like the money. Who will do the trick for you and who won't? And that obviously affects the top two or three [roles]. The thing that's most depressing is that there's a package before you, before you even start. Nobody says, "Did you see that tracking shot?" It's like the Bill Wilder line, about "Let's go see this picture, I heard it came in under budget." People don't go and see a script.

They do go and see actors. Somewhere in the casting, you try to find actors who will give you more than you put in. I see them a lot and I talk to them a lot, and it's one of the arrogances of our jobs, that you reckon that you judge people to an extent, and you hope that their selves will reveal themselves But then simply they have to be able to play it. They have to be able to do it whether they are educated or not educated, whether experienced or inexperienced.

There comes a point at which you do have to be able to say, "I back you, it's yours—I want what you are."

Every script requires different techniques and different sorts of actors, and there are all sorts of actors—I mean, they do fall into categories. The writer, who was a man whom I greatly valued and worked with immensely happily, said right at the beginning that he intended not to write anything that wasn't in the medium of jokes. We all know a joke will fall off its pedestal very quickly if you get it even slightly wrong. So it has to be very precise and had to be spoken precisely, and Hugh had the ability to speak it precisely and at the same time be believable.

There are an awful lot of actors screaming for love, and you can see it. You can see that kind; they're looking for lens the whole time, and when they find it, they start to make up to it. They start to kind of flirt with it. It's not particularly loveable, but it has to be lived with.

I talk to them to sort of get a sense of whether I'm going to be able to work with this person or not, but if someone's really going to be trouble, I think you can get a sense of that by bringing them in and meeting with them.

Oliver Stone

JFK

An actor cannot resemble a look, or wear the same clothes or have the same voice, as the person that is actually historically accurate. Therefore, a film is a fiction to begin with.

With this kind of movie, because we had to stay on the realistic side of the equation, we were trying to be believable. I tried to go against type. With Ed Asner—I mean, he's the sweetest man in the world, in person, but I wanted to make him as mean as he can be, and he did it. I tried to reveal something new each time with the actors.

I love Kevin Costner. I like his small ears that kind of like go back to his face. He's so cute. Let's be honest, you can watch that guy for three hours. It's a three-hour movie and, well, for me he anchors the movie. And he is so generous, because there are so many wonderful supporting actors in the movie, that he allows them each to have that moment. People think he has integrity and honesty, because he does, and it comes across.

Gary Oldman—everybody thinks that's Lee Oswald. They don't know that it's Gary Oldman. He just vanishes, you know. He's the most self-effacing actor I know. Amazing. He learned Russian for the film. Unfortunately, I ended up cutting out most of his Russian.

It's nice to hang out with people. It's nice not to have a formal structure, to take them to Las Vegas, or just to go to a movie. Talk to them as you're walking or doing other things, because then you get their real-life reaction. Take them out on the street, walk them around. Do other things—just don't make it a formal head on. But, alas, if you have 180 roles to cast, you do get into a formalized situation. And you do read [where an actor reads the lines from the script in a formal casting procedure]. And they come in—sometimes they come in five times. And I've learned a lot from the reading process. I have a casting director generally, and maybe a second party to read. Or another actor who comes back and helps with the reading.

Peter Weir
The Truman Show

I love the process. I mean, it is exhausting, there's no question of it, and you know it's sort of difficult when you do find yourself opposite somebody and sense their tension and nervousness in the casting. But I love to read all the parts. I'll tend to, at least in the final sessions, play the part off camera unless the actor objects. It's the most mysterious business. I sometimes think it's like a missing persons search. You're like a detective trying to find this person that exists on paper, and you're meeting people who claim to be the person. I think there's another mysterious side, some sort of other-than-verbal connection with the person — you feel you get on with them, and you're going to direct them, and you know you need that rapport. That's the most mysterious side of it.

I tend not to say much. I shoot a video — I love to shoot that wonderful system of recording and taking it home with you. Make it very informal, camera running all the time. I'll improvise sometimes. If I find somebody's interesting, but the lines are getting stuck, I'll interview them. I've done that a bit. I'll say, "Okay, you're playing the mother whose husband's just left. Let me talk to you as if I was a journalist." That sort of frees it up. I mean, what sort of life did you have, or why did this happen, or whatever. Sometimes I'll do that. Sometimes I'll ask them if they've got a scene in a church or something, and I'll get some music, put some music on.

The whole thing is, you're trying to take the dialogue down as much as you can and tell the story with the camera. I'll say, "Let's put some music on here, let's just have a quiet moment where you are just thinking to yourself." Or if it was a church scene, that you're praying or something. And then I'll move even that little camera myself and get some interesting angles. Try and break the formality of it, get them less tense.

In *The Truman Show*, the part of Christof, the Ed Harris part — somebody else was cast that didn't work out. So that was one of the only second time of my career in which a mistake was made, on my part. Differences arose, which can be very painful. That part wasn't fully realized. I think it's really fair to say this, the part of the villain as it were, in the story, was really a kind of stock character. It worked because the plot was moving at such a pace at this point that in a way, as long as the actor was competent and so forth, it would work. But I began to realize as we shot, because the villain, Christof's, stuff was to be done at the end of the shoot, that there hadn't been enough thought about this character. I began to make decisions on his behalf: Christof wouldn't do this. In meetings I used to say in pre-production, the first half hour we'll do it as if it were *The Truman Show*. And I'll be Christof, you know, we'd laugh and then get on with it. So we'd do half an hour as if I was Christof, and then I began to see — and, of course, the man's got an aesthetic, and once we'd chosen the town, it was a man who wanted a town that looked like this. Now I'd cast the part, but the character emerging through the shoot, via myself in a sense—at one stage I thought maybe I should play this. It was a joke, you know, but I sort of knew this man. You know, I knew his obsessiveness, and so I ended up with a part that really was very different to the part offered to the actor. I needed another—some other type of person. It was an awful situation.

Mel Gibson

Braveheart

Even a small role can really screw you up sometimes if you don't make a very careful choice. It took a good three months of almost on a daily basis for half a day, just looking. So I was very vigilant about going through that whole process with a very gifted casting lady who brought a smorgasbord of talent from the British Isles, and the decisions became so difficult because there were so many wonderful actors. I didn't read them or any of that kind of stuff in front of cameras. You just kind of sit down and talk to them for half an hour and just talk about anything. Talk about the story. And you didn't even know where you were going to place them. The guy that played Robert the Bruce came in, and I sensed in him an angst. He wasn't quite sure who he was. And I said, "Wow, that's kind of like what I want there." Later on, when we were talking, he told me that he'd only found out a couple of years before that he was adopted. So that there was this sense he didn't have a belonging—he was wandering. In the script, the King and the King's son were a little bit like some kind of goofy comedy team that they just put on the bozo wigs and come in and I wanted to have kind of intelligence and authority. Then someone suggested [Patrick McGoohan] and I thought, he's got this tremendous presence and he hasn't worked in forever. So I invited him to lunch and he did it to me over the lunch table. I could hardly talk to him, he was just staring at me. I said, "I know you haven't worked in a long time Mr. McGoohan, sir, does this idea even—would you have any interest—would you do this?" and like that—and he just looked at me and went, "Baaaahhahahahaha!" And I sat there and all the neurotransmitters were going, "What does that mean?" But it meant that he wanted to do it, I guess.

If my career had been dependent on reading, I wouldn't have gone anywhere. And sometimes when people come in and they give a great reading, they never progress from there. You can tell from talking to someone whether they're capable. There's something in their eyes. The guy who played the Irishman, for instance—he came in and I said, "This is the most lawless bastard I have ever met in my life." He didn't know what a chair was for! You could've lit matches in front of his breath. And he just didn't give a fuck about anything and I said, "This guy is just the kind of maniac I want."

Kid actors are tough—I mean, you meet the ones who have something natural going on and then you meet a whole other bunch, they're OK, but somebody got to them and gave them a bunch of bad habits. It's a tragedy, that they start so young and get the wrong information from someone. Some drama coach that totally destroys them so that they're like a bunch of little parrots.

This lady had a boy, who wasn't the young Wallace, but he was in a theatre group there and he was a very precocious young kid and we used him, he played the other kid. And he was funny and we thought, "He's a good kid for that part there," and we asked—she actually went up and said, "Do you know anyone—I'll give you a twenty if you dig someone up that looks like Mel Gibson." And he says, "I got your man." And he took her through the bowels of all these places and came to this kid's house and got him out from breakfast and said, "Here he is." And they brought him in and he was wonderful. He was wonderful.

Scott Hicks

Shine

Everybody said, look, it's a wonderful script and terrific, but who's going to play this so off the wall? At the top of the list was Geoffrey Rush, who I had seen in the early 80s in theatre. I'd seen him many times and I was dazzled by him even back then. I started to look at tapes of other more recent performances, and it was just astonishing. So I met with Geoffrey, and he's so different from the characters that he plays. He's calm and very centered and very intelligent and humorous. I was actually dazzled by these incredible hands that he has, which were marvelous because I was thinking that he's going to have to look like he's a pianist. We just talked for I suppose an hour. And at the end of it I offered him the role. The casting person was saying, "Don't you want to sort of test him or audition him or read?" I said, "Well, no." In a sense his whole body of work was his audition. And I said this is a part which will never test or audition right until all the work has been done to create this character. And you can't expect an actor to fully fashion this incredibly complicated character in order to do a screen test. And I felt it would inevitably be a disappointment and then cause me to doubt my own judgment.

Once I'd cast Geoffrey, it became the stumbling block. Who the hell is he?! Literally, someone said to me, "He's 40, he's made no films, what sort of failure is this guy?!" And everybody has their own agenda when they are getting involved with you on a film — there were these attempts to sort of shuffle Geoffrey out of the pack.

This process of casting is incredibly fraught with tension and this sense of your sense of the other person's vulnerability. They only get this little time to make some sort of an impression on you, and I find it utterly exhausting. And I'm still figuring out how it all works.

That ghastly process where you have dozens and dozens of children brought into you by parents. And each one of them thinks their child is a magical child. And indeed they all are, even when you can hear them tap dancing down the corridor on their way in. And most of the children had the worst thing of all, which is some experience of being coached or taught. We [with Alex Rafalowicz, who played the little boy in *Shine*] set up a chessboard and we played a few games with it. I would get him to close his eyes and I would shift pieces around on the board and say, "Tell me what move I've done." What I was looking for was his ability to play a game with me, first of all. Secondly, to focus on something that really mattered. And so I started to get a glimpse of just what kind of concentration he had and how he could keep the focus.

The approach to Sir John Gielgud got completely muddied, where I had a real sort of altercation with this particular agent who was determined to replace Geoffrey with a client of his. And I said, we've come to talk about the part of Gielgud. And we left, leaving the script for Gielgud there. And then learned two days later that he had passed, Gielgud had passed on the script, and I said that was a terrible shame. And months go past in which we look for someone else. All these desperate attempts to find some great theatrical knight! We came to a point where I sent the casting lady to London and she went to see someone else in the agency and told him what this role was and he said, "Well, this sounds perfect for Sir John Gielgud!" And she said, "Well, sadly, he passed," and he said, "I beg your pardon? Let me just tell you that everything that Sir John reads goes through me, so let's just start this conversation again." And within 24 hours he had accepted the role!

Steven Spielberg

Amistad

I had sort of built in for myself a golden parachute. I was a little nuts to have decided to make three movies in 12 months. After I had committed to *Amistad* and I had everyone to move over from one production to the other, I realized that perhaps I was making a mistake. So I set a very high water mark and I basically said that if I don't find the right power for Cinque, there's no reason to make the picture. Just when I decided I was not making the picture, along came this young man, Djimon Hounsou. He was homeless on the streets of Paris for a number of years and then was discovered by Herb Ritts, the fashion photographer. Then he found his way to New York, and then found his way to Los Angeles, and he answered an open casting call, which often happens. I wasn't looking for well-known actors to play the Africans. I wanted people who spoke all the different dialects. So the thing to do was to have open casting calls where you actually put ads in papers in Atlanta, Boston, San Francisco, Los Angeles, Chicago. And all the different African communities would come to those casting calls and they would be put on videotape. So, Vickie Thomas, the casting lady, and I looked at hundreds and hundreds of hours of videotape. What I do when I have an actor read a scene is, I never give them the scene out of the movie, because I get sick and tired of hearing the scene thirty times a day. I don't want to hear the scenes two months in advance and then have to hear them again on the day [of shooting]. So, instead, we'll just write a mock scene that has all the emotional beats of the scene that's in the picture.

This tape went into the player, and there were 20 actors on the tape, all reading for Cinque, and he came on the tape, it was a wake up call. It was probably the most phenomenal awakening I've ever had. Next to maybe discovering Ralph Fiennes for *Schindler's List*, which really woke me up. When Djimon came on the tape, it was the power of what he *didn't* say that made me say to Vickie, I pray he's in L.A., because I want to see him today. And he was, and he came in the day I saw the tape. And I interviewed him, or spoke with him for a while. The problem that I've had sometimes in the past is, certain actors that aren't actors per se, they're aspiring actors — they get in a room with me, and they get all clammed up, and I do a lot of work to relax them! And Djimon came into the room, and he was not intimidated by anybody. And it was really one of those things where after he left the meeting, the entire office was a buzz. He had left a real scent and a charisma behind him.

I had not worked with Anthony Hopkins before. I had always wanted to work with him, and one day I was presenting at the Academy Awards one year and I met him for the first time in the green room, and we were both rehearsing our presentation speeches and we did that thing that you always do in Hollywood, you always hear done . . . . you say, "Gee, I really wanna work with you someday." That happens all the time, actors and directors are always saying, "I love your work, I wanna work with you some day" . . . and I really meant it. But I didn't think of him as my first choice for John Quincy Adams. I had five other actors turn me down. I had five actors, that I thought I wanted, say no to the part for various reasons. Paul Scofield felt that he had touched on the tone of that character in *The Crucible*. Paul Newman just didn't want to work in that window [a specific time available for production]. I had one talk with Anthony Hopkins on the telephone, and he talked to me in the voice of John Quincy Adams. And it was a telephone interview — that was all we had together — and that was all it took for me to say, if he wants to still do it after my hesitating so much, I'd love to do it with him.

Saving Private Ryan

I got Tom involved from the moment I read the script. But the rest of the cast was a little more problematic, because I have a different kind of process for casting. And that is, I spend a lot of time looking at actors' reels—television, movies, whatever they've done. I find it more valuable for me to see someone's work before I meet them, and often I won't even meet them. I will just cast them based on something I've seen of theirs or a reading they've done on videotape for me. I don't like to read actors on videotape based on the screenplay I'm directing. Because in my early films, when I did that, I'd get so sick of the scene—you hear it 120 times, and then you really throw out the baby with the bathwater. Because you go back to the writer and say, I'm sick of this scene—write me a new one, because it's a test scene. So I usually write sides or have the writer construct sides that are completely different than the screenplay but still reflect the character. And I judge that way. In the case of *Ryan*, I didn't meet any of the actors until we got to Ireland. I just didn't want to. I had a couple of criteria for myself. One was, I'm a big collector of *Life* magazine. Because I've made so many movies that take place in the 1940s. and it's very hard to find faces today that look like the faces of 20-, 22-year olds back in 1944. So I was really in a face hunt before I was in a talent hunt. And when my casting director had brought me some sensational people—most of them, I said, they don't look like 1940s kids. They look like modern kids. So right away, that just brought down the possibilities to a select few, and then of that select few I was very fortunate that—with the exception of Jeremy Davies, who plays Corporal Upham, whom I'd met through my wife, who was co-starring with him in a movie; I met him on a location in Texas and cast him right there in Texas—aside from him, it was really an interesting experiment which I had never done before in that way.

Anthony Minghella
The English Patient

It came to the point of casting and Saul [Zaentz, the producer] said, "Where do we begin?" And what I said to him was that this is one thing that I want to do by myself. I think it was a great index to his generosity in the sense that he has been in every casting session of every film he's worked on, and this was the first time that he didn't come. I don't like to read with actors. It's a mysterious thing, and most of it has to do with the horrible, excruciating intimacy that you're trying to collect in a room with them. So I sit in a basement meeting actors for hours and hours and hours. Juliette Binoche was the first. Juliette Binoche was dancing through the pages of that book when I read it. And I had no idea why but as soon as I talked to Saul, the way I got him interested in the project was, I said, "There's a part for Juliette Binoche in it."

I use a casting person who's always worked with me as a writer and a director in London, Michelle Gish.

The interesting thing about casting this film is that the danger of being the writer as well as the director is that you have completed something too soon. You've got in your mind, particularly with me, the sound of a character. And then you can become over-proprietorial of each moment. The odd thing for me is that Kristin Scott Thomas is so far from the idea I had in my head when I was writing. And the reason it took me so long to cast that part was the Katherine I had in mind was as far away from Kristin Scott Thomas as could be imagined. The first time I met her, I think we both wanted to leave the room after about five or ten minutes. But we were locked into having dinner together, and it was an unhappy event. It wasn't because I didn't think she was a good actor—I thought she was a fantastic actor. It's just, the music in her was so far away from the music that I had heard when I was writing. When I went back to the screenplay, every time I tried to find an actor, her noise infiltrated my thinking. What happens is, the list gradually gets smaller and smaller until there's only one name there. Then what happens is that your evangelism for that person knows no bounds.

One of the things I did do—and this was a surprise to me; I think Saul prompted me to do this, I'm in his debt to this—he said, "Why don't you start to put people in a room together?" I did have a day working with Ralph [Fiennes] with the various possible people. Now I found that actually one of the most uncomfortable days, since I'm terrible at saying no and I hate feeling I've disappointed anybody. The reading that we did was really an excuse to see what alchemy there might be, and I think that it became very evident immediately to me, once we did that process, who was right. The danger is that while you're watching as a director trying to work out what's going on, the actor, too, is responding. And I made a pact with Ralph at the beginning of the day, which was, don't say anything to me until the end of the day—then we'll trade our feelings. And there were lots of very glamorous actresses in this room, and they all were ravishing, and Ralph seemed very interested in being ravished by them. And all I thought was, "Oh no, he thinks of them as so beautiful, he's bound to say he likes her," and it was so manifest to me instantly that Kristin was the right person. And he said at the end of the day, I know exactly who it should be, before I'd even opened my mouth, which disconcerted me. And thank God he felt as passionately [about Kristin] as I did.

Roberto Benigni
Life Is Beautiful

When I'm casting, the process in Italy preparing movies is much different than the United States, much different because we don't have studios. Me, I am an independent, so I'm preparing when I am casting the movie, there is something very much a mystery. How to choose? Something very "mysterical" because you don't understand exactly what happened with the face I am thinking or dreaming one face. Things change and it's like the movie is choosing, really. Like something happens, something strange inexpressible, unspeakable, inexplicable that I cannot to understand why I choose. But something happens and this is really very mysterical thing. And this is very wonderful—for example, the little boy, I was testing and he comes with an overcoat like a really little clown. And he told me, "I dreamt of you last night, Roberto." Because it was the movie like grabbing him. And sometimes it's so hard because in Italy we don't have such an amount of actors. I like actors very very much. For example, Danco (who plays the Uncle), he is a theatre actor, very old, and never did movies before, but what an elegance, what a man. He's such a wonderful actor, the face, and he could be the grandfather of the little boy and really my uncle. This was by accident. There is the Italian writer, Machiavelli, who said, "There are people who know everything, but that's all they know." Is very good, because when I learn that "everything," I am missing something.

For the female protagonist I chose Nicoletta Breschi because, Mamma mia, I love so much! I respect her as an actress because in my mind when I'm thinking about something feminine, her face comes up immediately!

Another example, my friend in the movie is very important because we are both together all the first part of the movie. He was bigger and taller than me. I shoot a lot with someone small, tall, and fat, skinny, like we call that August and white, no cloud. They have to work together. And also there is some chemical that happen. Chemistry. And this also is so difficult to understand. Because I called him and I said, "No, sorry, but you are not the right person," it's terrible. Then I shoot with some other actor, and then at the end by accident I put in the wrong cassette and I see again him! And it was momentous, it was the first one! And I called him and said, "You are wonderful, wonderful!" And he couldn't believe!

Clint Eastwood

Unforgiven

Well, the unfortunate thing about being an actor first, and then being a director later on in life, is that you've gone through the acting process. You've gone through the cattle calls. You've beaten your head against the door many times. So, it's very difficult for me to meet actors. I'd hire everybody that came in the room! But fortunately, now, with the videotape—and I have a casting lady now who is very sensitive to actors' feelings, so she will put people on tape so I can look at them without encouraging them falsely. Then when I've made up my mind, when I'm ninety percent there, then I like to meet them maybe and say hello.

I don't like readings a lot of times, because a lot of very good actors are not very good readers.

If I have the person come in, it's just to meet them, to feel how at ease they are. I'll maybe go into the philosophy about the part a little bit, but I'll try not to intellectualize it to death.

If you've seen the actor's work and know what they can do and they seem to be in line with the understanding of the character you're gonna ask them to portray, there's really no reason to beat it to death and beat them to death and make everybody all nervous and upset. Sometimes you go through many, many actors. On one occasion I looked at the tape of [only] one girl and I hired her. And my casting lady said, "Do you want to look at some more?" and I said, "No, no, this is the one I want, on the next picture we'll go through the other tapes, but on this particular one I want this girl." If you're in doubt, then maybe you should look further. But if you see something, you've got to say, "OK, that's the way I want to go." I'll tell you about an experience that happened to me once in Europe. I had someone send a tape over of an actor from Munich, and I said, "This guy will be perfect, yeah, this guy—I like his face, I like every-thing about him, hire him." When he showed up on the set, it was another actor! And I thought, it's not the same guy! So I kind of went off in the corner and sat there. What am I gonna do? How am I gonna handle this? Then I looked at the guy, and he had an interesting look, and a good face, so I said, you know, I'm not gonna tamper with this. I'm gonna go with this guy anyway! I didn't have the heart to come up to him and say, "You know, you're not the guy," and send him all the way back home.

Pictures are very important. A lot of times people send in the pic-tures, and I've done that same thing myself as an actor. You submit the picture and resume and you figure, that's gonna go in the waste-basket. But it is important, because sometimes you are looking for a face that is specific, because you have a certain kind of role and you feel that—that role is going to be reoccurring and that face has to be very recognizable, and the ability of the actor is important, but the look is very important, too.

Cameron Crowe

Jerry Maguire

When Hanks chose to direct his own movie rather than be in *Jerry Maguire*, I immediately wanted it to go to Tom Cruise. He was the "Magic Bus" to me.

Tom Cruise read it and called me and said, "This is a part I'm very interested in playing; it's different." He said, "I'm coming to L.A. in a few weeks—let me read it out loud for you to see if I'm right for it," which was great. I did have friends who said, "He'll never play a loser." And in fact he was dying to play someone who was on the ropes. And it all blossomed from there.

Once I had the actor, I wanted to surround him with fresh faces— you feel like you're glimpsing real life. That's the greatest gift of all, and so it was also rewarding to find newcomers and put them next to Cruise. And you start to forget that it's Tom Cruise. You start to believe that you're in another world.

I had a casting lady I really loved, Gail Levin. She was tireless and we basically saw as many people as we could. And Tom was very available to us. So he read with many, many actors from bit parts to, of course, his leading lady. And Renee [Zellweger] was the one that came in and kind of punctured everything that you expect to see in a movie starring Tom. She came in a number of times. The first time she came in, she had read the script and didn't really have a strong take on it. But this seemed like the type of person a character like Jerry Maguire would see around the office and not take that seriously, and her beauty or her depth would appear later. Then she came back and everything that was great about her the day before was sort of gone. She'd had a problem with her dog. She was in pieces and unable to really connect. Sort of an awful moment, when an actor leaves the room and hasn't quite lived up to the advance hype. And so for about a month we didn't speak to Renee. And then Gail brought her name up again, and she came in and nailed it. Tom was there. I actually had a video camera going. She flies into the room in all of her "Reneeness," and she's kind of spinning around and talking about things that happened to her that day. In the background you see Tom regarding her in that great way that Spencer Tracy regards Katharine Hepburn. Just someone watching this person who, as it happens, was going to play a big part in his future life. And it was all there in the first moment. She had the qualities that set him off both personally and in the character, and you just die for that.

The little boy was tough. The little boy was written to be a joyous little guy, but I sort of fell in love with this young kid who was quiet and sad. And I thought, well, this brings out a different aspect of the script. This is a kid who has truly lost his dad. This is a sad kid. And what if Jerry Maguire sees himself in that kid? And gives that kid a relationship that he hadn't had. And so I hired him. So I was trying to adapt to this sad kid and it wasn't working. He did not want to be an actor and wasn't an actor. And so three weeks in, we replaced him. And it was a very odd and terrible thing. Not to the kid—I think the kid was happy. A kid was found by one of our producers. And he was in fact everything that I didn't want in the kid that was going to be in the movie. His one experience was a McDonald's commercial. And to me that's the hellish version of kids in movies. So I kind of, in an exhausted state, went into the hotel room where the kid and his parents were staying. And I was really tired. I said, "Hi, how are you doing?" The guy said, "We think our child is a magical child." I said, "Great, great, great, great, where is he?" So out of the bathroom comes trotting this little kid. His hair is exactly as it is in the movie. His glasses are the same as in the movie. I would never make up those glasses and that look. That was him. The kid was on fire. Knew the lines, and said, "I've wanted to be an actor my whole life." He's five! He's great. And we took him to a set and put him in the room with Tom. And Tom started doing some scenes and Tom looked over to me like, "Whoa, this kid's pretty good." So we finished our little audition, and then the kid said, "I just want to tell you that my favorite movie is *Top Gun* and I've seen it twenty times." And at that point Tom turned into perfect profile and said, "I feel the need—the need for speed." And the kid just exploded and never came down. We hired him, and everything you see in the movie is his ride. That was a lucky break.

Robert Zemeckis

Forrest Gump

I've seen movies where there are two really good actors, acting their butts off on a screen, and you just say, "I don't believe this for a minute." And so in the case of *Forrest Gump*, it was like a rule that no actress would get the job unless she screen tested with Tom. I make actors read because I think there's a real method to the madness. I talk to them to get a sense of whether I'm going to be able to work with this person or not. But if someone is really going to be trouble, I think you can get a sense of that by bringing them in and meeting with them. I was fortunate to have Tom Hanks—he's a film actor, he knows the medium he's working in, so he's more willing to come in and read with potential actors. I'm a big believer in videotape, even though I have to make deals with actors sometimes to swear to them that I won't copy the tape and I'll let them have the tape so they can burn it after. But I believe in videotape for two reasons: I believe that something happens to performers—I believe in screen presence. And while I'm sitting there at the end of the day and I'm exhausted and I've seen twenty people, an actor might be doing the greatest performance, the greatest reading, and I'm not seeing it because I just got off the phone with the head of the studio who is just screaming at me over money or something. So I like to be able to have it recorded so I can look at it again and evaluate it at a different time. I screen tested the little kids for the movie, mainly because I wanted to make sure they weren't going to crack under the pressure of having a crew hanging around them. Once you walk on a sound stage it's a lot more serious than videotaping somebody in your office.

There's always that time when you'll see one person and you'll just get that feeling that, wow, they've nailed it. But in some cases, I see hundreds of actors. We actually scoured the nation to find the young Forrest and found him just wading through videotapes, and boom, he just popped off—he went into an open call in Mississippi. And that's how we got him. His mother had never been on an airplane until we flew him out for his screen test.

Rob Reiner
A Few Good Men

I actually read everybody, and I work with the actors in the readings at times. In certain films that I make, in the comedies, you have to have a certain rhythm and sense of humor, and there are certain joke constructions that only work if you perform them a certain way. You don't want to get an actor in there that isn't going to ever get that rhythm for you, because if they don't, then the joke doesn't work—

then the scene doesn't work. And this is not to denigrate drama at all because, that's hard to do, but comedy is way, way more difficult, and anybody who has done both will let you know that.

There are not a lot of good people who do comedy. That's why you have to see a lot of people, because somebody has to come in and just hit the right notes. It's like a great studio musician. You look at a great studio musician, and he'll hit every note right, every time. And a great comedic actor will do the same thing. But you have to see whether or not they can do it. If they don't have the rhythm, the instinct to do it, you can't teach them.

We got so much bad press on using these movie stars, and I kept thinking, well, wait a minute here—a movie star, well, where are they supposed to go except be in a movie? It's like, that's what they do! Do you remember in the thirties, forties, and fifties—you'd watch movies, you'd see Burt Lancaster and Kirk Douglas, or Jimmy Stewart and Henry Fonda would be in the same movie—you'd go, "Wow, isn't this great, I get to see a movie with two people I like!" Now it's like, how dare you, bastard, put these people I like in a movie! You got Tom Cruise *and* Jack Nicholson in the movie, what the hell is the matter with you!?

Tom [Cruise] was the first one I contacted, and he was the one I knew I really had to have for the film because there were so few actors who were the right age who can command the kind of screen presence and have power, that I knew was necessary to stand up to whomever was gonna play Jessop. And also could play this kind of glib wise guy thing in the first part of the film. Tom gets discounted for being pretty and sexy and original and stuff, but, the fact is, he's a great actor, this guy. Look at this guy's body of work—*Rain Man*, *The Color of Money*.

I sent Tom [Cruise] to see the play [*A Few Good Men*]. I called him and I said, "I'd be interested in you to do this," and he said, "I'll do it" And I said, "No, no, see the play—don't say you'll do it. You don't even know what it is yet. Why don't you go and look at it and you'll see. Maybe it's something you don't think you could do." But I knew he could do it, and he saw the play and said, "OK."

Kiefer [Sutherland], I had worked with before on *Stand by Me*, so I knew I wanted him. Kevin Bacon I didn't read because I had also

seen all of his work and knew. With Kevin Pollak, I did read because
Kevin Pollak had never done anything like this. He was a stand up
comedian. But, if you've seen an actor, you know what a guy can do,
you can see it in their work, so most of the time, I don't even read.
Sometimes I haven't even met the actor, I just call them up and say,
"Do you want to do this?"

John Madden
Shakespeare in Love

It is a very mysterious process. What is strange is, you're looking —
at least, you have a very strong sense, or at least you think you have
a strong sense, about who the person should be and what the person should be and what — usually the process I have is learning that
I haven't got the right idea, and when the person comes along who
is right, they tell me that person is right. But you have to go into it
with the apparatus of certainty, that this is what the part needs. And
you articulate that to producers and casting directors and to other
people. And it's mystical in many ways, because you frequently go
through a very long process — I've done this and then offered the
part to somebody and they say, "Well, I don't want to do it." Which
can be absolutely devastating, because you've gone through this
whole process only to find that actually you were wrong. Because
you are wrong if they don't want to do it. There's no point — I've
made that mistake, too — of forcing somebody to do a part when
actually they don't want to. I made it axiomatic that I had to read
everybody. It seemed to me that I was going to be doing the actor a
favor because it's very very unusual material. It's not that I wasn't
necessarily able to evaluate somebody who's work I knew, but I
didn't think I was going to find a Will or a Viola that way. Although
I have to say Gwyneth [Paltrow] was the first choice for that part.
But she wasn't initially available. I mean, I knew her from an earlier audition. But Will was incredible — that was quite a nut to crack.
I opened the book as wide as I possibly could. I was certainly considering everybody from this country or from any English-speaking
country. But I — in my heart of hearts I thought, he's got to be
English, surely, or I'll never be able to hold my head up in my own

country again. But I couldn't rule out the possibility that there was going to be a male Gwyneth Paltrow somewhere. It was a very very long process, in which certain actors simply ruled themselves out of consideration before the audition. Some during the audition, some immediately after the audition. Because it's the kind of material where the demands of the actor were quite extraordinary. I mean to be able to inhabit the language, the world, the humor—just so many things at once.

I went past Joe [Fiennes] the first time. Because I still had a kind of rigid notion and, frankly, I was beginning to kind of get despairing about whether or not I would ever find this person. That was such a sort of gut terror. I mean, for my own salvation, however wonderful the script was, I didn't want to make the movie if we didn't have the right combination. And I think, because of that, I was slightly blind, looking at who I was looking at. We got way, way, way down the line and I thought, this is crazy, this is absolutely crazy—I can't pass up this movie, it's too good. So I went back and I looked at the tapes again—I do the same thing and put everybody on tape. And I looked at Joe and I thought, this is, he's . . . it wasn't a good audition, in fairness to him. No, the opposite actually. It wasn't in fairness to me, it wasn't a good audition. But he . . . I looked at him and I thought, he's so—visually, he's so perfect for it. So I said, come in and don't prepare. Because Joe is an incredibly diligent and studious person who really likes to come prepared. And I said, don't come prepared—I said to his agent, have him come in tomorrow so we can just loosen up. But he wouldn't do that. And if I was going to get him back, he had to come in on his own terms, and he did. So we had to spend about half a morning deconstructing and just loosening up. I had a new scene that came out of the rewrites that we were doing, which was the scene between him and Marlowe at the beginning of the movie. Where he says he hasn't written anything, and Marlowe starts to spin the idea of *Romeo and Juliet* to him. And one of the things I worried about Joe was whether or not he would have the comic deftness that, of course, you can now see on the screen. And he just pulled this out of my bag. I hadn't even thought about it till just the night before, and I said, "Come on, let's read this. Let's work with this a little bit." And a sort of spark started to happen. Which he then—Joe's

instinct is to mistrust what he's just done and then go and do something completely different. So you kind of haul him back—and I put
all of this on tape. And I began to feel just that sort of tingle, thinking,
I'm sure there is something here. I found him tremendously attractive
as a person, very open and vulnerable and sweet. Everything that I'd
been looking for but hadn't quite been able to articulate. I needed
somebody who had the intelligence but also, you know, could play
Romeo at the end of the movie. And the movie's about first love, so
you need that sort of innocence as well.

   We worked on scenes, and we'd take different ways through the
scenes, I'd give him different actions to play—in particular, the boat
scene. You can play that scene, for example, as if he knows perfectly
well who he's talking to, which will reveal something about the
scene, or as if he has no idea, as if he's testing her. You shift the
actions around so that different things start to come out. And in that
process you begin to sense the kind of palette that he can work with
and you can work with. You find out also the most crucial thing of
all, which is whether you're gonna have a relationship there that you
can trust.

Quentin Tarantino

Pulp Fiction

Coming at casting from, like, an acting background, when I was trying to be a professional actor, I never found out a way to crack the
casting process. I always knew that I walked out of that room and
they didn't see what I had to offer. And it's like—especially when
you don't go on that many of them, all right? You can go on one, the
fucking weight of the world is riding on it, all right? And who can
give a performance when the weight of the world is riding on the
outcome? So, I had to figure out how I was going to approach this. I
wanted every single person to read. It's not that I want them to come
in and give a great performance—and some of them do—some of
them come in and they just kick your ass. But it's like, it's more—I
want to get a sense of their dynamic. What's *really* important is the
putting of actors together. You don't cast this person and arbitrarily
that person. They all have to go together. One of the reasons I cast

Maria de Medeiros in the part of Bruce Willis' girlfriend in the movie, was because I knew I was going to cast Bruce. . . . If I had already cast any other actor to play Butch, Maria may or may not have gotten the part.

When you're starting the film, you've got these lists of people and everyone is considered. One of the things that I do in casting is meeting the people, just kinda getting, feeling like you get to know them a little bit and everything. And if it's a situation where it's like, I'm starting to really think and starting to narrow it down, I make everybody read with me, all right? Not with anybody else in the room, even if it means they have to get drunk before they do it! I'm just at their apartment or they're at my house or something like that, and we're just gonna read it and it's not about performance. I did that with Tim Roth on *Reservoir Dogs*. He would not read. His feeling was, "I stand a better chance at getting this part, you judging my past work, than if I audition for you, because I know I won't get it if I audition." And so what happened was we just went out and had lunch, lunch turned to dinner, dinner turned into drinks in a bar, turned into 2 o'clock in the morning when the bar's getting ready to close and we're both completely shitfaced. And he goes, "I'll read for you now." And we read the whole damn script.

I very much believe in the idea of the director having a rep company. Most of the directors that I love have that. I wrote Pumpkin and Honey Bunny for Tim Roth and Amanda Plummer, and the reason that they're even in the film is, I bumped into the two of them one time at a party and they're friends, and I saw them together and I literally—it's one of the only times I've had it in my life—I literally had a director moment. I have got to put these two people together in a movie. In the case of Mia—she's my favorite character, I don't have the slightest idea where she came from. She's not me, she's not anybody I know. I didn't know what she looked like and I was going to find her. That was going to be my thing. I was going to find Mia and when I met her, I would know. I was very open—she could have been older, she could have been black, she could have been white, she could have been Chinese, she could have been English. I was interested in seeing all those different Mias, just knowing that when I met her I would know it. And what happened was, I ended up having dinner with Uma Thurman, and it was just in the course of having dinner with her that I realized, she's Mia. So what happened was, I went back and just started auditioning again, but now I couldn't get Uma out of my mind. So then we got together again in New York and had dinner. We're just sitting there talking, we're talking all this subtext stuff about the character. She was very scared about reading and it was very like, "Quentin, I'm a really good actress, please don't judge me by what I'm going to do here. It's not about being good—I don't worry about that, let's just do it." And so I had a couple of dinners with a couple of actresses, and I felt I was cheating on her.

When it comes to casting, I'll see people, I'll see people and then at a certain point, I can't see anybody else. OK? I don't care if it's my favorite actor in the world and they want to come in, when I get to that point, I've kind of more or less made a decision.

It was big deal getting Ving to play Marsellus, because there's a whole lot of males that will not do an anal rape scene. That was one of the things that when the actors would come in, we had to talk about it. And one of the things that Ving said and it was really cool, not only did he come and kick everybody's ass with his wonderful reading and I've always been a fan of his, we sat and started talking and I go, "How do you feel about the rape?" And we talked and he goes, "Well, you know, that's the thing I'm attracted to as far as this part is concerned." And I said, "Well, why?" And he goes, "Because the way I look, I don't ever get the opportunity to play very many vulnerable people. And this is the most vulnerable motherfucker I'm ever gonna play."

Michael Radford

Il Postino

The secret of casting is, once you've cast somebody, you forget all about why you've cast them, and you look at that person and then you build the part around them. Because very often you don't get the person that you want—and if you don't, the secret of making them look like "that was the person you wanted" is to recreate the part. That's what I did with the girl. If I had actually paid attention to her reading, I'd never have chosen her. Sum total of her experience was she had been in a spaghetti commercial. I must have seen every young actress in Italy. It was terrible. Day after day these beautiful women used to come past me, and in Italy you're an actress if you wake up one morning and say, "Hey! I'd like to be an actress." And you get a photographer and you take a topless picture of yourself, and that's it. You know you're in the profession. I mean, it was the most awful reading I've ever come across. But when she smiled, she lit up. So I just rewrote the part for her. She was the only person who'd come in who I thought was a real movie star.

The difficult thing was, I speak good Italian, but I don't understand the nuances of the culture. And I remember sitting in a café in the Plaza del le Coppollo, and I saw these two English girls come in and just order a cup of coffee, and I looked at them and in that one phrase when they said, "Could we have a cup of coffee," I knew why they were in Rome, where they bought their clothes, who their boyfriends were. Being amongst the Italians I would ask Massimo [Troisi, the star and his co-producer and writer], I'd say, " I really like this girl or I really like this actor," and he'd say, "Ma-es putinato." I went back to my assistant, I'd say, "What does 'putinato' mean?" And it means he's disgraced himself. What it meant was that they'd been in a film by a rival comic.

Some people just walk in and you say, "I just want to give you this part." I mean literally, I have done that on a couple of occasions. Even though they might not look anything like you imagined when you started, you think this person has something. For instance, the guy who played the telegraph operator. I do read people, but then I don't pay much attention to it. I read them mainly because I don't know what else to do when I'm talking, and sometimes it can tell you certain things. It can tell you, particularly with the character actors. I think this is the most dangerous area of making a picture, because a lot of character actors have basically done one thing all their lives and they get into terrible bad habits. I had to cast thin people in this movie, because in Italy in 1952, people didn't have enough to eat. Particularly in the south of Italy. And everybody in Italy now has a lot to eat, it's a rich country. So everybody's a fat person and to find thin people was extremely difficult.

The thing about Philippe Noiret is, one, he's a wonderful actor, he's made 117 movies and I never get bored of looking at him; two, he looks exactly like Pablo Neruda. So I sent him the screenplay. He got it on Thursday morning; three o'clock on Thursday afternoon, he rang me up and said, "Don't give this part to anybody else." And I never doubted that he was the guy to play this role. We then had to deal with the fact that he had to do it in French.

Frank Darabont
The Shawshank Redemption

You're just cruising on instinct and hoping for the best. Pinning the eight-by-tens [actors' photographs] up on the wall, playing mix and match. What if this guy plays that? Certainly in *Shawshank* there was sort of an ensemble thing happening. You wind up putting those faces up on the wall, and you wind up eating a lot of take-out food late at night with your casting director. All of our extras were local to Mansfield, Ohio, and surrounding areas, so there were a lot of unemployed steelworkers that were really happy to come work for the summer. We actually did have a few guards from the new prison up the road. We had them come in and audition, and there were a couple of them with speaking lines in the movie.

Sometimes the politics of things are such that you can't get certain guys to read — you have to make them an offer, so that was what we did. So we went in kind of with our fingers crossed. Our casting person would bring the actors in for specific roles, and there were a few cases actually where somebody would walk out the door and I would say, "What about this guy for that guy?" Blatch, the killer, he's on screen for like 45 seconds in the movie. He's the one who actually did commit the murder. This guy came in to read for one of the cons and he walked out the door and I said, "I have *got* to see this guy read Blatch." Sometimes there's just something about an actor that just triggers something. He came back in, he read for Blatch, and I was chilled and delighted. You take everybody that walks through the door. But, what you get actually on film versus videotape in an office is something else altogether. Sometimes you wind up with much more than you thought and sometimes you're watching dailies saying, "What were we thinking?" We were pretty much focused on casting for about three months.

Curtis Hanson
L.A. Confidential

I got this idea in my head that I wanted to cast actors that the audience was not already familiar with. That they did not already have an emotional history, the way that we all do with movie stars. We see them, and we immediately have feelings, based on past pictures. With Russell Crowe and Guy Pearce, my two leads in essence from Australia, most of the audience doesn't know these actors and consequently they don't know how they feel about them. They don't know who they like and who they don't like. This was obviously a hurdle, in terms of getting the financing for the picture, because normally we are all in the position of going to stars and saying, will you help me arrange the financing for the movie?

Russell Crowe I had seen in an Australian picture called *Romper Stomper*, and he had just knocked me out in that movie. He plays a neo-Nazi skinhead, and I knew that he could play the brutal side of Bud White. I then brought him over here from Australia and met him and worked with him and subsequently put him on tape doing a test to convince everybody that he could play the complete character. Guy Pearce, it was sort of a Cinderella story for actors. It was on a day when I was seeing an actor every 15 minutes and Mali Finn, my extraordinary casting lady, brought him in. He walked in the door, I had no idea who he was, and I could tell he was Australian when he said "Hello," and he sat down and just did a great reading. And I gave him some direction and had him just make some adjustments, and then worked with him and put him on tape.

The lesson that I learned is that I was then able to go to Kevin Spacey, Kim Basinger, Danny DeVito, one after the other, and say, we're starting this picture in a few weeks and I would love you to be a part of it, rather than asking them to be the locomotive that was pulling the train. And by being able to approach them as actors, instead of as, say, "the financing getter," they immediately jumped on board, and I put that cast together actually in just a couple of weeks.

I see actors more than once, and work with them and try to give them some direction, even if not the direction I want to go ultimately, but to just see how they handle the adjustments and also see how I get along with them.

And I think who would I like to see, and who can capture the essence of the character, number one—but also, who has the capacity to surprise me. And who can I maybe give an opportunity to that they haven't had before, where they can, in a sense, blossom.

Mike Leigh
Secrets & Lies

It's very important, the choice of actors and the influence that that has on what happens in the film. It would be quite wrong for anyone to get the idea that it doesn't really matter what actors I get, because I could make the same film no matter what actors they were. The choice of actors always, in a quite specific way with my films, goes some way to defining what the film is.

There is a particular kind of rapport which I like to have with each actor, because I do collaborate with each actor to create the character, and that rapport really moves in the direction of creating the character.

Marianne Jean-Baptiste, who plays Hortense, really embodies a new generation of young black actors in the United Kingdom who have the sophistication to be able to play black characters without feeling the need to act an agenda, and that is a great breakthrough. I had worked with her in a stage play a few years ago in London and I felt I just wanted to get her up there on the screen.

One of the things that motivates me is getting actors who are creative in their own right as artists and who are going to do something special.

I see a lot of actors. Because I can't say, "Well, we'll see all the heroines this week and all the old guys in the second." I just don't know who I'm looking for. And my worst problem is, I don't want to miss anybody.

I have a couple of casting people who are able to say, "You ought to see so and so," or whatever. And I have an assistant. But in the end

I have to sit in a room for a long time. And I see actors every twenty minutes, and I just talk to them and have them talk to me. The first event is meeting people, which is to say, I just get them to talk about themselves. I just find out about them and meet them a bit. And the ones that seem worth pursuing, I ask back, and I spend an hour and it takes me a hell of a long time! I spend a whole hour, one to one, with every actor that I call back. I do work one to one separately with each actor to get a character going, and broadly speaking, that's done by getting the character who in the end is based on a real person. I get the actor in and ask them to talk about and do somebody, do him or her "by themself" in a room, not doing very much. I ask them to think about somebody and talk about the person and to do that person. And then we may do a bit more work to develop what they did. Then we talk about it. It is all about an actor going into character and sustaining being a character in an improvisation and pretending that it's real. I'm asking you not to perform a monologue or a soliloquy, or to do an audition piece or to demonstrate. Some actors have an ability to be real, have a sense of what becoming somebody is, and others don't. The truth is that there are actors who have this natural instinct for doing real people and for what the world is about, and are turned on by that. And there are actors for whom it's all about showing off or performing in a quite obvious sort of way.

If an actor is half good, you don't need to know whether they can read. It's what they are all about which is the key.

Barry Levinson

Bugsy

I'm always amazed at the amount of people who turn down a part because they don't see what it is that you're making. So they read something in a different way, and they don't get it. I can't think of a movie that I made that somebody who I thought was perfect for it said "No, I don't see it." In the final analysis it's actually for the best, because that person would probably be constantly trying to do another film than the movie you're doing. There are some actors always saying, "I'd really love to work with you, I love your movies, I just don't see this movie, this character." I've always sort of found that happens along the way, and then I realize that it's actually for the best. Because then you end up with the actors that have the sensibility you have towards the work that you're trying to do. I've had cases where basically the agent will turn down the role for an actor, because he'll say, "Well, you know, they don't do ensemble work."

The process is tedious because I see an enormous amount of people for a lot of the roles—I will see sometimes hundreds for a small role. I'm looking for something that seems right. You've got this whole big cast and everything has to connect. All of these people have to sort of fit, all of their different kinds of energies and rhythms, because all actors have different rhythms. You're looking for a certain rhythm that fits, and you're trying to couple that all together. It's a little bit like putting the orchestra together. You need a little of this and a little of that. Sometimes somebody may be doing some great work, but it may not be right for the movie and it can kick the movie out of balance for me.

What happens is, you're always racing that clock. In *Bugsy* we didn't have a Meyer Lansky until a week before his role actually started. I had thought of Ben Kingsley, and he happened to be in town. He came in, and it's an interesting situation. You have a man who won an Academy Award, and he's a brilliant actor. Except he's supposed to be this New York Jew—and this guy was Gandhi. I, in the politest way, I tried to say, "Ben, I think you're terrific, but what do you think?"

I don't want to say "Would you come back and read this role?" Which is what I'm really kind of asking for. Because if he can't deliver that accent and that kind of character, we're going to be in trouble. And he said, "Why don't I come back tomorrow and read for you?" A very proper English accent, he had. I said, "That's a terrific idea." He came back and he read like two lines, and I said, "Ben, you don't have to go on, it's terrific." That's how that happened. For him to understand the dilemma and have the confidence in himself as an actor to suggest that—I was beside myself.

If the actor is right for the role, then you're really kind of working on all of the shadings of it. You're just tuning it and you're playing it, but you know that you've got it. You're just perfecting it. If the actor is wrong for the role, you're literally fighting just to get the performance. When you cast wrong, it's not an easy day.

James Cameron

Titanic

We had a hundred speaking parts more or less to cast, and there weren't really any star parts as written, and I didn't see it that way. I think it eventually took six months or so, going right into the start of photography.

I don't like to do ten or fifteen minutes with somebody, half of which is wasted talking about, you know—do you like to golf? Where do you live?— all that bullshit. What I like to do is, I like to pre-screen on video and get an initial impact from what that person presents to the camera. I trust Mali [his casting person] a great deal in terms of giving some initial direction in the way that I would do it, because I spend a lot of time with her on the script, talking through what the characters mean to the story and who they are inside and between the lines. So, I see an awful lot of tape of people, because what I want to do is, when I meet people, I want to spend an hour, hour and a half, with them. I want to try the scene different ways. I'm interested in seeing if I can work with them, how they are gonna respond to me and that sort of thing. So, I see sort of a select list in person, and I work with them and I often shoot it myself on video.

I make a movie every two years, approximately, and it's such a narrow window to see who's out there and what's going on. It's a big opportunity for me to meet actors and get ideas about who can do what. So, I like to take advantage of the casting process.

So we got down to a short list of actresses that we were considering, and rather than shoot them on tape, I decided to do a full-up film screen test, and we built a little set and lit it, and my DP [director of photography], Russ Carpenter, came in and lit the scene. And I wound up working with Kate Winslet during that day. I kind of was tending away from her, only because she'd done a lot of period films and because of the fact that it seemed like lazy casting in a sense. I wanted to explore other possibilities, and because she was English and I wasn't sure about the accent. Then she came in and just totally won my heart, and the hearts of the other people involved.

I worked with Kate for about three hours and we shot it like a scene—we did a master and a kind of two-shot, and I had a pretty good actor working with her, and I did some close-up stuff, and we did it in and out of accent. And she was actually just doing it in her English accent, because she hadn't worked with a voice coach yet. Subsequently, she did a tremendous amount of dialogue coaching to get her Philadelphia accent just right, which is actually harder than just kind of a contemporary American accent because it's a bit Mid-Atlantic. I had five actresses that day, but I spent the majority of the time with her, and as she left, I turned to the others and I said, "There's still people we need to see, but she's probably the one, unless lightning strikes." A couple of weeks went by and she actually called me from England and said, "Hey, what's going on? How come you are not casting me as Rose—I'm Rose, it's obvious!" And she was very gung ho and very confident about it, and in fact, I did decide pretty quickly after that to cast her.

Leonardo DiCaprio was on a list of names—I didn't know him. I'd never met him. I think I'd only seen *What's Eating Gilbert Grape*, and so I didn't know really what to expect. I noticed that when he came in for the first meeting—which was not a reading, it was just a casual meeting, you know—like my female CFO of the company was there, all the female executives of the company, some of the female secretaries were all in the room, and I'm, like, this is a little odd. So, Leo came in, and I wasn't won over right away. I saw how charming he was. I saw how he won the group very quickly, and was very calm and casual and had a lot of the qualities I would have wanted in a Jack. But I wanted to see him work. So, I asked him to come back and read with Kate. He came back and I got them in a room together, and he said he didn't want to read. I said, "No, you have to read." He said, "No, I really don't wanna read," and I said, "You are gonna read or you are gonna go home." And he went, "OK, let's read!" And I saw this glimpse of something totally amazing right in front of me. There was nobody else there but me and the two actors. He wouldn't let me tape it or anything and then he sort of left and so now I had to turn around to the studio and tell everybody else involved in the film and say, "I saw it! I saw it! It was great!"

Gus Van Sant

Good Will Hunting

The *Good Will Hunting* project always had Matt Damon and Ben Affleck attached as the two leads. They had cleverly put that in their contract. Which was sort of a thorn in a lot of the production people's sides. A lot of other guys were interested in the parts but, I knew them from previous tryouts. Matt had tried out for Jimmy in *To Die For* and he was really great. He was the best audition I'd ever seen for a part. So I knew his work and I knew he was gonna be great. I really like working with people that I've never seen before. When I met Ben and Matt, they were always expecting that their picture wasn't gonna be done. So when I first met them, talked to them and I left, they wanted to know where the Polaroid camera was and how come why I wasn't taking their pictures, 'cause they always felt they were gonna be cheated out of these rolls somewhere along the line. I've been very used to, through all my films, using a black-and-white Polaroid camera, an old camera. I take pictures that are about 4 by 5 of the characters when I first meet them and collect them and have like maybe these sixty pictures and sort of display them on the wall or use them almost like playing cards to figure out your cast. Play eight guys down and see, like, if they're working together. Like, take one out and put one in like solitaire or something. I can do that end-lessly. I can sit there and mix and match for days and days. We were looking for megastars that we wanted to put into the role of Sean — that was sort of the smallish role, kind of premiere role in the film for the star-to-be. And a couple of people looked at the part and decid-ed not to do it. And Robin [Williams] freed up at a certain time that we were going to film, and he said he'd do it. So he was slotted in. I don't really require reading, not like the top on my list. It's mostly the visual, like what the person is like. And then I figure I can get the performance out of them in some way. I trust that I can, usually, and the visual is hugely important.

   We were auditioning people for Skylar, and Minnie Driver came in one morning, it was like a Saturday morning and we'd all been out late. We showed up at my hotel room and she came over and she was presented with all these guys who had all gotten to bed at like five in the morning, had three hours sleep. She proceeded to read the lines with Matt Damon and she really blew everybody away like seriously . . . and left the room. And we just went, "Wow, how did she do that?" It was like magic, she sort of pulled this part out of a hat.

Andrew Davis

The Fugitive

It's the first time I've had an opportunity to really reach a broad audience in terms of having Harrison Ford at the center of it. And being able to reach an audience that encompassed grandmothers and their granddaughters, and allowed me to play in the major leagues. It's wonderful to have the support of a huge actor and have the support of a studio that wants this movie to get out very badly.

I have sort of a team of bad guys and cops from my tough-guy movies in Chicago, and some of them are not actors. They're real policemen and real characters. And because there's such a pool of talent in Chicago now, it was very easy to say, "OK, we're going to bring in certain people, but we'll have a core of our cast from Chicago," because we wanted people to sound and seem like they were from Chicago. I initially wanted Tommy Lee [Jones]. I went through the process of being fair to the rest of the actors in the world. And we actually did some other testing. And I just held firm and stuck with it. And the part is a much more flamboyant character. He's got all these marshals, and all the buzzers and whistles around him. And at the same time, if Girard [played by Jones] was not strong enough, the movie would die.

I like to have people read. I think it's important to see how relaxed they are when they're put on the spot. And it's also important to hear their voice, and just look at them. You have to remember, half the people who see this movie will not see it with the words of the people who are saying them, in terms of the world. So images and faces and textures and realities are very important. There's over a dozen actors in this movie who have never been in a movie before—the Polish lady in the basement, her son—they were people we would just meet on the streets, or people we'd meet at airports.

It's like decorating a room in a way, also. You've gotta have a balance between the different actors. The different colors and shadings, and textures of hardness and softness.

One of the joys is, the strange secondary character. I love secondary characters. Because everybody goes to see the stars. And they love the stars. And yet people relate to those other characters a lot. Those are the people they can identify with. The boy, for example, who plays the young Polish boy who gets busted and then turns over Harrison to the police. He was the son of a woman we met at O'Hare when we were out scouting locations. We were going down to look for a place for the train crash. And his mother worked in an *American Graffiti*-type restaurant. It was five in the morning, she was screaming at a couple of Italian guys, calling them "spaghetti-benders." And she was a great character. We said, "Maybe she can play the woman who runs the rooming house." And then it turned out she wasn't quite right, but she had this kid, who reminded us of Belushi. So he got the part.

Neil Jordan
The Crying Game

I had to get a guy who could be a convincing woman for 30 minutes of the film. And that was just a pure visual thing, really. So I saw hundreds of people, and the guy, he had to be either black or a mixed race, and had to be English. So I saw hundreds of people, and dressed them up, basically! I sent the casting director out to all these clubs in London, and in Paris and in New York. And I did video tests of everyone. And I did camera tests of everybody, a reduction of those, about thirty. And it really was finding somebody, actually, who could just physically carry the illusion. The thing really was to get that on a big screen and see, do you notice all this stuff? You know, the shoulders—that was it, really. Jaye Davidson was a very beautiful man, and had never acted before and had no desire to act, but had this obviously physical beauty and could carry the illusion of it, and you know, he was the only person who could actually do it. The problem in trying to find finance in America is, people would say, "Well, if you cast somebody that we know in one of principal roles, we'll give you money to make a picture."

One thing I like to do is find experienced actors who have got technique and have worked for a long time, and people who have never acted before. I've done that several times, putting the two together. It kind of "wrong foots" the experienced actors in some way — it stimulates them to be real, to be true, not to use technique to get them through a scene. I think generally, if you are casting a non-actor you get somebody who is bright. If you need to cast a child and went into a school, you say to the teacher, give me the four brightest kids in your class.

Barbra Streisand
The Prince of Tides

I couldn't have gotten this picture made, I don't think, if I wasn't in it. I couldn't have gotten to direct it if I wasn't in it. I remember the argument was that it was a famous book — and that seemed to be a detriment. I thought it was a plus!

Kate Nelligan wanted to play the role of the wife. She was spectacular, fantastic in this reading. But there was something about her that was too special. I had seen her in the theatre, and I was struck by her talent and her beauty. So then I thought, well, what if she plays the mother, because the mother should be very strong and very beautiful. Kate is both. I had been looking for two different actresses to play the younger woman and the older woman. I could never get them — two actresses that were either that good or that looked alike. And I just thought, well what if she plays both parts? She kind of thought I was nuts at first to suggest this. But then we did a makeup test with her. She's such a good actress and a hard worker, who has a great sense of detail — her southern accent was perfect; and the little things she did in terms of age — putting a pad on her back to make a slight dowager's hump, something in her jaw — she was extraordinary. So that's how that came about. First of all [with Nick Nolte], I ran everything he's ever done, every film he's ever made. And I saw some interesting things. I mean — there were never any real love scenes in his movies after *Rich Man, Poor Man*. So it was an area I was really concerned with, because I wanted a romantic leading man to play this part. And, as a matter of fact, one studio turned us down because Nick was playing the part. They had seen him in *Q & A*. Thirty pounds heavier, a big, black mustache, and they thought that's the guy I was going to play with. No faith, no faith. I said, "I want you to be this fantastic, romantic leading man." He said, "No, no, no — I'm a character actor, I'm not a leading man." I thought he had all the potential. I mean, he had the pain behind his eyes that I needed for this guy and the sexuality. And almost a mistrust, you know, of women, which was also essential.

In casting I like to break the pattern — if somebody has a reading in their head, I like to throw it out.

Casting kids can be a difficult problem. I didn't have them read. I played with them. I talked to them. I put them on videotape to see how they would react in front of the camera. Because sometimes a kid is great in real life, and then you put this camera on them and they stiffen up. I believe in casting people who have a quality that you want to capture for a part. Like this one twelve-year-old kid came in and I said, "How did you get your tooth knocked out?" And he said, "Oh, this guy smashed me over the head with a chair and I took this guy and punched him in the stomach." I hired him because he *was* the person. He wasn't an actor really — when I was actually directing him he would laugh all the time. But, he had the true essence of the character. I did a lot of improvisation with Nick and different children. Because even though I might have cast one girl I liked, she had no connection with Nick.

James L. Brooks
As Good as It Gets

I wanted Jack Nicholson for the part, and we're friends, and I went to see him and our conversations tend to be very truthful with each other. It was Jack Nicholson very much as a character actor that I wanted. It was Jack Nicholson with his craft that I wanted. The movie star part would only get in the way.

I had another actress in mind for the female lead, and this was true throughout the process at the time — every negotiation that went into the studio, it was "the check's in the mail"—for months and months you never knew what would happen. There was an absolute loggerhead on the negotiation with the actress that I had offered it to, and they asked me to at least consider others. And now I'm really this many months in, maybe the movie won't happen, so it was a request that you took seriously from the studio at that time. And about the fourth person through the door was Helen Hunt and she had spoken with a mutual friend of ours who contacted me and said she'd like to come in. And, very quickly, she was an actress who I really wanted to work with. The age disparity was something I had to deal with because at a certain point I just wanted her to be this character. Okay, you're four years older than you are, okay he's four years younger.

I think it's so important that you have a casting person who, when you're into your fourth month of looking and you've looked at hundreds of people, that they not make you feel like a fool, that they stay in there with you and try—because you can start to think that you're crazy because you haven't found it and you don't know why you haven't found it. And you've already dealt with actors who you respect who under other circumstances you'd kill to work with. The part that Greg Kinnear finally got, was very late in the game and his name came up and he was shooting in San Francisco, and he couldn't come down and so we went up and for what seemed like an odd choice at the time. And he'd finished shooting and it was around 2 o'clock in the morning, and he read beautifully and then he came down two weeks later and he read again with Jack and it was that much better.

The Crew

Clint Eastwood

Unforgiven

You really are only as good as the ensemble you gather. You cast the crew exactly the way you cast the cast. You try to get people whose work you respect or who you've worked with before. Some of the people I've used are brought up through the ranks, and some of them are new. I had an art director that I'd used before, so I knew that a town could go up in a certain period of time. It went up in thirty-one days, that's interior and exterior. So I knew he could deliver in that fashion, but if it had been an art director I'd never worked with, that might be a little bit dodgy. You can't tell by meeting a person how they are going to be over a two-month period, but by and large you can get a feeling of a person. If I was using a cameraman for the very first time, I'd probably talk to another director who I respected who had worked with him before and ask, first, how fast he is. And secondly, does he like the mystery of it, or does he like to get right in and put it all together?

Rob Reiner
A Few Good Men

The most important thing is to get people that you like to see in the morning. When you come to work and you've got a long schedule and it's nice to say, "Hey, it's that guy again that I like" and, "Hi, how are you?" So the most important thing is people that you can get along with, that you enjoy spending time with. The film itself is for the public, it goes out there. But what you have is your experience of actually making the film. And that's what you take with you through your life. So you want to surround yourself with people that you enjoy being with. Now, obviously, hopefully they can do their job as well, and they're not just your friends and family. Start with a group of people that you feel comfortable with and that you can communicate with. That you can talk to, that understands what you are saying. You try to build a family that way.

I find for most cinematographers, they don't understand the film because they're involved in images mostly.

Mike Leigh
Secrets & Lies

I'm lucky, now — there is an ongoing crew who, for the most part, comes with me from one film to the next, like my cinematographer on a number of projects, a production designer, the same gang of

sparks [electricians], the same grips. What happens with my projects is, we're in a constant touch and as soon as we get anywhere
near a green light we're calling them and they're doing their level
best to juggle other offers and other films so they can be there with
us. I think that's a very important part of the chemistry thing, to
have a crew that was completely with it and able to be sensitive to
those moments.

It's important for both the production designer and her team and
the costume designer to be around way ahead of the shoot, not only
to inspect the location, but to be part of the creative process as the
film starts to present itself.

The only thing I really think is important is the collaboration
between myself, the production designer, and the cinematographer.
So that in the case of *Life Is Sweet* we collaborated in a very specific
way about the look and the color. It seemed to make sense to choose
a particular type of stock to shoot it.

Curtis Hanson
L.A. Confidential

The same way I look for actors who can capture the essence of the
character, I look for crew members who I think can capture the
essence of the particular thing that I'm hoping to get from that particular department.

In terms of the cinematographer, I wanted somebody who could
capture the lighting and style and again, put the characters and emotions in the foreground. You start thinking of film noir, and all those
great movies from that period, and I wanted to make sure that Dante
Spinotti, right from the get-go, was not thinking that way. I spoke
with him about a photographer named Robert Frank, and I said,
"When you look at his pictures you are struck by the emotional
power of the pictures and it's only on a closer look that you see they
were taken in the period." I did this little photo presentation with
him of archival pictures that I had put together that represented the
look and feel of the movie for me and he just got it immediately and
we built from there. I used to take pictures as a still photographer, so
I'm very comfortable with cameras and lenses and visualizing. I'm

one of those directors who is, to some cameramen, a pain in the ass, in that I like to look through the lens at every shot. But it's a collaboration. I want them very much to understand the emotion of the scene and contribute ideas of how to shoot it.

Neil Jordan
The Crying Game

I find the thing that defines the cameraman is his ability to maintain control over the look of the entire film. That's what seems to me to distinguish great ones from kind of good ones.

Anthony Minghella
The English Patient

You end up with the best people you can find. They become like your family. They are your family. At the same time the jarring and disturbing notion is that, if *you* don't know what you want, absolutely nothing happens, and that's terrifying.

With John Seale, the cinematographer, every Sunday in our six-day week, the seventh day we'd spend the afternoon together worrying and fretting over the next week's work and trying to work out how to achieve it.

Barbra Streisand
The Prince of Tides

I used to describe the scenes to the cameraman and sometimes he'd say to me, "I can't imagine what you're talking about until I see the actors in the room." That was really hard for me because I imagine them all in my head beforehand, but it doesn't mean he's wrong and I'm right. It's just a different way of working.

Working with cinematographers, I show pictures and paintings. Before *Yentl*, I went to Amsterdam to see the Rembrandts and discovered the paint was dark brown not black. The edges of the faces were soft, not hard, and that affected the look of the film I did with David Watkins, who is so gifted.

Oliver Stone

JFK

I've done six, seven films with [cinematographer] Bob Richardson, so we talk in shorthand at this point. Basically he comes in very early, reads the early drafts, gives me his version of reality. We argue, we debate, we talk about colors, palettes, looks. He likes still photographs, I like paintings. He does his own version of shots, I do my own version of shots. There's a natural flow to a blocking that occurs, and often that dictates to me the camera.

Andrew Davis

The Fugitive

You look at their work, you find out what their schedules were like, you talk to other people. I've been very lucky to work with some wonderful cinematographers. It's all about lighting. Totally the most important part to me. Because I'm not worried about how to place the camera or what lens to use. Then it's how fast and what approach you take to get there.

Steven Spielberg

Amistad

I was very fortunate because I discovered something about the old-fashioned studio system that we don't have in place any longer, but we used to have in place forty, fifty years ago. And that is I simply took my entire crew, and moved them off of *Lost World*, and onto *Amistad*. I'm talking about everybody, and it was remarkable because it was as if we finished one story and we simply came to work the next day and began a new story.

James Cameron

Titanic

Peter Lamont had worked with me on *Aliens* and on *True Lies*, so we had a pretty good history. I knew him as a good kind of old-school

English production designer, which means that he's the general that oversees a vast pyramid of people underneath. And it's run like the federal government, but that's what it took to do those previous pictures. We had made the decision to save money on construction and all the thousands of crafts people that were working on the set, sculpting everything and carving everything and all the wood and all that stuff in Mexico that he knew how to use the Mexican infrastructure. And for the first time, I think in fourteen or fifteen Titanic projects that have been put on film over there, over the many years, for the first time Harland and Wolff actually opened their plans drawers and we got the blueprints to the damn ship! And we actually worked from the plans of the ship. And he had an interesting challenge, because I would not let him diverge from what it was. If you are gonna flood the set, it has to be built to a structural integrity about four to five times normal for a set, because of the massive water. So there's a tremendous amount of engineering that went into the sets.

Cameron Crowe

Jerry Maguire

The main guy that I've always worked with is, he's sort of a legendary assistant director, Jerry Ziesmer. And he's retired and comes back more than Sugar Ray Leonard. He's a real partner and an inspiring guy. He's also an actor and he pops up in a lot of the movies that he ADs [assistant directs]. He was AD on *Apocalypse Now* and he's the guy who says, "Terminate with extreme prejudice."

Gus Van Sant

Good Will Hunting

The designer was Missy Stewart, who I've worked with many times. She is a good friend and she was familiar with the locations and with Harvard and we shot half of it in Toronto, interiors were in Toronto. [Because of the value of U.S. currency and what some believe are very unfair labor practices, over a billion dollars a year of American film business is going to Canada.]

James L. Brooks

As Good as It Gets

Bill Brzeski [the production designer], whom I'd worked with on television, had begun his feature career. When we talked for the first time, he showed me a book, and this was the most ridiculous "Eureka" moment, because he showed me an old hallway with a staircase in it, which gave levels. I just embraced him.

We built everything. I wanted the picture not to be about New York, but to be about two blocks of Manhattan and three blocks in Brooklyn—that's what I wanted the picture to be about. We were having lunch at this café, and suddenly you just looked around and you say, "It should be this." We built it in downtown L.A. in a welfare hotel, we took over the lobby, and one of the most difficult things were those crosses [on buildings] they have for earthquakes and how to disguise those, and how to make them look like they're in New York. But that's what we had to do, financially we had to do it there. I like being on location. I like that everybody is away from home. I think that even though it makes for great trials in everybody's personal life, it gives a focus and a kind of respect for what you're doing. It's less a job, it's more a calling.

I'd worked with Michael Ballhaus on two previous pictures. We've had great times working together because we each had a love of actors. We'd be in dailies, he'd be cinematographer and he'd be talking about performance width, which is great for me. We complemented each other and I love that he operates the camera himself because when you have a picture that's going to have close-ups like this, to have your DP [director of photography] have his eye in there as long as yours isn't—it becomes important. He was slated to do a picture with Redford and they were on location so he was unavailable and then the picture fell through. And on the day that it fell through, he had a friend who was doing *Air Force One*, and he had me who had been talking to him for two years, and he had called my office, and the person who was answering the phone that day, for some reason, volunteered that I wasn't gonna be doing the picture for a while and the next phone call was *Air Force One* and I had lost Michael Ballhaus, which was a huge blow to me.

Then I began a search. The way I do it is to get a cinematographer's pictures and mix all the reels up. Usually if you do that, you can separate out the cinematographer from the director, because you're just taking odd reels with no sound and you begin to pick up a style. Then production design was everything for me on this picture, the details of it, because we were going to be so interior, and because the problems I worried about were — I had really over forty pages in doorways.

John Madden
Shakespeare in Love

I took the whole production team from the last two or three films that I've made, and I felt really strongly about that. This is a twenty-five million dollar movie as opposed to a one-point-five million pound movie. And there's a feeling of, you know, are these people up to it? And I always felt, well if I'm up to it, then they certainly are, because they've made these movies with me and they are my collaborators and they're the people on whom I depend. It's very important to have people around you who you know and who support you. You develop a language with them, and I had a kind of messianic feeling that their time had come as well, and I'm so happy they've all been acknowledged because we've all done it together. Film is always collaborative, so much more so than people outside the business realize, but I've never been on a film where the collaboration was as crucial as this one.

Design
Rob Reiner
A Few Good Men

You key off of actual locations — in this case it was based on an actual true story that happened in Cuba in 1986. I went down to Guantanamo Bay, just looking around and seeing what the base looked like, the way in which the Marine barracks were laid out there. Very similar to what we built. And also the topography, which we shot down at Crystal Cove down in Laguna. It's virtually the same as what's down in Guantanamo Bay, Cuba. You can see the guard towers across the way that are anywhere from 300 yards to a $^1/_2$ a mile away, depending on what part of the fence line you're looking at. So we tried to recreate that.

The courtroom we took a lot of dramatic license with, because the actual JAG Corps in Washington are small there. And since, again, we knew we had to spend a large portion of film in the courtroom, we felt that we could take some license and make it a little better. We actually fought about the courtroom quite a bit. The story, the theme of it is big, because it's about following orders and where you draw that line of morality. But the actual scenes themselves are intimate, because it's a man on a witness stand and it's an attorney and they can't really move very much. And your jury is fixed and your gallery is fixed and the judge is fixed. So, the courtroom should have some size to it, to give it a little bit of a look, but also again, it couldn't be too much, so we actually cut 20 feet off it, after it had been built.

Obviously, if you can shoot something in a controlled environment, it's better, as long as you get the reality. I thought that by shooting scope [CinemaScope, a wide-screen process] it would make it a little more cinematic and not so claustrophobic. *A Few Good Men*, it's basically a courtroom drama, it's all interiors and stuff, but I thought that giving the scope might just make the picture a little bit more pleasing to the eye.

John Madden

Shakespeare in Love

My kind of tutelage in movies is excessively low budget, and I feel comfortable trusting a real environment as the source of the feel and look of a film. And I don't mind — in fact I welcome the kind of restrictions that that brings. If it's a very small room, it forces you to shoot in a certain kind of way; if it's a very large space, you can shoot that way. And I kind of nurtured that — I would find something that would pass for Elizabethan England. That kind of Elizabethan England simply doesn't exist anymore, even in England. I was coming back from the Cannes Film Festival, and I stayed overnight in a place called Toi, which is still a medieval city, and I kind of really began to think, maybe we can do it here. The streets started to feel right. I was staying in a hotel that was exactly like one of those little innyards where Ned Allen's men would have been performing and so forth. I was digging my heels in against the idea of building. Because it's not a way I've ever been able to do it before. I've built sets before, but not an entire environment like that. I knew we would build the theatre and that, oddly enough, was the other way around there, because everybody was always saying, "Why can't you shoot in the Globe?" Which was the wrong theatre, and it's in the middle of London, and it looks very disappointing for me. I mean, not as a theatre, it isn't, but it didn't have the feel or the look or the world that I wanted. And I began to realize—right, we're going to have to build the whole thing. And the river was the main kind of nightmare. And that my location instincts won out. Because the idea of shooting that on a flooded soundstage would look so preposterously phony, and it may sound odd because the whole movie is dealing with a very nonliteral realm, you know. It's dealing with a realm where the imagination is free to make up its own mind what it wants to see. Shakespearean theatre was based on that idea. And yet, I felt that if the movie were not really grounded in a kind of grubby smelly muddy reality, the transcendence of poetry and of language and the kind of transport and transformation that obviously happened to audiences would not mean anything. And I felt that the whole piece could sort of topple over into artificiality unless I could find a way of grounding that. So we set about the process of building the theatre, which we built on a soundstage. That was kind of an archaeological process. The remains of the actual Rose still exist.

We had to go belting into production as you always do, earlier than we thought. Like two or three weeks chopped off the preparation time, and this extraordinary kind of monster, like the ship I guess in *Titanic*, was just kind of growing as the nightmare of preproduction kind of engulfed you. I used to go down at the end of every day and spend the last three hours of every day walking around on this thing as it evolved. It took, of course, the entire process of the pre-production to evolve and was only ready like the day we started shooting. But it became incredibly crucial in the whole conceptual way that the film evolved. Because it's an amazing space—it's such a cinematic space. I couldn't believe how cinematic the space became. One of the great worries of it was—of the movie, for me—was, you know, that people would use the word "theatrical" about it. Which is really a no-no word in the movie business. If it's theatrical, it's bad. And theatre on film is not something that really has worked very often. The magic of theatre doesn't transfer very easily. But as I began to see this space—first of all, you have this amazing discovery about why they built them like that. It's the most brilliant performance space—the actor's never more than this row away from you, wherever they are in the theatre. They're wrapped right around you. You just get on the front of the stage and you feel like turning a story. It's just an extraordinary space. But particularly what was wonderful for the film was that it had three distinct realms. Physical realms, which you know fed and reflected the realms of reality within the film. A backstage world where one kind of reality existed, which is already an overlap of two, a real world of these people scratching their asses and getting their clothes on. But also a preparation for a fictional world, which then became the world that you found onstage. The camera, of course, was free to move between in a way that would never be true in a modern theatre. And that in turn gave way to a different world outside, beyond that. The world of the audience where they are interpreting that reality. You could put the camera anywhere in there. I just couldn't find a space where the camera wasn't interesting. In particular, I suddenly realized that the division between the place on stage and the place backstage was exactly where the whole movie took place. And it became a kind of guiding principle of freedom of movement between those two things where the real goes over into the imaginative and so forth.

The town was another matter. The town was completely constructed on the back lot at Shepperton. I'm a great believer in not having too much money to spend, because it forces you into solutions that are much more interesting than if you had the ability to build an endless town. So what we did was build a small labyrinth with a theatre at one end and a theatre at the other end. Which were half theatres, because the two theatres in the movie, the one theatre we built, we rebuilt. They were just a series of labyrinths, really.

Some outrageous duplication goes on all the time in the film, but you don't really notice it and you don't feel it.

Andrew Davis
The Fugitive

I think my instincts are always to try to make it real. But what does "real" mean? Sort of a heightened reality is what we wanted. I wanted it to have qualities of the old thriller. With shadows, and this kind of Hitchcock look of things. Very contrasty. And at the same time, we wanted to feel that we were involved in real life, and in real situations, where things were not glamorized. So the contrast between the life of Richard Kimble [the lead role played by Harrison Ford] and this beautiful, tuxedoed couple, versus him on the streets buying a janitor's outfit, was important to me. The aerials were important to me, in terms of the idea of a nest. Of being lost in a haystack. Which made the city a character in the movie.

Originally I thought they would never let me go to Chicago in the middle of winter. This would be suicide. They'd had some trouble on a film the year before. But Harrison was very smart to say, "Let's not make it a road movie. Let me come back and put myself back in the cauldron of tension here." So it was very easy to conceive the life of a surgeon, because growing up in the city and knowing doctors, and making available the University of Chicago Medical Center to use, we quickly invested our self in creating the life of the doctor. From meeting other doctors by accident, and going to their homes, and looking at their art collections, and designing the inside of his house to match somebody's house.

The train sequence was probably the most storyboarded, because we actually had to create our own train. We had to find an empty locomotive and push it from behind. We had to have a side railing that we put in. So it was very complicated. We knew from the beginning that we were going to crash a real train. We were not going to rely on miniatures or process to make the sequence work. We would shoot as much as we could real. We actually did have models. For example, the plate of the train chasing Harrison is an Intravision shot that we created with a model. But at the same time, we did have a shot of a real train running into a camera in North Carolina. So the combination of the two of them together made it work. Intravision is a special-effects optical process that allows you to look through the camera, and see exactly what you're going to get. You can adjust the lighting while you're doing it, so you don't have to wait two days to see what's coming back optically. We'd do the shot list, and I'd say, "This is what we need to see," and then we'd go about talking to our special effects coordinator, and the whole team would work together and try to say, "Okay, how are we gonna do it?"

The river was an important element, because it led down to running downriver, and getting to the dam and the tunnels. There was a continuity, and a sort of baptism of Kimble's jumping off the dam and surviving.

We took over a grammar school on the south side of Chicago, that turned into a jail, police station, hospital, and some interrogation rooms. So that became like a mini-studio. We took over another warehouse. A huge warehouse, a former Westinghouse plant, where we built one of the tunnels of the BAM tunnels. We built the elevator shaft for the end of the movie, we built Kimball's house in. So there was some major construction. At the same time, we were on location a lot. We were in neighborhoods, we were in real basements. It was a production that mixed both types of challenges. Being on location in the middle of winter, in ethnic neighborhoods downtown. I have a deep feeling for that area, because that was the area right by the steel mills, where a lot of kids from my high school grew up. It's sort of an abandoned, desolate area. And when we first looked at it, everybody got real concerned. They said, "My God, it's so small and crowded and tight. It's a mess." And that's what I liked about it. That it was going to be confining. And we weren't going to take walls out and put the camera places that it shouldn't be. And we were going to be able to make it very real. The problem is, you've got all these reality television shows where video cameras are running and chasing everybody all the time, and that's the level of reality that we have to accept these days.

I've been lucky to sort of create a family, a little repertory company of technicians and actors, that just really like being together. And they're very supportive. I'll take recommendations from everybody, and I actually love it. I've gotten some of my best ideas from team-sters and craft service people.

Michael Radford
Il Postino

I love working on location. I don't like working in the studio—I always feel slightly fake in the studios. On this film it was impossi-ble, really, and as Massimo [the star] fell ill, it became even more impossible. We had to shoot as much in the studio as we possibly could. The problem about finding locations in Italy is that it's such a beautiful country that everybody goes there for their holidays, and the entire coast of Italy has been built up. And to find somewhere that even resembled the 1950s, we finally ended up finding this island called Selina, in the Aeolian Islands. There's no airport or any-thing there—it just had the feel that I wanted. I didn't want this to look like a kind of pretty Mediterranean film. I wanted that sense of the landscape somehow is a metaphor for the interior stage of the characters, and I wanted something that was both beautiful and oppressive to this guy. He was going to have to discover that it was beautiful. So you have to feel that sense of oppression. I love those kind of big mountains and those cliffs, and we built a small fishing village. I have to tell you that I can thoroughly recommend location hunting in Italy. It consists of going from one restaurant to another restaurant, and sleeping through the afternoons.

Anthony Minghella
The English Patient

The first time I drove anywhere near a location and I saw how many trucks there were, my stomach just churned and churned. Because it was massive. I think we had over forty trucks that went from here to the desert. We had to build roads! We had to build a road into the Sahara because, funnily enough, there aren't any roads there. I went to the desert a year before we started shooting, and it was so gor-geous to be there, and it was so cleansing and so extraordinary. Then when we went back there a year later, I loathed every single second of it because it was so inhospitable and cold, bone-chillingly cold. It was also totally against the spirit of making films, which is repetition. If you ask Ralph Fiennes to walk up a sand dune and he does it too quickly, you're stopped, as we say in England; because when he comes back, there are the foot paths of the first go-round—and so, you know, the insanity ensues very quickly. The day we were there we were rained out, so that the place we went for was completely gone. When you're trying to roll a truck down the side of a hill and they discover they can't do it and you've moved all the equipment there and you can't do it on that hill, then you try and use what you have. You try and live in the moment that you have.

I drew every shot in the film repeatedly. Partly because I was terrified of the scope of this film—and so I thought, the more I know, the more I'll feel like I'm not a jerk when I turn up every day. And I'd rather have that than the screenplay.

We built tons of stuff—the church which Hana is flown round in, and most of the monastery. We built the exterior and the interior of the cave in the location. Stuart Craig [the production designer] said, "What do you want to see at all times? My job is to give you that back." So, I'd go and I'd say, "I want to see that, but that's not right." And he'd say, "So, then, we'll make that bit, and if you want that ravine to lead into a cave, then we'd better find some way of doing that." You're the sum of your own decisions.

James Cameron

Titanic

The biggest challenge in making this picture was to get past the technical challenges, which were so enormous and daunting for everyone concerned, because they were an order of magnitude beyond what we had done previously. We started doing a lot of testing. We did a lot of previsualization. We got a model of the ship, and went around it with a little lipstick camera, making hard copies of that, drew on them, and that sort of thing. We did a tremendous amount of figuring out light placement, and how much of it would have to be practical and built in. We'd do a lot of camera tests, especially with Kate and Leo, to really find out what focal length lenses worked with them, what types of lighting worked with Kate, especially. But also what types of lighting suited Leo's face. Eventually we just decided: We are trying to take the audience into a time period and let them inhabit that and live in it. We want it to be rich and not desaturated. We want it to look like Kodachrome. We eventually wound up opting for very little filtration and going for strong colors as much as possible. Then, of course, that impacted the costume design and the production design as well.

We never really used storyboards that much. We built a twenty-five-foot-long study model of the ship. We built models of the interior spaces based on old reference, used a small chip video camera, so we had several weeks of previsualization. We had the luxury on this film, because we were dealing with a known and defined space. If we were doing a science fiction film, we would have had to do rough production design drawings, some kinds of storyboards, and then convert that into models or maquettes. We took the twenty-five-foot study model, drove down to an empty field in Rosarito Beach, stuck it out on a bluff, and watched what the sun did to it during the day. We kept turning it and moving it and finally said, "OK, this is exactly where the thing should go. Now build it here—except, 780 feet long." We actually worked from the plans of the ship. And he [Peter Lamont, the production designer] had an interesting challenge because I would not let him diverge from what it was. I said, "I want the Titanic, and I want it exact." *The Guinness Book of World Records* called us up and apparently it's the biggest set ever. But we only built one side and the whole top. And for the first time, I think in 14 or 15 Titanic projects that have been put on film over there, over the many years, for the first time Harland and Wolff actually opened their plans drawers and we got the blueprints to the ship! Because it had always been kind of a black mark for them . . . which frankly it shouldn't have been because there was nothing wrong with the ship, they just drove it into an iceberg! You drive a Volvo into a bridge abutment, you are gonna get the same effect!

We went in with a very, very clear idea of the game plan. At the time that the film was greenlit, all the sets were blueprinted, all the tank and riser systems were all blueprinted. To achieve the time scale which we had set out to do, which was to do the entire thing including building the set, then shooting the movie, posting [editing and mixing music and sound] and delivering it, was supposed to be 13 months. In that previsualization phase, we sort of merged together, figuring out the effects. If the *Titanic* really existed, this would be a cool shot. OK, now, how much set do we need, how's it going to be done with a model, how much of it is CG [computer graphics], CG water? And you eventually realize—if you try to do all the effects, it's going to cost you even more, because the effects are not cheap. At a certain point as a storyteller, you go, "My god, I've got to have something to work with. Something that I can see, because I've got to react to something, too, because the actors need it and I need it as well." You can't preconceptualize everything.

Scott Hicks
Shine

The design side of it was quite tricky. And the location side, because I had made repeated pilgrimages to the Royal College of Music over the years, developing the story and planning to shoot the film. It was essential to me that we shoot there, just to get those little bits of connections with what was outside the window as much as anything else.

The only other thing we built was the bathroom. And it had to be that appearance of being in that tiny room and that period, and overseas it was just physically impossible. The house, particularly, a family house, was an empty and somewhat derelict place that we found months ahead of time. And that enabled the designer to do wonderful things as far as I was concerned. She was able to put all of the ingredients that were part of Peter's landscape—you know, the bottles that he'd collected that we see him doing on his collecting rounds—and let the grass grow through them and dig the vegetable ground and make it appear as if things are growing. To really give the sense of a place that was lived in and had a life. And it made for those usually enormous logistical difficulties of shooting in tiny spaces, the enormity of the camera and the crew around. It's extremely restrictive, but at the same time it does add. I remember when Armin Mueller-Stahl walked into the set on the first day that he was involved in and he said, "I know what this is telling me, this is good." He felt the authenticity of the environment in which we were going to make this sort of extraordinary family setting. And so that was the positive element, if you like.

Mike Leigh
Secrets & Lies

Now, finding locations for my sorts of films, even though they are, ultimately, quote-unquote, "ordinary places," is a difficult one. Because what happens is that, this day looms on the horizon when we will go out to a location that has been dressed and prepared, which is one of the series of locations, and we will start to shoot a coherent picture. We not only talk about where it might be, but we choose the whole world, the whole those, the whole spirit of the film as it's growing. Now when there is no script and story and I don't know the locations, the speed with which that date races towards you is terrifyingly quick! What happens is, we tend to arrange one or two main locations. Usually one location is booked for the entire shoot, so you can start there and go back there, and it's a sort of fail-safe. And there are other locations that are found spontaneously, because I'm still making it up as we shoot, and we go and do things as we go.

When we came to *Naked*, it began to appear to me what kind of film that I felt I wanted to make. We talked about color and tone. We shot tests. We decided to shoot AGFA [a film stock like Kodak] and used the bleach process and all of those things. And that still without having started to make the film or know what the film really was. In *Secrets & Lies*, we took as a point of reference the quality of high-speed photography and chose Fujicolor for that reason.

Quentin Tarantino
Pulp Fiction

I don't storyboard, because I can't draw and I don't like anyone else's drawings. They always get the framing wrong, as far as I'm concerned. But I can light, so I describe everything in great detail.

We didn't have enough money to build what Marsellus would call his house. I had a budget of 8 million dollars on *Pulp*, and I knew — wow, this is the first time I've had some real money to make a movie. And, I was like, okay, I have a lot of money, but I don't have that much money. So I'm going to give myself one big Hollywood thing. And that was Jack Rabbit's Slims. Everything else was like a little independent movie, if you look at it, but that was my big thing. So I created this restaurant.

Peter Weir

The Truman Show

Dennis Gassner got involved very early on. I needed a top person and I was familiar with his work. We met and got on, and he was hired truly months before the start of pre-production, in fact. To do research and so on. The key was the town — we had to find the town. First, I thought of doing it here and joining up the key back-lots of Universal and Warner and a little bit of Paramount. I was going to sort of construct a town out of the existing standing sets and streets. But it would have tipped the film into a more theatrical comic direction, with a Western street, or the Paris café corner. But it was tempting, and so I photographed it all, and we were looking at that. Wasn't right. And then it was suggested to me — there's this little town in seaside Florida. And it was quite a remarkable exper-iment, really. Architectural experiment where the people had built in the style you might say of the Southern vernacular of the United States. These little clapboard houses. So of course I sent a camera crew — it looked interesting. I then began the difficult negotiation. These people were very sensitive about what we were going to do — obviously physically, but also in terms of how the town was portrayed. Because part of the architectural community, of course, condemns what they're doing as sort of retro and Disneyish. In fact Disney came down and had a long look at it. The kids play in the streets, and they live the life that we all lived from my generation. Where kids could go out and play in the streets in safety and live in this very pretty seaside town. The great thing was, in the end they decided against cash and they said, "We haven't got a school —

build us a school." It was great to go back recently and walk through the school.

As with many things in this film, it had to be done with an apparent effortless quality. This film is in danger of being something that would be too much of a brain tease for the audience if they couldn't just relax and go with it. I had to, in a sense, subvert the form of the movie. I wanted to turn the audience into viewers of *The Truman Show*, just like the characters we see from time to time within the film. And I wanted them to assume that they knew all about it. They knew they were in a dome, so I would just have to give you a little glimpse here, a word there, a phrase there, rather than the awful feeling that I, as the filmmaker, am telling you information.

It was really an aesthetic choice. The wide angle and the minuteness of cameras was done to occasionally give the audience a reminder that they were being watched. I liked very much from the silent era where they would have all kinds of frame shapes around the lens, and were free to experiment. Sometimes triangles and all kinds of things to focus your attention on what you're interested in. And so we would shoot a lot of them and then I decided it was too risky. We made up a number of gobos [devices covering part of the lens] that we would be able to put around the lens or have the lens shoot through. Then I decided it was much better to do it optically. I had a lot of fancy stuff in the film that I took out, finally. Again to make the audience have a cinema experience and then reveal all that was to be revealed, but not to in a way to distract them.

I don't use storyboards very much, although I did for the critical sequence, the storm. I like to draw them myself, though. I find I draw almost everything. I keep saying, I've got to go to a drawing class. These stick figures are becoming embarrassing. But I love to draw little frames. And sometimes I'll give those to a professional to have them drawn up more fully.

James L. Brooks

As Good as It Gets

I always like storyboards, because if you hand them to somebody, everybody will go away and look at that, and then you can figure out what you are doing.

Curtis Hanson

L.A. Confidential

I do not storyboard, unless it's a situation for a stunt in order that everybody can see exactly what the shot is and anticipate what to build for safety reasons. In terms of communicating, with the cameraman, I prefer not to storyboard. Unless, for example, the shootout at the Victory Motel, I actually did a list, a shot list, it wasn't storyboarded until again, for safety sake, we storyboarded certain aspects of it so that the effects people could see exactly what the expectation was.

I grew up in L.A. and in a sense feel as though I've been researching this picture all my life. And I've always wanted to deal with the city of my childhood memory and it was very ambitious logistically in that we had 45 locations to find, and my dream was to do it all on location. I wanted to actually find real locations and shoot in what would appear in a casual way, as though we were not interested in the set dressing. There's always a tendency I feel, as a movie-goer, when one looks at movies that are period pictures where the movie somehow becomes about the period instead of about the story and the characters. I screened a number of pictures that were shot in the fifties. Pictures by directors who had a very lean, no-nonsense style, like Robert Aldrich, and Don Siegel and Sam Fuller and so forth. To show that when they shot the scenes on the streets, there was almost a semi-documentary feel to it. It was as though they'd put the camera down and shot because they didn't care about the cars or any of that because it was all ordinary.

Mirrors and reflections are a thing that runs through *L.A. Confidential*, with this theme of illusion and reality, image and reality, in the city of illusion, in Los Angeles. It was constructed in such a way that several of the characters have moments of truth. For instance Kevin Spacey in the bar looking in the mirror at his own reflection and seeing it's like looking at the portrait of Dorian Gray. His eyes become filled with self-loathing and he sees what he has become. The character that Guy Pearce plays in the beginning of the movie—he's behind the mirror watching as Kevin Spacey is being interrogated and in the middle of the movie, Guy's on the other side of the mirror doing the interrogating, and at the very end of the movie, when he's finally telling the truth, so to speak, all the cops are outside looking at him, and he then looks in the mirror. . . .

Roberto Benigni
Life Is Beautiful

This is my first period movie. But I must say each story is a contemporary story, so we are talking about the present always. And my production designer is Danilo Donati, really one of the oldest and wonderful. He's very old and really a genius. And the director of photography, Tonino Delli Colli, who is very old. And they are like two little boys. They fight all the time. For example, when he chose the grand hotel, we discussed a lot with Danilo Donati about this grand hotel. So big and wide with gigantic stairs, very strange. I was really scared by this idea, because a grand hotel like this in Italy doesn't exist. It was really worrying me, this big white. . . . And you know the director of photography, they hate white! Stay away! "You can't do it white!" And then Danilo Donati decided to put in mirrors, white mirrors! And Delli Colli left the crew. Because they are very old both, and they are two geniuses. And they are really like little kids. "Tomorrow, it will be red. Because your blood will be there." And also because Danilo Donati was thinking about the green horse. And the light, I like very much what Delli Colli did, because the light is like the sky and the reality. It's like the world, the sum of the movie. Everything, the light. And they did it with the light. In the hotel I told them to try to put a dramatic light in the first part of the movie, of course. And to try comedy light in the second part of the movie. So this was very difficult to explain. And the second part of the movie, the extermination camp, we discussed a lot because this is not a true story. But we had seen a lot about all the extermination camps. But I didn't want to put the idea of a precise extermination camp, because I was not telling a true story. So I try to give the idea of the extermination camp. For example, in Italy, we have only one extermination camp in the north of Italy. It looks a little like this. But for example there is never mountains. And I choose this place because it was completely different. I didn't want to put something real. It was a question of style. And we really lost a lot of time about this, between the first and the second part of the movie, so to combine something real with something completely invented.

Steven Spielberg
Amistad

When I read the script, I pretty much knew that I wanted the film to have a certain look, and I wanted the look to be Goya, especially in his late dark period. And when we looked at those pictures and we saw some of those paintings—we knew what the mood of the film was going to be. The production designer [Rick Carter] did a lot of conceptual paintings with some illustrators he brought in, and I'd be up there on a stepladder with a Panaflex inside the mouth of a *T. rex* and he'd be trying to feed me these big pictures up a second stepladder! But a necessity of the schedule created a kind of spontaneity that actually benefited the movie. I didn't storyboard *Amistad*. I didn't storyboard *Schindler's List*. But I did storyboard all of *Lost World* and all of *Jurassic Park*. The size and the logistics of the film kind of dictates what we need to share with every member of the crew.

We principally shot the movie in Newport, Rhode Island, and we used all the old seventeenth-century houses and squares and courthouses. That was all very authentic, so most of the light, even though it's augmented by units coming through the windows, or by hitting grifs [gryflon is plastic reflective material] and bouncing into the windows, I'd say the movie was about ninety percent about location.

Saving Private Ryan

I didn't do any storyboards for this movie, because those soldiers and those cameramen didn't have any storyboards to key off of in 1944, and we took a kind of method actor approach to directing and to performing in the picture. We just used each day to kind of inform us where we should be and who we should be.

The design, once again, came from history. I hired Tom Sanders, who was an assistant art director on *Hook* in 1991. I liked him a lot. Then he went on to become a production designer—he did *Braveheart* and some other wonderful pictures. We just basically got all the American, the British, and the American flyovers of Omaha beach. Because they did a lot of flyovers before the invasion. And when they were building the Belgian gates and they were building all the tank traps and all the barbed wire, all that was in construction, we were photographing it up and down the beach, months before the invasion. So we got hold of those key kind of aerial reconnaissance photographs. And basically, Tom Sanders simply duplicated what was once a part of reality. The same thing with the town of Vermeil and with the central town in the story. Those were actual pictures of Carentan and pictures of Sainte Mère-Eglise and a lot of the French towns that had been devastated and had been kind of denuded of trees. That was just part of history, and those still photographs helped Tom to make his determinations of how he was going to lay out the sets.

We did a lot of camera experiments. I had seen the Robert Capa [shots] — all, there's eight of them left. Robert Capa was the photo-journalist who took three hundred or four hundred shots of first-wave D-day Omaha beach, and the lab in Britain had melted all the shots. The developer was so excited to see the shots and made key mistakes and ruined all but eight stills. Those eight stills have survived, and they've been printed again and again in magazines, in history books, and those eight stills totally told me the look of the movie. I showed those eight stills to Janusz [Kaminski, the cine-matographer] and I said, "How do we get this look? What do we do, because it's all blurry, it's got stuff on the lens, and it's right, down low." And we began to do tests on the back lot at Universal. I'll never forget our first test. We took a camera and put some extras in Army uniforms and we lined them up and we photographed them. And I took one of those huge drills, those big industrial Black and Decker drills, took the bit off, and instead just used the drill as a large vibra-tor. And basically had the on/off switch and I would hold the drill up to the camera and when I pressed *on*, the camera would vibrate, and we'd turn it off, it would stop. And we realized that when we saw the dailies the next day, it gave the most neurotic affect to the movie. The vibration was subtle enough to create a subconscious neurotic feeling to it. And we substituted the Black and Decker for an actual device called Lenshaker that you actually put onto the lens and it does shake the elements of the lens. And there was another technique: I saw hundreds of hours of documentaries and I always wondered, how come in those WWII black-and-white documen-taries—when there's an explosion, you can count each piece of dirt that goes into the air? Whereas in a modern action movie, when there's an explosion it's a beautiful flower eruption, it's a beautiful orange yellow black and white flower erupting, and it's just kind of like, glamorous. And Janusz was saying, "Well, I think it's because the old Bell and Howell cameras had an open forty-five degree shut-ter. So there was no blurring possible." So we took poor Panavision, we took their camera and deconstructed a Panaflex. Totally decon-structed it—stripped the lenses of coating, 'cause lenses are coated, you know, to make me look good. I mean, if I was in front of the cam-era. And we took all that off and basically opened the shutter up to either 45 degrees or 90 degrees, as opposed to 180 degrees, and when you do that, there's no blurring. It almost looks like every frame is a machine gun, like every frame is a bullet coming from a machine gun. And that combined with intermittent vibrations to the lens and just the way the camera was handheld and where it was placed. Several times I actually put a blood pack with a squib on it and I would put the blood just under the lens and I would trigger the squib so simply the lens would be splattered with blood. Because I wanted to deconstruct the look of the picture. I didn't want the pic-ture to look like a slick, glamorous John Wayne war movie.

Cameron Crowe

Jerry Maguire

Well, we built a lot just because it was a complicated movie with a lot of scenes. The porch where the kissing scene took place and everything is on a stage. A lot of care was put into making it seem real. But the jewel really is, of course, the set you don't see a lot, which is where Jerry works. Every desk in that place is unique, spe-cial to the person that works there. One's a punk rocker, one is very angry about certain things in his life, and all the photos on the desk are very specific to that person.

The house was supposed to be Jerry's soul in a way. At the begin-ning he's sort of "shoplifting the pooty," as they say in the movie, but by the end of the movie this place that he was kind of rushing out of to move on with his life is where he has to go to begin his life. And for that you've got to have, I think, the perfect kind of place. Where you stand on the lawn and look in the window and what's inside is your future. That is how we designed the house.

Mel Gibson
Braveheart

The battle scenes were the only sections of the picture that were story-boarded because of the massive amount of people and logistics and you had to have some kind of bible to fall back on when it all got to be too much. You can see the chaos that it looks like, in fact, it's not. And it was very carefully planned around a table with people's imaginations running riot about battles and tactics. There was one storyboard artist. There was myself, there was the guy doing line producing, and the camera guy and the first AD and the stunt coordinator. And we were all in there sort of cracking the whip and coming up with all kinds of ideas for what this battle could be and how it was to be done and we had a table with egg cartons and stuff with cloths and stuff drenched over it and little plastic soldiers—and lots of cigars being smoked.

I wanted rotting carcasses and I wanted to be able to smell it—I wanted it to be really funky and down, not what people expect from the thirteenth century. People think they had castles. In fact, there was a lot more wood. They were going from wood to stone, and the wood fortresses that they built really served as a kind of inside scaffolding for what would eventually become the big thick stone walls of later on. And as you went further south, there was more stone used. But it was pretty rough and primitive, and we did aerial photographic scouts of what had been. We developed a little Scottish town from that, very similar to Native American dwellings, just no chimney or anything, just a hole in the roof of a rock teepee.

Clint Eastwood
Unforgiven

With the art director, I walk over the spot, and I say, "We'll put this building here." We sort of kick around ideas. He'd say, "How about this," and everybody would contribute; and then somebody else might say, "Well, the stable would be better here, because this is the way it would be in life." I wanted the town on 45 degrees, so that I could have upwards and downward angles, and so that I could look out across the valleys. I told him I needed a mezzanine thing and I needed separation from the girls upstairs, but at the same time, I wanted it all connecting. Then the art director will design the buildings on paper, and you start going through it and imagining how you would shoot it.

I wanted to shoot it like a black-and-white film. And so I even had the costumers working accordingly. There's a lot of coal oil lighting, there's no real big illumination for a building, so you have to make the interiors look like their actual coal oil lighting of the day, and as you know, everybody can shoot exteriors, but interiors are what separates the players in cinematography.

Gus Van Sant
Good Will Hunting

We talked about the design, but we [Missy Stewart] kind of had enough of a camaraderie that she sort of went off and did it, and I would often be surprised just sort of showing up and seeing what she had done. One of the issues was trying to match the Toronto interiors with the Boston exteriors. Usually when I go into a film, there are a lot of styles that are in your head, and you're looking at films with the cinematographer. We were watching these sort of examples of films that we were kind of trying to get ideas from. One of the things I'd always try to do in my past films was to try and get a sort of natural light going so that the natural light from window is lighting the scene, and you don't have to do much interior shifting of lights, which usually takes up a lot of time. You know, like the changing of an angle can sometimes eat up thirty or forty minutes of time for the cinematographer. I've always tried to get this going with cinematographers, where you just sort of light the set and then you can move the camera around within the set. And it usually never works out that way when you're there doing it. I told Jean-Yves [Escoffier, the cinematographer] this, and he did it. He knew what to do and what we wanted to do. He accomplished that, so that our turnaround time for cameras was like, five minutes, which was pretty amazing—and it made it so that the actors worked harder, because they couldn't really take breaks. It made it so that I was shooting twice as much film as any other film that I did.

The first film I did was completely storyboarded with like 500 pages of drawings, and I used that in a "Hitchcockian" sense. And that was a very low-budget film. We could handle all those different drawings, we could get the shots. Then when I did *Drugstore Cowboy*, I was faced with an eighty-person crew. I realized that just changing your shot became a huge ordeal, and I couldn't keep with the story-board I had drawn; so I got used to shooting a scene after rehearsing it and getting the action down, choosing the first angle, and then deciding what the second angle is.

Neil Jordan

The Crying Game

We built that glass house, because it seems an odd thing if you capture a hostage and you want to hide him and you put him in a glass house. But I had a situation where this entire thirty pages of dialogue had to happen between two guys. You were told, if somebody were hostage, you would hold them in a dungeon, wouldn't you? But if you are in a dungeon with a camera, you are finished, aren't you? I mean, what can you do? It's dark! So I said, "OK, we have a glass house adjacent to the little farm house. OK, they're in the glass house, so you've got to obscure what they see from the outside." So I say, "OK, it's a dead glass house where all these tomato plants are hanging down so all these vines cover—obscure your view from the outside, which then creates the impression of heat, like you are in a jungle or a sweaty sit-uation." The demands of the action plot create the design. Designers love to do things, don't they? You know, they like to create arches and curves and stuff, and you say, no, no, it's like that. And then you have to persuade the guy that he came up with the idea. That's the most dif-ficult thing! The main problem was to create the sense of space within confined spaces. To make things that did not look too large for the characters or for the actions. But actually gave me some space within which to compose the film. You get the set built and you bring the actors in and maybe it's not right, maybe things are not right. You sit somebody down here, and you say, "Well you can't see this guy from over here," so you get the designer to change that.

We had to create some rather little sad glittery fantasy in a bar that was in a workable shape. It was a dreadful shape, but it was the only one. The only place you could put the camera, actually, was behind the bar, so it was a nightmare. I couldn't afford to—we couldn't build anything. You're in a real location, so your choices are limited. And sometimes you come up with some interesting things—you can use mirrors, or you have to organize all the movements of the people through the only place you can put the camera.

The film that we were doing was mostly between two people, and I—the audience is with two characters for the first third of this movie. And if you use that big wide-screen format, it means you don't have to cut all the time. You can have one of their faces there and the other face there, and if it had not been wide screen, it would have been cutting from face to face to face a lot more.

The problem was, you know you are going to be in this room for at least thirty pages of script, so you better make it interesting. And her bed—I wanted to surround it with curtains. Her bed had to be about sex. The bed had to be the center of the flat, really. So I just came up with these series of curtains that surrounded her bed. It was a bit like a boudoir kind of situation, but yet it was a one-room flat, it was a loft. So I tried to build in things like that, that can actually create some mystery, so you can see the character behind the curtains, or she's behind the curtains, or she's looking at something, which adds to the sensuality of it.

I mean, we had so little money that we had to achieve these solutions. I prefer to be in a studio, generally, because you can control everything—the lighting, the colors.

Rehearsal
James L. Brooks
As Good as It Gets

I love rehearsal. I've had great rehearsals where I don't even touch the script. I think that what kind of rehearsal depends on who the actors are. When you have something called a rehearsal, basically all you are saying is the system goes away and lets you talk to the actors for a certain length of time. And that's so hard to come by, and it means everything. It means how you communicate—it means what you know about them, what they know about you, how quickly you can talk to each other when you're filming. I just think it's everything.

Rob Reiner
A Few Good Men

I do a lot of rehearsal—I mean, some of the pieces I've done are like theatre pieces. Particularly *A Few Good Men*. It's a courtroom drama, it's like theatre. And I go through the whole thing in a two-week period, and I rope out, tape out all the sets on a sound stage.

I find that the fear is always that you are gonna lose spontaneity. And the fact is you do. You lose it in a big way. But then you regain it. You have the spontaneity right away, at that first read-through, and you hear how it sounds, and everybody sounds good. Then you put it on its feet and it gets worse and worse and worse, and it's really starting to stink. Then it turns the corner. If you stay with it long enough, you get something a little bit better than you ever had before, with a little greater understanding and a little bit more depth.

[On *All in the Family*] we'd read the script around the table Monday morning. We'd be hysterical laughing, it was great—we'd put it on its feet, and the first couple times it was funny. By Wednesday or Thursday these jokes are lying there, I mean they're just dead. We've all said them, and we've all heard them a lot, but we kept saying, have faith, stay with it. The audience is going to hear it for the first time. They haven't been through this process. And if you can find a new way to make it fresh, not only will you have preserved a well-crafted joke, but also the audience is hearing it for the first time.

[In *Misery*] Jimmy Caan didn't like to rehearse so much. And Kathy Bates is from theatre and she loves to rehearse. So, that was difficult. I had to wind up rehearsing a little less than Kathy would have liked, and a lot more than Jimmy would have liked. Jimmy was frightened he would lose the spontaneity, and he had to use a wheelchair in that film. And he would say, "I want to see what it's like when I first get on the set and just feel what it's gonna be like and experience it." And I said, "Jim, you've never been in a wheelchair before. If you have to get in a wheelchair, it's gonna take you hours, you're not gonna be able to do it." I said, "What you gotta do," and he knew it, I said, "you get in that wheelchair, and spend a lot of time in it, so that you can get that wheelchair to do anything you want, spin this way, turn that way, move back," I said, "then you can make it as awkward or as easy as you want it to, rather than always be struggling with trying to make it work."

[In *A Few Good Men* in the rehearsal] I had the luck of having Jack Nicholson there. He knows what he's doing, and he comes to play, every time out, full-out performance! And what it says to a lot of the other actors is, "Oooooh, I better get on my game here, because this guy's coming to play! So I can't hold back, I've got to come up to him," and he sets the tone.

What you are trying to do is get to the point where you are realizing the script as best as it is, and maybe adding just a little bit more spin to it, just with their performances.

Steven Spielberg

Amistad

I don't like rehearsal. I can generalize one thing on most of my movies: I don't rehearse unless the actor truly needs the rehearsal, because that's what the actor requires. I'll read through a piece, but I don't do it often. I've done a number of readings to determine for myself whether I should direct the movie. I've never committed to a movie based on one of the read-throughs—I don't know what that means. On *The Color Purple* we did a read-through with all the actors, and there were fantastic moments that evolved and existed and dissipated in my conference room and never occurred again anywhere on film. And it was a brutal lesson to learn, that sometimes you cannot capture lightning in a bottle. Sometimes you really have to trust that when the mojos are working, there's gonna be some kind of magic happening on the set that day, and it's all gonna happen when the cameras are moving.

I think an actor really needs you to believe in him and her. If you simply believe in him and the actress, it's amazing what they can do for you.

Saving Private Ryan

In this case there was really nothing to rehearse. There was another kind of rehearsal. All the actors went to basic training and became soldiers for a week. Capt. Dale Dye, who was our technical consultant, took Tom Hanks and the other eight actors and brought them to a small bivouacked area near where we shot the film, which is near British Aerospace, outside of London. And he put them through six days of grueling, treacherous, torturous training. And it was a bad week. It rained every day and every night. And the actors all wanted to go home. And they wanted to quit the movie about the second day in. And Tom called me one day in the editing room and I was cutting *Amistad* at the time, and Tom said, "We're losing our entire cast. They're walking out. They're calling their agents. They're saying it's humiliation, and they're being humiliated every day, and people are yelling at them. They haven't been yelled at since they were children at home. What do we do here?" And I just said, "Well, Tom, I'm here and you're there. And you're a director. You just did *That Thing You Do*, so do that thing you do and save this cast." And he did. He rallied the troops, and from that kind of near-disaster came a real bonding of the entire cast, to the point that when I showed up, I was the outsider. Because I hadn't been yelling at anybody, and I hadn't been in their lives, and I only met about two or three of the actors anyway for the first time. And they weren't listening to me. They were listening to Dale Dye and Tom Hanks. And I showed up, I had my name on the back of the chair and everything—they didn't care about that. And I had to win my way into their hearts and minds, because they weren't accepting me right away. When I'd say something, they'd all look at Tom Hanks, or Dale Dye. And so I had to kind of prove myself, and it took a while. But it was a great experience to know that they went through that experience. Because what they really brought out of it, even though it was only five days and not the ninety days that most soldiers spend in basic training, in much worse conditions — they brought with them a respect of the combat veteran. And they came out of it really understanding that we weren't just making an entertaining, escapist kind of summer action movie, but we were making a movie that was really meant to memorialize the WWII veteran. And I don't think any of them realized that's what we were determined to do, until they had gone through that process.

Anthony Minghella
The English Patient

I rehearse. I come from the theatre, and I think the actors need to rehearse, and they get better through rehearsing, and I get better and know more about what can be done and what can be eliminated.

Quentin Tarantino
Pulp Fiction

I do two weeks of rehearsal. It's the time we talk subtext. And that's one of the great things about rehearsal, "Why don't you go over there?" "Why would I go over there when we can stop and talk about it for an hour about why would you go over there?" That's great. When we're actually doing it we've reached a certain point with each other and I try to keep it pretty precise and I'm trying to say something actable.

Neil Jordan
The Crying Game

I find the most important moment is when you bring the actors onto the set. Because you know they've imagined the scene in their minds and you've constructed the set, where the door is or where all the pivotal important objects are — that's when I rehearse.

Oliver Stone

JFK

I rehearse a lot—it allows us freedom. Once you have developed in a rehearsal an attitude, then we can go against it. And I find that very valuable. But the movie is a debate. The debate starts with the rehearsal.

We budget usually three weeks in advance. We do one week in wherever most of the actors are. And the second week we move to location and we rehearse on location as much as we can. Not all the sets are ready, obviously, but we do the best we can. Then I stop and I do some rewrites.

Whenever we start a new scene, we rehearse it again, only with the actors—I ask the crew to leave. And I take the set with the actors and we work it out. We agree to agree, synchronize our watches, so to speak. We block it out. And often it's quite different than what we did several weeks before. But we've now done it three times. This is the third time. The crew comes back. We show them the rehearsal, often indifferently, because we want to save it. And then we go and we shoot. We had the liberty of going through it three different times and trying three different things, or maybe three similar things. But it becomes a payoff. We've made an event—we've built up to a moment.

I believe in rehearsal. But I believe in going against the rehearsal, too. As I believe in preparing the script, but also going against the script, too.

Peter Weir

The Truman Show

Rehearsal? No, I don't at all. It doesn't all happen until everyone's in costume and props. The invented world, the magic world, it comes alive. I come alive. I can't draw chalk on the floor, that kind of thing. It seems sort of comical to me. I must say it's my own approach. I have trouble sometimes with actors. Jeff Bridges, for example, said to me, "Boy, I'm really nervous about that." For his sake, I did set up a rehearsal. But I said, "Rather than do the lines from the film, let's improvise the rehearsal." And we ended up really, I think, just laughing.

In terms of the friend, Noah Emmerich, I cast him firstly because he is such a warm personality. And then I said, "This is breaking your heart. You hate what you're doing. You grew up with Truman, as a kid." And we worked out backstories, always working out back stories, which I often did, by the way, with a more conventional film. I loved to talk about who they were and where they came from. We worked out that he'd been told at twelve the truth of his situation. He moved to the town when he was seven—he was told to make friends with that little boy over there. "Truman, he's your kind of boy—go and make friends with him." So at twelve, his parents said, "We want to have a talk with you, and sit down." He thought it was going to be about sex. He said, "I already know all about that, Dad." And he said, "No. This is, you know, television." "Sure." "Do you like television?" "Yes, I do." "Well, you're on it." And he said, "That day, I lost my innocence." With the parents telling him. So he had all that kind of backstory. So there was emotion for him there.

Barry Levinson
Bugsy

The first screenplay I wrote was . . . *And Justice for All*. And Al Pacino wanted a reading of it. I wasn't the director, I was just there. They had a bunch of really terrific actors. And what happened was Al Pacino maybe not wanting to give a performance and every other actor not wanting to upstage him—they are doing a little less. And everybody's doing a little less. And the point is, I had no idea what anyone was saying—I didn't know what the movie was about.

The idea of putting, like, twelve actors around the table is the most petrifying thought to me. I kind of hear a movie in my head to a degree, and so I'd rather just put it on the floor and work it out.

In a sense it's like a constant rehearsal on film that you keep shooting. A lot of times you're looking for the imperfection of it. Because sometimes what happens is you get a nice piece of professional work, but the professional work doesn't give you that surprise.

Sometimes there's a struggle to say the lines, maybe a struggle of not remembering what to say, that is the same as not knowing what to say in life. That may be good. And those are the moments that you kind of treasure.

Mike Newell
Four Weddings and a Funeral

We rehearsed for a couple of weeks, and I like rehearsal, because I enjoy the whole business of acting. We tried all sorts of things, and a kind of chemistry emerged. There is rarely such a thing as natural chemistry. There is mostly people who must make a chemistry together, and because they are actors, they get on and do. There's that phrase that people use, "You've got to get good performance," which I rather mistrust. I don't think you *get* performances, I think actors *give* performances, and what you have to do is sweep the ground in front of them so there's nothing for them to trip on. I mean — of course, you have to set guidelines and you have to be clear with them about what's necessary, but if you've got the casting process right, it should work, so long as they don't stumble.

Barbra Streisand
The Prince of Tides

I knew I had to have a reading, because I needed to hear this piece and I needed to see it read. And I was devastated by what I saw. I thought, this piece doesn't work. But I learned a lot from it, and the script changed a great deal from hearing that reading.

In terms of rehearsal, I only like to rehearse certain things, things that have to do with technical stuff. Otherwise, I like to capture the actor's spontaneity, his first instincts, on film — then go from there.

Andrew Davis
The Fugitive

There was rehearsal time in the sense that I did go around with Harrison [Ford], for example, and with Tommy [Lee Jones], and showed them where they were going to be living and working. I wanted their feedback on dressings, and character things that they would want to have. "What kind of personal items, things that would make you feel better about this?" Actors like this are very resourceful — they'll come up with wonderful ideas for you.

You rehearse to find out what you have to change. And I haven't done a dramatic piece where you're sitting in a room for six minutes talking to each other. There's hardly a scene in these movies that are longer than two minutes.

Certain actors do not want to rehearse. Certain directors don't want to give scripts to people. And there are advantages to not letting people know too much. They can get stale, they can preconceive things, and then they get upset when it doesn't work. At the same time, it would be wonderful to have somebody rehearse and really know what they're doing. I think that both techniques are viable, and valuable, and should be used within one movie.

Michael Radford

Il Postino

Philippe Noiret is a great, great movie actor. He knows precisely what to do — you don't have to have any great discussion with him. When I first met him I said, "I think Pablo Neruda this, Pablo Neruda that," and I went through a whole kind of spiel of about what I thought he was — and he looked at me and he said, "Hmm, I find that very interesting, what you said. You know what I think about Pablo Neruda?" And I said, "What?" He said, "I think he's a man when he sits down, he sits down like this. He doesn't sit down like this." And he had it. He had it absolutely down, because he was an extrovert, he was a generous man — so he never crossed his legs throughout the entire picture, and that was the only real discussion we had. In terms of dealing with his performance, he has in the film a very small space to move, a very small arc of character. The balance to achieve with Philippe was how cold he would be towards the guy, so he could just warm up enough to feel that this guy had touched him. What I did basically with Philippe was to shoot practically every piece of dialogue that he had in two different ways. We'd do a colder version and a warmer version, because I knew in the editing rooms I would be able to judge it, but I couldn't quite judge it on the set, particularly as he was doing it to a blank space. [Massimo Troisi, his co-star, was seriously ill, and so wasn't there to act with Noiret.]

Mike Leigh
Secrets & Lies

What I tend to do is to have a sort of pyramid, where we start rehearsals with two or three people and it builds up. People are contracted to join in as it develops. And their contracts are constructed so that they are contracted to drop out during the shoot, but with an extension which has to be taken up before the beginning of principal photography. It's a curious combination of being creative and mathematical.

Mel Gibson
Braveheart

Ofttimes we rehearse the last thing of an evening, or a day when you'd know you'd have to come in tomorrow morning and you'd have an idea of how you wanted it to go during the rehearsal. Sometimes you end up ripping pages out and say, "Hey, we don't need that."

In between takes you'll stand around and yak about it—who the person is, what's his particular dilemma, and why? Just a lot of questions, and sometimes I pose the questions, and sometimes they pose the questions, and you're just talking in kind of abstract terms. And you can reach for all kinds of situations, from stage plays you've seen to old movies. Nothing's out of bounds.

Gus Van Sant
Good Will Hunting

I'm used to about two weeks of rehearsal time. It'll be, say, two hours in the morning and two hours in the afternoon, pretty short periods, where we're reading through it and acting out scenes and we're probably trying to get to know each other. Sometimes there's some going off the page and just doing the character without going from the script—just inventing things. Also during that time there's costuming and gearing up and getting ready. I'm totally in favor of keeping out of the way of the performance, because you can definitely jump in there and screw things up. I always let the actors sort of come up with a bunch of things, and maybe there's an editing process or advising process, but there's not a whole lot of monitoring the performance or the actor. Unless they really want it. Sometimes an actor will really want you to sort of explain exactly what to do, and you can do that.

James Cameron

Titanic

I don't like to over rehearse. You want to give the actors a sense that they are gonna be able to explore on the day. So what I did with Kate and Leo was, I spent a week a couple of hours a day, two, three hours a day, and it was mostly improv [improvisation] work—it was mostly just figuring kind of who their characters were to each other and working on that chemistry. Leo was still struggling a lot with his guy and how to play him, just because he always sort of looks for a dark side, and that's really not what the character was all about. Finally I said, "Look, it's a lot easier to do the stuff you've been doing than to be Jimmy Stewart." Because to have so little of what I think of as flashy stuff in the part, and to be mesmerizing to an audience a hundred percent of the time that you are on the camera, is a great acting challenge. Once he realized it was hard, then he was down for it! It's only when he thought it was too easy that he didn't want to do it!

Curtis Hanson

L.A. Confidential

Rehearsal to me is invaluable. I use it: I don't think of it as rehearsing for performance as much as I do rehearsing for content. To me it's the opportunity to be with the actors, read through the script without them actually acting it, but just kind of reading it—and maybe they go up to, let us say, second gear, just to kind of feel what it feels like. It's the time where, in a relaxed mode without the crew, without the pressure of time, you can talk about the scenes, and talk about the intent of each line, if need be—and with some actors it's necessary to talk about the intent of each line, because they want to challenge it and feel it's right.

The rehearsal period on this picture was unique in that I had these two Australians, and they both have Australian accents. So, I brought them over actually seven weeks before we started shooting. I wanted them to become comfortable with the language so that they wouldn't have to be thinking about it when they were performing. But also comfortable with me, and I felt the picture rested on their ability to pull off these parts. So I went through every day with them for however much time it was necessary, given scenes, and then gradually I would feather in the other actors.

— 4 —

Production

The Shoot

Barry Levinson

Bugsy

You may spend twelve hours a day, and out of that maybe walk away with two minutes of usable film. So the concentration of the director on the set has to be very, very focused. You can't miss a moment because you never know when those "two minutes" will happen.

Sometimes the blocking [the actors' movement] is not clear, so I'll just let the actors keep playing around with it as we keep evolving into some kind of blocking that begins to make sense and feels comfortable. When you approach a new scene, there's always a certain amount of trepidation. Just really be very comfortable with it. Try the blocking that makes sense, like you might say, "It'd be nice if we went over towards the window," rather than saying to the actor, "Why don't you go to the window." Otherwise they say, "Why do I have to go to the window?" It's better that they went to the window and got there by themselves. It's a little bit like trying to get what you want and at the same time not wanting to be so demanding that you're restricting the process. I like to give an actor as much room as possible to explore anything that might come up. And the performance may change radically as we begin to play with it.

It's not always the words themselves. It is the struggle to say the words and what they may represent other than the actual words.

And that's kind of what I'm trying to evolve to in the easiest way of sneaking up on the performance. You have to work in different ways with different actors. I did *Good Morning, Vietnam,* and I had a class-room of all of these Vietnamese—none of them could act or knew anything about it. So what we did was just try to keep the camera on and hide it. You don't say, "Action," you don't say anything. You just sort of launch them and somehow they don't even know that they're being filmed anymore. There's a cause and effect that's taking place, and yet the script is being serviced to some degree, because a lot of times they will say different things that may be better than what we have and they're not even aware of it. You have to find a way to get their behavior on film without intimidating them.

Sometimes it takes longer for some actors to warm up than others. Some of them are there in that earlier take [each time a scene or par-ticular shot is put on film is one take], and others are fourteen takes in—that's when they're starting to cook. That's a dilemma. You have to find some way that it's going to start to work.

Certain blocking suggests certain things. Between the blocking and some ideas you have in terms of visualization, you will find the day's work and how it should take place.

In *Bugsy* I wanted to end up with Bugsy and Virginia behind the movie screen, because they were sort of like these people who wanted to be movie stars but never were. I knew I wanted to get to that. I didn't know how to get there. When the actors were kind of playing it, all of a sudden I said to Allen Daviau [the cinematogra-pher], "we'll pick them up from the time they come through the door." They go around the room, we go behind the screen, one's behind the screen, one is in the clear—and it suddenly evolved into the entire scene as one take.

I like to use two cameras a lot. I'll put them anywhere, maybe at very odd angles to one another. A lot of times I find that the B cam-era, which is supposedly in the wrong place, is actually better than the one that's in the right place. We don't want to compromise a shot and the look of the film, but at the same time I think you can find cer-tain parameters you can work within. Sometimes that second cam-era, which is slightly off, may be more interesting in a way, because it can't give you all of the information. I found that a lot of times not having the total information engages the audience slightly more than having all the information.

Most scenes in the film are two-cameras, unless you've designed a specific shot for one camera.

I like to mike [putting microphones near] everyone, whether they're on camera or off camera because sometimes things happen. It has to do with rhythms. When I was doing *Diner*, we got into the diner scenes — I had not directed a movie before — and we started to shoot, we're looking this direction, and the actors are talking, and then the sound technician says after the take, "You've got a problem because we've got these overlaps." I said, "Yeah." He said, "But they're off camera." I said, "I know." He said, "But they're off mike." So I said, "Why can't they be miked? Why don't we mike them?" He said, "Because you can make the overlaps later in editing." In real life when we talk we overlap one another, all the time. So, I prefer to struggle with the overlapping in the editing room rather than try to invent it.

> **Barry Levinson:** I basically just mike everybody, whether they're on camera or not. They're going to have a wireless [microphone].
>
> **Barbra Streisand:** They're the worst. I can tell you that from the actor's point of view. They're horrible.
>
> **Oliver Stone:** My people don't like wireless, either.
>
> **Barry Levinson:** But it works extremely well. I did it in Thailand with all the people over there, and you're able to use it. I like to mike everyone, whether they're on camera or off camera, because sometimes things happen — because when we talk we overlap one another, all the time.

Oliver Stone
JFK

People will tell you that my set's pretty wild, it's chaotic. Which is good, because each day is the day of birth. No matter how much you rehearsed it and how good it was in rehearsal three months before, it doesn't mean shit when you're out there. That's when it starts.

We had five cameras on certain days: we were running around between cameras. So many angles suggested themselves naturally at Dealy Plaza that a storyboard [drawings made of all the intended shots] would've minimized the scene. Why limit yourself?

On the day of the final rehearsal, I might change the position radically and say, the point of view is totally wrong. It really should be inside this person or inside that person, or outside this. Or the entire movement of this should not be six shots. It should be one shot. And that will happen right then and there, and he'll [the cameraperson] go crazy because the lighting scheme has to change. But better that than shoot it and not be happy with it.

I can't sit there and wait for two hours while the cameraman lights. I just don't have that kind of patience; certain directors do.

I usually get out in less than six takes. Could be the script, could be an actor, the camera, the lighting. I occasionally go seventeen, twenty-seven, but very rarely.

How do you deal with the actors that start late? And I've had that problem many times. Huston had a great solution. He just announced that he was doing one or two takes. And the actors realized that it was for real. He did both and he walked away. There is some truth to that because it does force them to concentrate. I don't admire people that assume that film is free. It isn't. It's a privilege. I don't like people that just sit there for seven takes and warm up. It's a waste of everybody's time and energy. The crew is trying from take one. I want it to work on take one.

I encourage my actors to overlap all the time. I love the Wellesian technique. But there are certain actors who really—a line of dialogue is sacred to them. There are some actors that don't like to be changed at the last second.

I torture the sound man. Because I often like to do extreme close-up with an extreme wide at the same time. And they hate that.

Barbra Streisand
The Prince of Tides

I like to know what I'm going to do, then throw it away. Because I get bored easily, too. I don't like to do that many takes because I come from the theatre, where things are done without cuts. I like to stage things in just one shot. I kind of enjoy living on the edge, the risk factor of having the take fail if all the elements aren't right—it keeps everybody on their toes.

I have a video 8 camera and I go around and do the shots that I see in my head.

At times I have models near the sets. I like to know what I'm going to do with the camera. Does a wall have to move? What has to happen to get this shot?

I always imagine how I want it to be. But, I don't want to impose that on actors at first. I impose it if they don't come up with something better. I like to use reality, and use what is: use the day, use something the actor does in real life and be open to the moment— be present in the moment.

I do find it fascinating that most actors would like to be told what to do.

But, I do like it when the actor has very definite opinions, because again it forces this debate, the energy, and the aliveness.

Storyboarding that rape sequence, I had done way before I had a set. So one reality exists on paper, the other on the set. I don't look at storyboards then.

I love being able to be flexible and bending to what is, the reality that exists.

On *Yentl* David Watkins [the cinematographer] lit the set so you could go anywhere. So that I could do ten-minute masters and have two cameras that had to be choreographed to avoid each other.

John Madden
Shakespeare in Love

We rehearsed for about three weeks. Which is much longer than I would ever normally do. Gwyneth, for example, had never actually performed Shakespeare, so dealing with the language, and understanding how the language works and so forth, was part of that. It was also building a life for the actors. And so much of the time, I knew I was going to have to rely on the core group of players in the movie, to have a life that was going on at the edge of the frame. Because it needed to feel real all the time in order for something to come out of it. For something to transcend from it. And we had dances and we had fights and so forth. And the movie is extraordinarily patterned. It's not something you necessarily spot the first time around, but the balcony scene happens three times in the movie, and the people are changing places all the time, and changing sexes all the time. There are all kinds of patterns going on. So it's a matter of working those out so that the actors understood. The physical stuff between Joe and Gwyneth was something that we, I wouldn't say rehearsed, but we certainly talked a great deal about what that would be. I don't like to rehearse too much for movies. I operate on a sort of touch-and-go policy, in aeronautical terms. Where you just kind of land on the material for a moment, just to prime it, so the actors are aware of what might be in the scene, and then you take off again quickly. So that when you're there, in the white heat of the moment, trying to decide exactly how you're going to shoot it, and how it's going to be played, there's still something left to discover.

The camera is an accomplice to the language. You have an instinct about when you want your camera to move and when you don't. When you feel that movement is going to generate some visceral sense—when that moment is right, and when it's right for the camera to be still and just observe. Usually that's when you hear music, or when you know you're going to be using music. And I have this bizarre habit of sort of humming whenever I'm doing a moving shot, or sort of thinking about a moving shot, which is a strange sight to behold. I find that what I do is I try and prepare as much as I possibly can—think about everything, every possibility, so that I can throw everything out when I get there and then do something else. Which is where the anxiety comes in for me. In certain sequences, you do exactly what you intended to do.

It seems to me that you don't want to have a method of working. A director's responsibility is to be able to pull completely different sensibilities into the service of the story you're trying to tell. And that involves, I think, being sensitive to and recognizing a particular route that people have to take to get there. Gwyneth and Joe, for example, totally different actors. Have totally different ways of working. Joe's very, very, very exploratory and has a tendency, almost as soon as he's found one thing, to distrust what he's found and want to go find something else. That's partly his own nature, partly just where he is in his profession, I suppose — still searching. Gwyneth, by contrast, is extraordinarily accurate, and very instinctive about where she's going to go. She doesn't want to land at all until the camera turns over. I think she's frightened the genie will get out of the bottle. She perhaps doesn't trust herself as much as she could. What I think I have to do in that circumstance is to create a kind of bridge so that I can negotiate the problems one actor is having with the way the other actor might be receiving it. And I always do that with the text or the scene or whatever, to create an imaginative world that they can all believe in. And somehow, then, you've got a way of negotiating what's going on, rather than saying, "Gee, are you having trouble? Do you want to take an aspirin?" You can't do it that way. If you go back into the world that you've created, the imaginative world you've created, and that you're all engaged in, trying to create for other people. But it's difficult. Sometimes an actor will get trapped. And, of course, you go through the process of a large number of takes. Which seems to make matters worse. Often I just walk away at that point. Often I'll even shoot something else. Come around and shoot the reverse again. That's another thing I did a great deal in this movie. I'd say, "Let's go on," and then we'd shoot something else, and then I'd go back and shoot the reverse again. Because with this material it was so strange how elusive it could be. Every actor would come up and go, "I don't know, was that all right? Did that work? I didn't quite feel that was right—was it funny?" And we all knew what he meant. It was just very, very hard material to target. I have to restrain my instinct not to want to go again, because I am so committed to this idea that there might be something I haven't yet discovered. Which is a pain in the ass for producers who work with me. I'm not saying I want to do thousands and thousands of takes. I gave every actor a rule that they could call upon, which was that if they ever wanted one more take when I had called it a day, they could have that. The interesting thing about a movie is that, of course, you learn about what it is as you go along, and it has things to teach you about what you're doing and the way you're approaching it and the way you're telling the story as you go along.

Clint Eastwood

Unforgiven

Some people perform at their very best early in the game, and maybe they'll disintegrate and you can bring it back up. I like to set the atmosphere and just kind of go through it, and as we're going through and setting cameras, I'll just have the actors just talk through it, "Don't try to put too much into it." And in *Unforgiven*, I had Gene Hackman, and I had Morgan Freeman, two of the fastest startup actors I had ever worked with. Gene is one of those guys who — I think he is one of America's best actors, he just is ready to go immediately. You start the rehearsal and you're going, "My God, why aren't we rolling?" And so what I would do is start rolling early. I'd say, "Let's just rehearse this on film."

I like improvisation, I must say, I like that feeling of that first time. And I guess a lot of the directors I've worked with out of television and everything, didn't have the benefit of rehearsals so you become kind of . . . you want to expedite things fast. Jessica Walter, in the very first film I ever directed, she was one of those kinds, who loved to rehearse on film, loved it, that first time out of the box. Now it isn't always ideal and sometimes it won't be as good. Sometimes you may do three or four takes. There may be something in that first take, though, that's great. There may be a section of it that is just fabulous, and you may never recapture it again. I think that's the advantage of film — is, you can try things and see what happens and you don't have to use it.

I think a director's most important function is probably a comfort zone that he can set up for the actors, because every actor has a certain insecurity level when they first come on. It's a very frightening experience: you are up in front of a lot of people you don't know, and all of the sudden you are going to start spouting dialogue you've thought about, but you've never heard it come out of your mouth. Then, you set a comfort zone, try to make everybody feel very, very much at ease, and sometimes you can do that by saying, "Well, here are all the props and stuff, and you walk around and you do this, and the cameraman will be here, we'll be lining up some things," and you give the actors a chance to be free and wander about and get it, and all of the sudden — boom! — they're ready to go.

The main thing I always tell other directors is, "Get more sleep than anyone else," and so I go to bed relatively early and try to get a decent night's sleep and go in with absolute will. You are gonna will these shots. They're going to be made. Never look back and never think negatively that, "Oh gee, what happens if . . . ?" I hate the expression a lot of times people use—"Oh, I'm afraid of this, I'm afraid that won't work." If you are afraid, then you shouldn't be there.

With the actors, I kind of start out kind of gradually. Sometimes a European technique, where the director shows the actors what to do, is effective only if the actor asks for it. I remember Vittorio De Sica [Italian director of such masterpieces as *The Bicycle Thief* and *Two Women*] insists on acting out every part for every actor. I don't do that unless the actor gets "salty" with you. I had one actor once who insisted on going into a corner, and we were trying to stage a scene in his room. It was an interesting room—it had a lot of nice set decorations put up there—and he says, "Well, I feel better over here in this corner." Well, there's nothing more dull than shooting into a wall that's flat. I kept saying, "Well, you know it's such a bad place to be;" and he says, "Well, this is where I feel it." And I said, "Well, I tell you what—why don't you try it where I feel it out here?" And he's going, "Well, how would you do it?" And so I thought, I've got to appeal to this guy's ego, so I walk over to this window and say, "You feel this light coming, see this light coming through the window, see how it hits? Now it's really dramatic, it makes your face look sensational." So all of the sudden, this guy's going "Yeah, yeah, that's OK, that sounds good!" So pretty soon I got him out into the room. Sometimes you have to be a little bit of an amateur psychologist or psychiatrist.

My first three or four films, I shot exactly what I wanted. Then later on as time goes by sometimes you give yourself a luxury of shooting a little extra footage or extra angles that you think might be effective, but you have some sort of doubt about.

The first two films that I did I used video [connected to the camera that shows what the camera sees and can be replayed with a VCR]. I found it helpful in some ways, but I found it also something that could be very abused. A lot of times I'd see the shot and we had to put the video player in a trailer. So I'd go back to the trailer and I'd hear this rumble behind me, and I'd look and here's all the actors and half the crew, everybody's come and they're all going to see the shot. And after a while the actors are saying, "Well, I could do one more and could I have my hair fixed and makeup?" So I finally would only use it on my own close-up, something I was in doubt about, or crane a shot or something like that. And then in recent years, I've just discontinued using it all together.

I know there's a lot of precedent for actors, dating back since the beginning of filmmaking, actors who have directed themselves, but I don't recommend it as a usual way. Sometimes you'll say, "Well, wait a second — I'm in this scene, but I'm only about forty percent in here because I'm really thinking technically and I'm worried about the other actors, the light on them." I remember years ago, I was doing a film with an actor, an older actor, and he was having trouble with his dialogue. So I started kind of rooting for him, and we'd have the camera over here, and I'd be kind of mouthing it along with him. When the camera came around here, I was mouthing along with him again! And the camera operator said, "You know, you were mouthing his lines with him." And the shot was on me!

Nowadays television has trained the eye to look at cinematography differently than when we grew up, because we grew up looking at Ford pictures and Welles and various people that would do some very bold work. And nowadays sometimes people are afraid, a little more cautious. I'll look through the lens at times, I'll have a stand-in go through it if I have to be in a shot or if it's a sequence. Naturally films that you're not in are much easier, but I'll look through the lens maybe on a rehearsal of some kind or maybe it's a simple shot and I know what the lens is and I know what it's seeing.

Neil Jordan
The Crying Game

First of all, you've got to put the camera somewhere, you know, and I'd say, somewhere around there, and it was not specific enough. They used to call me "There'ish" because they'd say, "Where would you like me to put the camera?" And I'd say, "There'ish."

People think if they are doing loads of things that they're actually acting. Very often it's just to get everything simple so the only gestures are the necessary ones.

With Forest [Whitaker], the main thing was to get his accent right, because he's from Texas. So, I found this taxi driver in London, and I heard his accent. I was in the back of the taxi, and this guy had slightly a bit of Caribbean and the North London accent. And I thought for Forest, the way was the Caribbean accent. So I got this guy to read the whole script into a tape and he became Forest's driver. And this guy then came to drive me insane because he'd be sitting at the back of the set, and we'd be doing the little scenes and Forest would look and say, "Was that OK?" When people get a hint of power, they really take it!

The first day is a disaster, generally! Everybody is nervous with each other, and the actors are nervous, and generally I end up redoing it.

The night before, I write out everything I want to get in the next day. Like I'm my own mother, saying to me, "You have to get this tomorrow or when you come home, you're not going to get any dinner!" And I just write out the shots I want to achieve. And it's a strange thing if you want a certain bit of emotion at a certain moment. I try to make a list of what I actually want. I even write out what I want the weather to be like. And then you get to the next day, and everything changes. I go out and talk through the scene with the actors. It's a bit deceitful, really, to say, I want them to move from here to there for the purposes that I want, but I want to get them to do what I want them do on their own accord. But sometimes I'm wrong. Sometimes they would move places naturally and it is perfect for the scene.

I try to operate the camera, you know, on the rehearsal. And sometimes I try to give the operator shots that he can't do! Because you do see things differently when you are looking through the lens. I don't believe anybody in the world can draw what happens through a specific lens through a moving camera with a moving object.

When you do long takes that are like 2 1/2 minutes long, and when you are putting a lot of film through the camera, and you have to do that twelve times, that is exhausting for everyone concerned.

I think acting is a mysterious thing. Sometimes when you get non-actors—Jaye Davidson was a non-actor—and they're doing this stuff and it's terribly leaden and you're saying, "Well, OK, if I get it a bit faster I could use it or maybe I cover [shooting the same scene from different angles] it in these different ways." And then suddenly one day the guy begins to act and you say, "Why is he acting now, not before?!"

You hope the spirit of the roles is going into the actors. You hope the actors are being as generous to the characters as you were when you were writing them. And you hope they kind of get involved in the emotional traumas of their characters.

I think the danger with me is that sometimes I like excessive performances. There's something in me, and I have to watch it, that likes bigness; and I've come to realize that that's a dangerous tendency of mine in part.

I try to work at the rhythms of the whole, of what the finished film will be. And in the scene, let's say, of dialogue, where there's progressive intensity between two characters, I try and design it so that the broadest thing you see is first, and the tightest thing you see is at the end of the scene — you know, the closest thing you see is at the end.

You try and work out how you want it to be seen. [In *The Crying Game*] we've had all this tranquil, but, terribly tense kind of moments between two men. I want this gunfire to come from nowhere — it's like demonic, it's like vengeance of god or something. So I don't want you to see the source of the gunfire. Or perhaps just want to see the helicopter up there. So I just draw out the different shots that I want and give them to the special effects people to work out what to see: the glass house, to see every pane just explode. And you say, "Can you do this? Will this be the most effective thing?" Maybe there's something else to come up with more punch. And are those stunt scenes you work out what you want to see? But you're in the hands of what actually can be physically done at times.

A main problem was — could you look at a man with a hood over his face and could he engross you? Now Forest took care of that problem just because of his emotional power and the way he uses his voice and his language, or the way he struggled with this, or the way he went into exhaustion. I wanted to see his mouth, the little bit of humanity that Stephen Rea exhibits towards the character is, he rolls up the hood and holds it up to there. Now you can write that down, "he rolls up the hood and you see his mouth," but try doing it. The thing keeps slipping literally, and when he struggles to get it up to

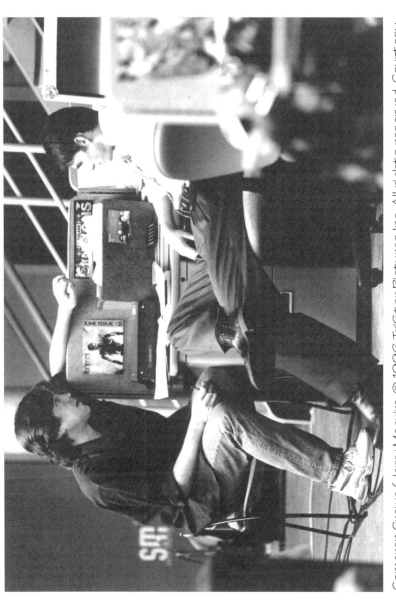

John Madden (*Shakespeare in Love.* © Miramax Films. Photograph by Laurie Sparham)

Anthony Minghella (*The English Patient* © Miramax Films. Photograph by Phil Barayowitz)

Mike Newell (*Four Weddings and a Funeral.* ©1994 Polygram Filmed Entertainment. All rights reserved.)

Rob Reiner (*A Few Good Men.* © 1992 Columbia Picture Industries, Inc. & Castle Rock Entertainment. All rights reserved. Courtesy of Columbia Pictures. Photograph by Sidney Baldwin)

Andrew Davis (*The Fugitive.* © 1993 Warner Bros., a division of Time Warner Entertainment Company L.P. All rights reserved. Photograph by Stephen Vaughan.)

Peter Weir (Courtesy of Paramount Pictures. *The Truman Show.* © 1998 Paramount Pictures. All rights reserved. Photograph by Melinda Sue Gordon)

Roberto Benigni (*Life Is Beautiful*. © Miramax Films. Photograph by Sergio Strizzi)

Curtis Hanson (*L.A. Confidential.* © 1997 Monarchy
Enterprises B.V. and Regency Entertainment (USA), Inc.
All rights reserved.)

James Cameron (*Titanic.* Lightstorm Entertainment ©
1997 Twentieth Century Fox and Paramount Pictures.
All rights reserved. Photograph by Merie W. Wallace)

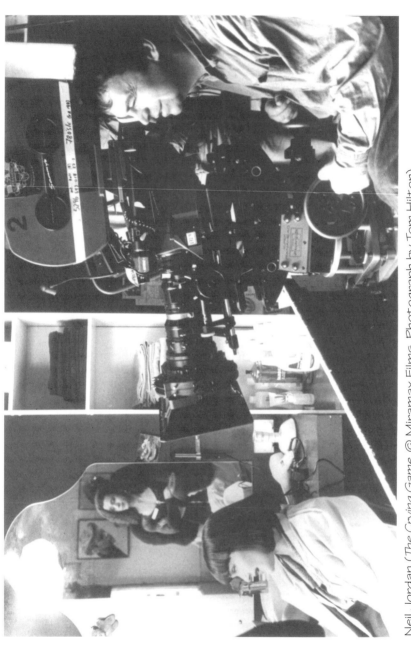

Neil Jordan (*The Crying Game*. © Miramax Films. Photograph by Tom Hilton)

James L. Brooks (*As Good As It Gets.* © 1997 TriStar Pictures Inc. All rights reserved. Courtesy of TriStar Pictures.)

Quentin Tarantino (*Pulp Fiction.* © Miramax Films. Photograph by Linda R. Chen)

Steven Spielberg (*Saving Private Ryan.* © 1998 DreamWorks
reprinted with permission by DreamWorks, L.L.C. Photograph by
David James)

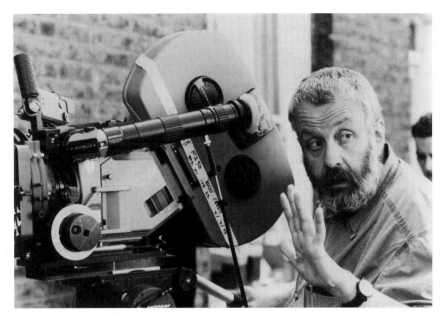

Mike Leigh (*Secrets & Lies*. ©1996 October Films. Still courtesy of October Films, Inc. reproduced by kind permission of CIBY 2000 SA. All rights reserved.)

Michael Radford (*The Postman* [*Il Postino*]. © Miramax Films.)

Gus Van Sant (© Eric Edwards/Sawtooth Film Co. Director Gus Van Sant, Actor Bill Richert)

Mel Gibson (*Braveheart.* © 1995 Paramount Pictures. All rights reserved. Courtesy of Paramount Pictures. Photograph by Andrew Cooper)

Clint Eastwood (*Unforgiven.* © 1992 Warner Bros., a division of Time Warner Entertainment Company L.P. All rights reserved.)

Barbra Streisand (*The Prince of Tides.* © 1991 Columbia Pictures Industries, Inc. All rights reserved. Courtesy of Columbia Pictures.)

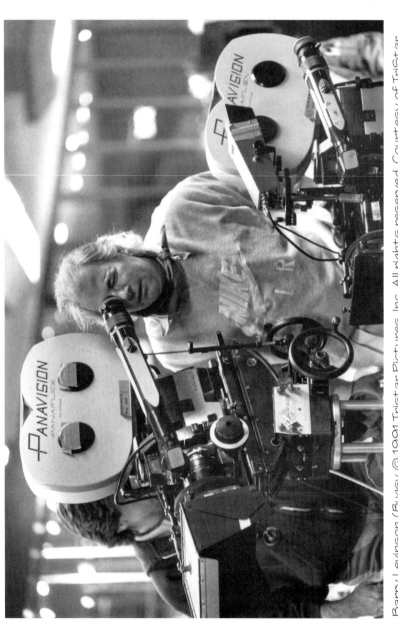

show his face, he'd do it once or twice and the whole thing would
come off! So the take would be ruined.

Roberto Benigni
Life Is Beautiful

Working with the little boy during shooting—it's like working with
a giraffe with an oak tree—what can I say? I put the camera there
with a sea, what can I say to the sea? "Go home?" No! The little boy,
was a very poor boy, very wonderful, pure really, but because it was
first time for him, he couldn't learn by heart, his lines and the concentration was one minute and a half. He thought to shoot a movie
it takes daylight two hours, like to watch.

In order to protect him—he's not an actor. I couldn't shoot with
him together a master. Because only he was imitating me. Like a little monkey. He's full of energy and he was just imitating me. But
when I was acting with him it was impossible to because he didn't
know his lines. I was just telling him. So I adapted to the boy direction. It's a kid direction.

For me, I don't sleep the night before. And my dreams, they are
directing, maybe my unconscious. I am dreaming somebody is
telling to me, "What are you doing? What are you doing?" Very
directly. And I can't sleep during the shooting, because I feel that I
don't know where I am going. Like Columbus, maybe I think to discover India, and I find America. I am sure that I am going toward
something, and then I discover another direction, and I won't discover India. When I read the diary of Christopher Columbus, the
crew wanted to come back, and I feel sometimes that I am never
sure. A lot of the time, I'm not certain what to do. And the crew, they
feel everything, and this is good. The director makes the feeling, and
that's very good. And when I am only actor in movies, I like to have
this feeling very much. I can feel very much the director. And so I'm
thinking, when I'm directing, maybe I am doing this. And that's
good. And I feel when the ship is going in another direction, or it's a
moment when I'm not sure about what I'm doing, everybody, actors
especially, they feel it. So I'm inventing. Because art is something you
feel, but you cannot explain. And actors, they have to feel. I think

this. So when I start to explain, "You are bourgeoisie," I feel like a real idiot. Because the script is there. I so offensive to explain.

Rob Reiner

A Few Good Men

Jack Nicholson has one of the biggest laughs in the picture, when he says "Hi, Danny, how is your old man?" and he [Tom Cruise] says, "He passed away seven years ago." And then you cut to Jack and he says, "Don't I feel like the fuckin' asshole," and he didn't get it right at all. I'm one of these guys that gives line readings most guys don't do—they hate it, actors hate it. I find that, if you don't give them a bad line reading, most actors will take it and then make it their own anyway. That's the easiest way to communicate. I would say to him, "Jack, what you gotta do is hold the smile. Hold the smile in your face. Let the line break the attitude." He would always break the attitude, when he heard that the guy passed away. I said, "Your attitude is what's delivering the line. You have to let the line deliver the attitude, rather than having your attitude drop, because then you've already delivered the line—the line, then, is anticlimactic." And he finally got it. He did it, and it's right.

I do have a cinematographer come into the rehearsal period after I've worked a little bit with the actors, so at least he gets a sense of where people are going to be moving. At that point, I'll make a shot list up for the day. I'll sit with the script supervisor and I'll tell her I want all these shots, and she writes every one of them down—and then as you go along, as you're working the scene, sometimes another shot will make itself known to you.

I don't like a lot of takes, because that's what the rehearsal period was for: to know what we're doing. And then we're out there, and let's just go for it. I mean, obviously, if it doesn't work, then you got to do it over, but I rarely see double digits on the slate.

I'll help actors out—I mean, some actors, like Kathy Bates [on *Misery*], she said, "Tell me how you want me to do it." And I'd act it out for her. Or Tom [Cruise] would say the same thing: "What do you want me to do and I'll do it." And I would just act it out for them. I'll show them. It's not a great way to do it, if you can't act; but I can act, so it's a tool that I can use to communicate when I want and then I say, "You've got to obviously make it yours and do it the way you would do it."

I don't stage for the camera—I let the actors do what they do, and then I photograph that rather than determine that this is the way I want the camera to move and I want to place the actors in it. You go in there and you rehearse the scene once the cameraman and all the key department heads look at that, send the actors off to get made up and all, and then you do your work and go about the lighting and try to avoid the craft service table [where food is served] as best you can! Because it's very dangerous if you start in early in the morning, I could be 100 pounds heavier by the end of the picture and I have a problem with that!

Anybody who's been with a director during the making of a film and had a relationship or marriage, they get a lot of gold stars, because it's all-consuming. You're working twelve-, fourteen-hour days every day, and you basically don't have time for anything except to have dinner, go to sleep, and then get up the next day. And I always tell the people the toughest thing about directing is the physical part of it. Get as much rest as you can, and sit down as much as you can during the course of the day.

Andrew Davis
The Fugitive

The real challenge for me was to keep the balance between what Tommy [Lee Jones] had to work with and what Harrison [Ford] had to work with, which is really the much more difficult part. Harrison had nobody to talk to—he was left alone, he had to play everything on his face, which is really difficult acting. And I was trying to create the balance between these two characters.

Tommy Lee Jones was very concerned about shooting a gun in a public place as a U.S. Marshal probably would not do. And rightfully so—he was concerned about it being irresponsible. And yet dramatically, for the film and the kind of entertainment that that gave us, we went ahead and did it anyway.

If it involved stunts or anything dangerous, it was all very storyboarded and very exacting. But in terms of things that just felt like we needed to do something—for example, the end of the sequence in City Hall where Harrison runs into the parade—we met Mayor Daly before we started shooting, and I realized the parade was coming; and so this opportunity became available to shoot the actual parade, and we basically winged it. We had some hidden cameras, and we had a great Steadicam [a portable camera allowing great freedom of movement], and we prepared it, but it needed that kind of spontaneous, anything-could-happen quality to make it be believable.

There were no parts for Joe Pantoliano. But Tommy [Lee Jones] needed somebody to play with, a really solid actor to improvise with, and to be the straight man to. So I said to Joey, "Listen, you're gonna have to make up all your own stuff." He created that part and gave great life to that group of marshals, and they hung out together.

We started shooting with Harrison's beard, for continuity. And we started in jail, then we went into his apartment. And we had enough for a forty-minute movie on the night of the fundraiser, and the murder, knowing that we were never going to use it in continuity, knowing that it would be long and flaccid. But the reason for doing that was to be able to keep the memory of his wife alive through the whole movie. To keep that kind of emotional pulse alive.

We built a set-piece on top of a two-hundred-foot dam that was about twelve feet long; and we created the actual scene where Harrison turns around, looks down, and we were two hundred feet up, wired on our ankles. It was freezing, it was blowing, very dangerous. And we took a couple articulated dummies and threw them over the camera. We dropped a couple out of some helicopters, and somehow magically it worked.

Usually the first day of shooting is easy because you've done so much planning. The fifth day, forget it: you don't know what you're doing. But the first day, everybody's been so wired, and the shot lists, and going to bed early.

Tom Mack was the assistant director, and he is a great guy. This guy knows how to take two hundred extras and set them into a scene, and give them life, and work with his assistants to make it work depending on what the details are—of propping people, and dressing people, and lighting the set. It takes a lot of energy to get what you need in front of the camera.

We were actually writing the script, staging it, rehearsing it, and shooting it all at once. I was very concerned we would have a ten-minute trial sequence in the movie and it would be very boring in the first reel. One of the two actors with Harrison is a sergeant in the Chicago Department, the other is an actor who's had an interesting background with the police himself, and so both of them have a certain reality to what's going on. Harrison was wise enough to say to me, "Andy, don't tell me the questions. Just let them interrogate me. I don't want to know what they're going to ask me." And so it was totally improvised. We had a Steadicam and another camera working, or maybe two cameras, and we would do the scene a couple times, and then we would revise the questions a little bit. And it was the end of a very long day, and I said, "Harrison, great, we're done." And I was just going to stick around and shoot a couple cuts of the cops talking. And Harrison was on his way to his car to leave, and he said, "What the hell are they doing up there?" And the next thing he was back, sitting next to the camera, playing off-screen for these guys. And that's the kind of actor he is. And I think somebody said to me, "What are you shooting those extras for? Why are you doing coverage on those guys?" And it was only after they saw the film that they understood that you needed these two cops to indict this guy, and it was their mistaken judgment that caused him to be sent down the river.

I shoot two cameras all the time. I make it very, very difficult for the sound man. Who, in spite of all of his complaining, has been nominated twice now for the last two films. But basically, because of the improvising we do, it's very important to me to be able to have two sizes of the same performance so I can get in and out, to have cutaways of other people reacting to things. The Steadicam operator is a real artist. I don't think I could live without this type of talent and the equipment. It's given the ability to be fluid and to not have to do so much coverage and cutting. So we always had three cameras available to us to shoot at any time.

It's better to try to find a camera position or move that takes you in one piece, one fell swoop, right past and you're into it. And it was important for me to keep the camera moving, whether it be cutting, or panning, or actually moving, in order to keep this search. There's a lot of point-of-view shots in this movie. It's Harrison looking, people looking for Harrison. And to make you feel like you're in the middle of the movie, rather than standing back and observing it.

I just think that you can get more out of yourself and the people who are there contributing if you open it up and say, "What if?" Come with an idea. There are some days on this movie that I was lucky to know in my head what the one-liner on the strip board was. "Harrison rents an apartment," that was what I had to do. And the details of how people spoke to each other, it was all worked out. In the basement, as the room was being lit. Or as this woman, who had never been in a movie, got past being with Harrison Ford, and started talking. She came in, she was chewing gum. And I didn't tell her to take the gum out of her mouth. And that was something I never would have thought of. And so those kind of things make it real.

Did I know exactly how I was going to shoot a sequence? No, I did-n't. We, for example, had to experiment to see what kind of rig we could use that would allow us to dolly fast enough for Tommy and Harrison to run full speed, and still keep in front of them and turn corners. So between the grip and the Steadicam operator, we actual-ly put the Steadicam on a dolly and used it that way. At the end of the movie, when everybody left, we had some short ends [unused nega-tive] left, and I took some shots of the city off my balcony while everybody was going home. And those are some of the cut-aways of Jerome Krabbe looking down as Harrison's pushing him over.

Peter Weir
The Truman Show

What I do is use music. I'll go home and I'll have a quick bite. I find Japanese food's the best to eat in a shoot. Easily digested. And I'll play music for an hour or so, and do all my thinking for the next day on some level. Not sort of literally. But I find that music stops me thinking. Because we all know jobs are mostly practical. And necessarily so. And the danger is that you won't have the door open to the inspiration. How do you keep it open? So for me music is probably one of the key ways. A good walk and so forth is good, but it stops the intellect. And you switch on to some other thing as the music goes through your head. And then I'll go, "Oh God," and write something down. It sort of almost works as simply as that for me. I have certain pieces to get me into certain moods, that relate to the film. And then next morning, going to work sometimes, which is a very difficult time, that first approach to work, just getting every-body going. And so I'll play the music often very loud to myself. Because when you think about it, imagine you can cram your trailer with Gauguins and Van Goghs and all the great art of the history of the world, and Michelangelo's sculptures, and walk through your trailer and feel all this stuff, and go out and direct—but you can't. You can with music, the treasure of the world.

Mike Newell
Four Weddings and a Funeral

We all know spontaneity is the pearl without price, and how do you produce spontaneity? There are times, at least, when the spontaneity is out of kilter with what is needed. And then you're dealing with nuance and trying to produce a whole different atmosphere. And sometimes you don't talk sense to them at all. Hugh Grant tells a story that I once said to him, "Hugh, it needs to be a little quicker— thus, I feel perhaps a fraction slower." Now, that made absolute sense to me. What I was trying to do was produce nuance in him. That's my torment, is to try and get spontaneity with nuance.

There's a scene in the film after the funeral where the leading char-acter makes up his mind he'd better marry somebody. The whole scene floats on the brink of sentimentality. And so what I tried to do was to find a way of him not being sentimental. So I got him to be harder and harder, and what happened in fact was, he simply came out lunatically neurotic and angry, and people looked at the scene and said, "What on earth is it he's angry about?" I can't remember how I cured it. I suppose we looped it. But it was raining and rain is some-thing that drives rationality from your head. Water and celluloid—

they don't mix. Part of the reason why I got it wrong was that it was raining and I lost my reason. And people just want to be somewhere else. That's when the mistakes happen, and that's when you start to chase ideas that you should never have chased.

I suppose the thing's that's most frightening about acting is that you constantly think to yourself, tomorrow I might not have an idea. It might not happen tomorrow. Because whether it looks self-evident or not, acting does need, actually, a lot of ideas. I always try to read what I'm going to do the next day before. I have a kind of superstition about that, that it'll never go right if you try to do it in the car on the way out. I try to get there and hour or an hour and a half before everybody else starts to do their work.

Robert Zemeckis

Forrest Gump

My preparation is—actually, I don't write anything down until I'm in the car, that's when I start doing my shot list. But I think about it the night before. I dream, I have nightmares about it the night before. It's kind of broken down into the days when I can go directly to the set and the days when I have to go to the hair and makeup trailer first, which is the place I always hate to go, because I know they're always gossiping. But on the day that I have to go in there, then that's the day I'm not quite sure about something and I don't want to ever, in front of a crew, act like I'm not quite sure what we're going to do that day. My feeling is that you always have to act like you know what you're doing, no matter if you have no idea what you're doing! The scene in Jenny's dorm—I never knew how it was going to work and I was very worried. And Tom [Hanks] and I sorted that out on the day. The problem was, after he had this premature ejaculation, it was written that he got very disturbed and distraught about it. And Tom realized Jenny should have the punch line in this scene. Jenny should break the ice. And then we wrote that right there and that's what made the scene work. The days that are terrifying are the ones when you've cast this day player [an actor who works only one day on the picture] and a great actor, but you cast him four months before the day he works, and here you've got this whole film company who's been making this movie for four months. Everybody's got a short hand, and he walks onto the set and he's in a completely different movie. And those are the days that I know when we make our salary, because then you've got to step out away from the monitor, go up there in front of the camera and say, "OK, that was really good. Can you try this for me? Just try this for me." My job is to sit there and say, "You're feeling really angry here—well, not that angry, little less angry." It's a level thing. I don't try talk in any kind of mysterious psychoanalytical way to the actors at all. Kurt Russell, when we were doing *Used Cars*, by the end of the movie said, "I got to the point where I could hear how you'd say the word 'cut' and I would know whether we'd be doing it again or not."

The actor that played Bubba [Mykelti Williamson] said, "I want to have my lip look like this." I didn't think of that. He thought of that and I immediately said, "That's great. Go ahead!" Because usually actors are always saying the opposite, "You mean you want me to look like my lip's sticking . . . ?" They always want to look beautiful. But Mykelti is a very handsome guy, he really wanted to find that in the character.

Quentin Tarantino
Pulp Fiction

I very much, as far as shooting is concerned, believe in the "robbing Peter to pay Paul" principle. This scene needs four days to do, but I'll make it up because I'll do this scene in half a day, because I'm gonna nail it in rehearsal and I'll be able to take care of it that way. That ten percent that I'm wrong is always the worst day on the set. All the stuff that we had at the pawnshop—that was one of the practical locations, and I was just really abusing the crew that day because we only had one day set aside for that, when we absolutely, positively needed two. It was Monday and we're going really late. I tried never to abuse the crew until Friday, and that's cool, because that's no problem—they're going to have two days off and it's going to be cool. But you don't want to have them go until 4 o'clock in the morning on a Monday. And then you have this scene coming up and my first AD [assistant director] actually describes it—I've never heard this term before—"fear of shooting." This thing coming up that you were so dreading about doing, it's going to be so sensitive and everything that you do everything so you don't have to shoot.

Apparently actors hate it when you say, "Just have fun with it." What's that mean? The thing is, just trying to give them little minute adjustments.

[In working with one particular actor] we show up, and I just want to do a run-through, without the crew, just the actors sitting down, me, and the first AD. And I'm like, "Is he going to be able to remember his lines?" And he couldn't do it. In fact, not only could he not do it, he started to almost have a nervous breakdown. He was—that was due to age and fear—and then one by one the other actors couldn't deal with it anymore, and one by one they started leaving, and all the crew sees is, outside, the different actors walking through the door. I'm like, "Oh my God! I've got to rewrite this whole scene. What am I going to do?" And it was the only time I had like, complete despair, and actually my first AD saved me. She said to me, "You know what, Quentin, I think you just need to start shooting with him and it'll work out. Give him a chance." I don't very often use two cameras, but this time: I want a camera here on him and I want a camera here on him. And I said, "What we're going to do is basically, we're just gonna go through the speech until he forgets his lines." And he ended up doing great. It was start, stop, start, stop, start, stop.

On *Pulp*, whether it be the adrenaline shot scene, the whole thing where they're trying to bring her back, or any of the cinematic stuff that's got to work, that's always kinda scary that day before because if it doesn't work, it didn't work because I didn't do it right. Maybe another director would've.

Frank Darabont
The Shawshank Redemption

In anybody's working life is going to be a wave pattern. We, all of us, had what we would count as bad luck as well as good. There's another kind of luck, which is very important. Which has to do with intuition. You could have a lucky day of shooting, and I think that you're best not to ask questions about that. I think you are best to let that be, and let it happen to you, because it will happen to you. But it isn't going to happen to you if you look at it, and if you worry about it, and if you try to produce it. I find a lot of working is actually about not thinking about it, hammering at it—not trying to dissect it.

Oh, the actors, boy—sometimes they make you feel like Lillian Gish on the ice floe. I find myself being Zelig [a Woody Allen character who is a living chameleon] a lot. I'm the human barometer. Every actor is a different person and every different person needs a different thing from you, so I always find that I'm trying to be all directors to all actors. I'm always trying to assess an actor. Morgan [Freeman] is a very intuitive actor. Tim [Robbins] is a very cerebral actor. They both wind up in the same place, which is a very good performance. I think you need to know when to get out of their way as much as when to be in their face. I always talk individually and always in whispers. I'm the antithesis of Dick Donner, you know, Mr. Bullhorn Voice. I love watching him work. He's such a thrill to watch. He's like a force of nature. He will talk to the actors in the back of the auditorium, he will tell them what to do from there. And he makes it seem intimate—I can't do that.

Mel Gibson
Braveheart

I try to know what each scene means and why I want it there, and how to tell that story the best way. It's not always with action and dialogue, either. Sometimes it's just, "Where do you throw the camera?"

I'm not too good at articulating what I want, sometimes. People on the crew would sometimes be, "What is he doing?" And sometimes, I couldn't explain it. It's kind of like—you're doing a million things at the same time, and you think they can read your mind. But I think the key is to be open to things that other people see. Like the cinematographer [John Toll], because he made some tremendous contributions, as did the first AD [David Tomblin]. I thought, "That is a great idea, I'm gonna take it."

I'd have to do a lot of technical things like, they had to sew this damn thing into my head everyday, not a brain, but the wig. And I actually had to have some kind of closed-circuit television set up on two screens to see the kinds of things they were doing.

I rarely lost my temper or anything. It was one of those things that I thought, "I can't lose my temper"—I've seen guys do that and it just destroys everything.

The battle sequences were six weeks. It's a 22-minute sequence and I had eight cameras going some days. As an actor, I don't like the multiple camera thing at all. I don't know what to work for, because I think, perhaps vainly, that you're using a specific viewpoint, and that you show what you want, and you can't do that for two viewpoints.

I remember a few times in particular, I just couldn't get what I wanted. I think it was the largest amount of takes I did, partly because I wasn't quite sure what I wanted. It was a little bit of hit and miss for a while, and then I started getting in there with the actor and talking in between takes. Then he started to get freaked out, because we never did this many takes. And I said, "It was my fault, because I don't know what I want yet." I did want something different from him, but I didn't want to go up there and dictate things to him, and we talked about the oddest things. We eventually got to this discussion about something else we both had seen, and that sort of got a meeting of the minds going, and this guy who was wonderfully talented came in and just knocked it off in one take. And it was just perfect and it was worth it.

One of the things I learned early on from Peter Weir [director of *Year of Living Dangerously* and *The Truman Show*] and it's just a general thing, is that you take a scene and if it seems lifeless or it's not working, you do it twice as fast as you think you need to. And oftentimes, that's when it comes to life.

Some actors I've worked with have very different methods. There's no right way to do anything.

There were 3,000 [extras]. That was the largest amount of people I had to deal with. There was a huge system set up with loudspeakers. I felt like I was some kind of fascist in Spain. There was a delay on everything you said, but then you could hear it echoing back off the hill and stuff. They were getting it loud and clear. There was a whole lot of time spent in amping everybody, because I think that there must be something very distressing and I've experienced myself, you know — when you're in a scene where they stick you out on a hilltop someplace and they got like long lenses and everybody looks like an ant and you think, "What the fuck are they doing?" It's kind of — you're not connected to it somehow. And it's very important to give someone something that they can hook onto emotionally, so that they do their best, and that they have a sense they're a part of it. One time I remember — it was the last shot of the film, when they're all coming down the hill in slow-motion and stuff, and I had three cameras. They all ran down. It took a long time to set up. They ran down and did the whole thing and then I watched the video monitors back, and some of the guys coming down are horsing around and laughing and all this kind of stuff. This is one of the times when it backfired on me, when it was toward the end of the shoot and I was pretty cranky, and this is one of the occasions I lost my temper. And I just like, I said, "We saw that on the video monitor. Some of you are horsing around and laughing." And it went from, "I'll find out who you are, from the picture." By this time I was totally insane. We were eighty-five days in and I was pretty ratty. And it ended with insulting all their mothers, collectively. It stirred them up — and I'll never do anything like that again, because I had to pay the price for that two weeks later. And I didn't even think about what had gone on before, because you're so busy. And it rolls off me, like water off a duck's back, because I'm just single-minded and insane. But these people really got offended by that and they think, "Ah, we'll catch up with him one day." And they did. I had another scene where it was in the London town square where there was always not enough extras. We got these army guys to fill up all the spaces, and they remembered what I said on the hill that day, and we armed them all with turnips, potatoes, and every conceivable fruit. So there I am like Bozo at the fair, big goofy target, being wheeled through, and these guys decided to practice their cricket on me. A 19- or 20-year-old arm going for all it's worth with a turnip — this is not funny, this is an instrument of death.

Some of the pressures, of the financial and time pressures, will force you into decisions, frantic decisions, and you'll just do the most incredible things — like you'll have to shoot in the rain, and it gives the film a wonderful look. I learned that from George Miller [who directed Gibson in *Mad Max* and *Road Warrior*]—just shoot no matter what.

Michael Radford

Il Postino

We had this terrible problem of Massimo being mortally ill through the shoot. Any preconceptions, any idea I had about how I would shoot this picture, went straight out the window. Under normal circumstances, I don't rehearse. What I tend to go for is what I call "the tingle." It's like, when you're on the set you feel the chemistry of the scene, and suddenly it happens. It's very hard to put your finger on what it is, but you know when it's not there. Now very often that actually only happens when the camera is running. I also feel the same thing when I set up a shot—I find the tingle to feel, yes, this shot is the right one. So the night before I'm usually having some food, relaxing and not really thinking about the next day. I tend not to be very good at night, because I tend to drink a lot. It helps you sleep and I wake up very, very drunk. It helps you unwind and stuff and this particular film was particularly difficult—if I'd wanted to rehearse, I couldn't. So I'd wake up the next morning—I'd wake up very early in the morning, then concentrate the mind, and I sort of think through the scene, and I think approximately the parameters of it. I don't storyboard things—maybe if it's a big crowd scene or a big scene. I'll have a storyboard to make everybody else feel confident, but I very rarely stick to it. But it gives you somewhere to go.

[Each] morning I'd have to see how Massimo was. He would come onto the set about 5 o'clock in the afternoon. He couldn't go to any of the locations which I had chosen, so I had to redo everything, rethink everything. Every day it was another day where I had to rethink everything. He could only walk three steps and he'd have to sit down. So, we had to find places where we could shoot him sitting down. I don't shoot master shots quite often—I don't work that way. For me, there is a shot which is at the center of a scene. That shot I would shoot at the end of the day when Massimo came on board.

I discovered that actors spend an awful lot of time on the set, sitting about or feeding lines to other actors, or waiting for the lighting, or doing shots in which they're not recognizable—and if you cut all that out, you've got that hour or hour and a half with an actor when you're going to do his close-ups.

Now, Massimo was a brilliant, brilliant comedian. And comedians have exquisite timing, and what it meant was that usually on the first or second take he was at his best, he was cooking. And if you started to repeat too often, it went away, and then you'd have to do fifteen or twenty takes, and he wasn't physically capable of doing that. So what I would do is, I would make sure that by the time he came on the set, this main shot we were going to do would be technically perfect.

Massimo was a comic, not a dramatic actor. And all I knew was that I wanted to pull him back. This is often really basically what you spend your time doing with actors. This is what I could bring to the film, as slight resonance in the way that he behaved. He was used to making comic movies, where he would take the script, he would sit down and he would just improvise. He'd never learned lines in his life before! He started to learn his lines, he said, "God, you know, you're making me learn these lines," and then he would come up to me and he'd say, "You know, I just got this urge to do a little something in this scene, would you mind?" And I'd say, "A little something, as long as it doesn't last too long." Then he would come up with a brilliant piece of improvisation, absolutely brilliant.

After about three weeks into a picture, the picture is your life. You wake up and you see the characters in front of you—you don't see the actors.

The whole film is handheld [the camera is held by the operator rather than being locked down to a tripod or dolly]. We had a Movie Cam, which is not designed to be held on the shoulder. I said to Stephano, the camera operator, "I want this to be handheld for a number of reasons. One, I feel it gives the sense of immediacy to the picture. The second is I know that you're going to be able to adjust instantaneously and improvise if Massimo does something, so we won't have to reshoot it." And he said, "OK." And it was unbelievable, he was so strong. All the tracking shots that we did, I would sit him on a dolly with a camera on his shoulder.

I used to say far too much in the old days. I try to avoid that now — it confuses an actor. An actor is reaching out for something, and if you're as clear as possible, even if you don't quite get it right that time around, you've got another take. You let the actor do it, and then you adjust it again. If you say too much, it's confusing. I always avoid acting it out in front of them. I think that to me, if you can't find the words to express it, then you don't know what you want. But then again, these are not hard and fast rules — these are just things that make me feel good. So I try to find an adjective which basically characterizes that particular moment.

You don't get any atmosphere on a video [assist, used to see what the camera sees], and I tend to work a lot with atmosphere. I tend often to just listen with the cans [earphones] — I shut my eyes. I often listen rather than look. Particularly towards the middle of a picture, when I know pretty much what the actors are looking like. You stand where the script supervisor is standing. She or he always finds the best spot, so I stand back, I watch, and then I walk up to her and say, "Get out of the way!"

It's about creating the circumstances in which something untoward can happen, because that's when it comes to life. You have a screenplay — but actually, what you're hoping for is for something else to happen. In the movie there's a scene, a long scene, which is my personal favorite, when he discovers the poetry within himself and he starts to record the sounds of the island. Now, I'd written that as the central moment in the film, but the interesting thing is, I couldn't shoot it with Massimo. So, at any spare moment, I would start to improvise scenes: the sea would be rough and I would get the double [a look-alike for the actor, used usually to stand in while lights are being positioned] and the telegraph operator and we'd shoot. We had about eight little scenes. You just see a hand coming up from behind a bush or something like that. But it lacked the presence of Massimo — it lacked his presence, and I knew I wasn't going to get away with it. And on the last day of shooting, when I thought he was going to go for his heart transplant operation, I just went up to him and I said, "Massimo, these are the shots — just read the shot list that we've done." And he sat on the bed and he read this shot list. And when we got into the cutting room, it was the most powerful thing

I'd ever seen. I actually had tears in my eyes when I was watching it. And it was better than I could have ever imagined.

Scott Hicks

Shine

I wanted to create around the camera an environment that I thought was going to be really conducive to getting this character of David. Particularly with Geoffrey Rush being nude in the filmmaking process, the last thing I wanted was this cut and thrust that can go on around the camera. Geoffrey Simpson [the cinematographer] has a very centered, calm personality. He works with a crew that again invites a good mix of genders.

[Another issue was that] John Gielgud doesn't travel these days and so it was important that we had somewhere in London. He comes up from the country. He works for four hours a day, which by the time you take your lunch break out and make-up and wardrobe, it really boils down to about two hours in the day that you're working with him. So you have to use that energy that's available very carefully.

We decided to start shooting because I was in mortal terror of us running out of money. If we started shooting in Australia, I thought, there won't be enough to afford going to London at the end. I mean, the whole film was shot in forty-two days, and in London we were there for a total of seven or eight days shooting, in which we had to get quite enormous elements of styles as far as the film is concerned. It's a small film, but the big concert scene we saw is a central piece of it. And in the end, it was put together in one of those wonderful sort of movie things where we shot the concert, as it were, in the Royal College of Music with their orchestra and all the rest of it. But to me it was like some doughnut, because there was a gigantic hole in the middle which was all of Noah Taylor's work at the piano. And that was all shot on the stage in Adelaide. It had to be shot on the first day of shooting, because we then had to cut Noah's hair for the second half of the shooting. And the concert pianist whose hands were doubling for Noah was in London. So he flew to Adelaide for a day. He got off the plane and was led to the set. We did all his stuff and wheeled him back to the airport and put him on a plane. We didn't even know if he survived. And that was just symptomatic of trying to put something together on two continents on a very slender budget.

Anthony Minghella
The English Patient

Saul tells a story about me, which is entirely true, which is that he left the filming for one day, and I fell over and broke my ankle. So his diagnosis of the whole film is that the minute he turned his back, I couldn't even stand up by myself.

Walter [Murch, the editor] gave me this totem every day. For the 127 days of shooting, he gave me 127 mottoes. They were extremely deep and aphoristic: "Remember what you've forgotten and forget what you've remembered."

One thing that I try to do is never take the screenplay with me when I'm shooting. Because I don't want to be the writer on set. And so I try to leave that behind and learn and be surprised by the day.

It was a road movie of epic proportions. You take everything with you and throw as much of it away as you can and focus on the real thing which is the human being. However beautiful the locations we had, however ravishing Tuscany is or Africa is, I'd rather watch a human being against a wall. In the end, you're there for the actors, who are wonderful and give you a commitment.

What you're looking for is to eliminate forgery because audiences can smell it from a thousand miles away. They want to feel as if they're somehow invisible participants.

When you make a scene about sexual behavior in films, it's the most difficult thing. Not because we're embarrassed by sex, as we are, and I'm a particularly prudish personality; but because, it's like a required scene and so you don't want to do scenes of people who pretend to make love to each other, because it's the moment where you most see the artifice. You want to get as far away from dealing with the mechanics as possible. And particularly in this case where I wanted the electric charge of the film to really be something. I wanted you to feel that these people were resisting emotion, unwilling participants in this event, rather than running into each others' arms. So everything to me was how to set up a dynamic when they finally came together.

The job, as I understand it, of directing is to create a space in which actors feel empowered — and the more space you take up as a director, the less room they've got. If you push them and pull them and tug them, they are just rocked around by you. At the same time, if you do nothing, they can't see the space they're working in.

Cameron Crowe
Jerry Maguire

I was able to direct rather quickly and enjoy the process more than I ever had before because of the time I'd spent directing it in my head.

Renee [Zellweger] does have an utterly real quality. And you find that you torture an actor like that sometimes because, say you have them do a break-up scene twenty, thirty, forty times from different angles, and they're in shreds, because it's real — they're breaking up every time.

James Cameron
Titanic

I was dealing with a large number of actors, a lot of ensemble scenes where everybody was gonna be watching each other work. I made a decision early on to just say to everybody going in, "We're gonna shoot a lot of takes, so you've got a lot of room to figure it out." We gave everybody permission to explore, to screw up, to find different ways of doing the scene on film in case there is that lucky accident early on that is something that you could not have predicted. Fortunately for me and my working process, Kate [Winslet] and Leo [DiCaprio] especially were very much the way I like to work, where they just get into the scene and just work and start playing off of it. Really, take six was always better than take five, and take seven was always better than take six. In fact, we were doing Leo's — Jack's death scene, and I had done a lot on him and we both felt really happy with it. And I turned around on Kate, and Leo was giving Kate what she needed and doing better than when he'd been on camera! I said, "Leo, you son of a bitch, you're better off camera than you were on camera!" He says, "I know, I'm always better off camera!" And Kate laughs, and then Leo says, "And so are you!!" When Kate finished that scene, she went off and cried for an hour in the arms of the makeup artist, who was kind of her confidante on the set—just to come down from the emotion of having done the scene and keeping it at that peak for so long. It's not a question of the director pulling the plug. It's getting the actors to stop once they've got the bit in their teeth. Because they feel that they are closing in on something. They don't want to stop. And I like working with actors like that. I feel like we don't want to leave that space. We've spent all these months, and in my case maybe two years, to get to that moment—hours to light it, all this preparation, months to build the set and all the costumes and everything—to get to that moment and to walk away from it without it being the best that everybody there can do is foolish.

The way I approached all the scenes on the film was, I worked with a thing that my brother invented, which is a video viewfinder system. It sends a video picture to the monitor station, so I can actually kind of line up the shots by holding the actual lens that we're going to use for the scene or for the shot. But I don't go right to that. What I like to do is get the actors into the space and get some lights on. The lighting, especially on the interiors of the ship, was primarily done, or was meant to look all "sourcey" [more realistic], from the practical fixtures, and so then I asked the crew to step out of the way and the actors were like in sweats and stuff. And on a particular scene [at the table scene] we might spend an hour and a half just figuring out who was sitting where and what are the currents. The dynamic of the scene changed the seating around a lot. We had to play it—we had to see what it meant to everybody. And then once we had that sort of roughed in, we started figuring out the angles. I decided to move the camera in virtually every shot of the film and to impose a kind of sort of semi-modern style on 1912. I wanted to give it a vitality and a life and an energy. When you start moving the camera, it starts to get in the way from an editing standpoint, so I had to figure out when in the moving master [a shot that covers the whole scene] exactly camera cutting, what lines I wanted when I was likely to be wide, when I was likely to be in close, and make a lot of those decisions before the fact.

And sometimes I would even say, "OK, I wanna do a couple of different versions of this." One where the moves start a few lines earlier, just in case, because I'm thinking editorially I might come off him, but I might wait till she answers. I'm thinking editing-wise as I'm shooting. So you let them run with the line for a while, and if you don't see anything that you like better—and this is a subjective area, I mean, sometimes your own preconception is so in place—but I try to be very open like that, and if the actors can come up with a better way to say the words, then give them the space.

Leo and I were talking about a scene the night before—it was one of those rare occasions where we actually did think, "We've got a big thing coming up tomorrow, let's sit and talk about it." I'd done a little rewriting on that scene, and Leo said, "I'd like to try something to make contact with Cal, you know, throw him something or something like that." I said, "Let's have him smoking a cigarette," and he said, "Yeah, I could throw him some matches, because I was smoking in an earlier scene and it came out of that." And then the question is, OK, now where are we going to do it? And then finding the right line to put that exclamation point at the end of. And I think it landed in the right spot, but that was a collaborative effort. Leo is the kind of guy that has a lot of ideas, and I like that. You know, some actors have a few ideas and they really hold onto them. It's like if you don't use it, then you don't love me. But I think the actors that I feel most comfortable with are the ones that have a lot of ideas and just spew them out there, and they are gifts, and if you want to use them, use them, and if you don't, don't.

Gus Van Sant

Good Will Hunting

You are channeling everybody's energy—the cinematographer's, the actors', everyone else involved in the production coming together and kind of trying to channel something to make the scene come alive.

I'd often find out that you'd put the cameras say, in point A, and since you couldn't stand in point A, you'd have to stand over here.

But during the shooting, you'd realize that point B was a better angle! Then, you'd move the camera over to point B. It was really frustrating. Then you'd realize that, OK, you have this side and that side and you're sort of starting to create like a philosophy of that particular scene which you're drawing from sort of a history of all kinds of things: storyboards that you've done in the past, films you've seen. There's sort of a dictionary you've built up in your head by the time you've done three or four films so that you start to be able to think on the set pretty fast. And you can do pretty tricky things, even though you are just thinking them up on the set.

I think for me, it's mainly keeping everybody comfortable, very comfortable, where they can make a mistake and it's OK to try something new, or don't be afraid to goof because you can always roll again. And once everybody's really comfortable, the different styles and the different experiences kind of equal out, and then people can have fun together. I like to do just a couple takes if it's appropriate, depending on the actor.

There's the curious thing of the mojo being right the day that's kind of a hard one because from the first say, week or two weeks of shooting a film, hopefully you've gotten it, you've gotten the mojo right each day and you sort of brought something in focus in each scene. And by the third or fourth week, you have to match yourself because you've done this day in and day out. And a Monday or Tuesday or Wednesday or Friday, there will be a scene, it could be a small scene, and there's a sort of helpless feeling that the director has because they know they have to once again bring all the forces that they had on all the other scenes together and you just try and do it.

The least experienced actor on *Good Will Hunting* was Tom [John Mighton], who was the assistant to Lambeau and probably one of the most experienced actors was Stellan Skarsgard, he was playing Lambeau, so, they were really interesting, and they were very comfortable playing across from each other. Tom, I think, had never been in a play or a movie or anything. He was a real mathematician, though . . . so he sort of had this whole presence that he brought to the screen. He could ad lib, he could do all these great things and Stellan would just be amazed.

James L. Brooks
As Good as It Gets

I tend to have insomnia when I'm shooting.

On a lot of days, you say, we are all here to serve the actors, and that's your message to the crew. I think the most exciting day is when you change your mind and something totally different happens. On *As Good as It Gets* there were two examples: one was the hospital scene, where Greg Kinnear was beaten up and scarred. There were a few jokes in that scene I thought to relieve the tension, with the idea to play it almost farcically, and we were able to take the scene in a new direction and have pure fun. I do do a lot of takes. The other one—there was a letter in the script, that Helen Hunt's character wrote to Jack Nicholson's character. Helen said, "I'd like to know what was in the letter." And then I wrote the letter. And I wrote a lot of pages about what she wrote—it was sort of fun. And then she handwrote everything I typed. So now he had this great prop. He had 20 pages of this prop and it was never intended for her to read the letter. And it was a very problematic scene from the story point of view for me. And then, it's just one of the great days where, "What if you read the letter to him," and that became the solution to the scene. I was always worried about these three people going to Baltimore—how do we justify it, how do we get there? How do we believe it? And somehow that letter got me over a huge hump.

What you are asking the actors to do is to lose self-consciousness. It's a very difficult thing to do. Sometimes you're asking them to risk being bad, which is the hardest thing for anybody to do. Stretching, testing your limits—it's a very scary place to be.

But I think the big responsibility you have is: let's move on. "Let's move on" should be your pledge to the actors that you really have it. That's what that should mean.

The last scene in this picture we had to do within the first days of shooting, and it was ludicrous that we're out there doing the last scenes in the picture, especially for somebody like me, because I tend to be linear in my thinking. We did it and there was a moment there, because he wasn't supposed to kiss the girl, and I said in the middle of the take, "Kiss her." It was a good kiss and we went home and, I don't know how many months later, the scene wasn't right, because it was glib with that kiss. And it wasn't played correctly. There was too much emotion in it. It was a cranky kind of scene and it was based on stuff that I believed in when I was writing it. And that didn't turn out to be true. And we went back and the performance became simpler, and we solved some choreography. And that was an example of not getting it right, and going back.

The worst moment was one day, when it just wasn't happening and it was serious, it's embarrassing and it's frustrating to the actors out there when the director's saying, "Do it again," and it's some indication that he didn't do it right. I think the great thing about Jack is his willingness to humble himself. I had to send the crew home and I was a little behind schedule. I'd never done it before, and I hope I never have to do it again, but suddenly it was just the two of us. And we talked for four hours. And Jack can remember what we said and I can't, because I felt it was just that we gave ourselves the time. And we just sent everybody away and it was just a matter of respect — respect for the process, that we're not machines.

Curtis Hanson
L.A. Confidential

I try with every scene to form a visual key, that I don't want to lose sight of in terms of the visual telling of the story. For instance, in the liquor store where Russell Crowe sees Kim Bassinger for the first time. To me, the visual key of that is this moving point of view that reveals her. And because that's an image that he's going to carry with him for a long time. So, I have that in my head, going to the set.

In *L.A. Confidential*, there were so many sets it was usually a matter of going to a new set each day, so I would get there first and I would meet with the cameraman and the first assistant director, and talk about the general thing that we hoped to accomplish. Then when the actors would show up, get everybody else out. Then it would be just the two actors and me and I let them just kind of do it, and see what's comfortable for them, and then I would try to sort of nudge them into a situation. Working with the actors is, to me, the fun part actually of directing. Because I think that's where the magic happens. I find each actor is different, and I think that my job is to create the environment in which that specific actor can shine. Some actors really want very specific guidance—as much as saying, for instance, "When you say this line, in the next take, I want you to look into his eyes." And others don't want or need that. Some actors obviously need a lot of takes, and some don't. I do as many takes as it takes. I've found myself caught in the middle, certainly as I think we all have, with actors who sometimes give it all, that first time, then you get diminishing returns as they need more. As you get to know the actors and again this is something I try to achieve in rehearsal period. I start then having a plan that when these actors are working together, which actor do I shoot first? Let the actor who likes a lot of takes—let him be off camera, for instance, so that he's kind of warming up through the early part of the shootings. I try to do as little coverage as possible.

It's interesting, we're dealing with a time period, that of course, was before Russell Crowe and Guy Pearce were born. Number one, they're from another country so there's the cultural thing to deal with, and the language and also as it happens, neither of them is a fan of old movies. That they didn't even know much about. So it was a laborious process and different with the two of them. Russell was somebody who had a dialect coach and broke down his lines phonetically each single line. Whereas Guy Pearce has a remarkable ear and what he did was imitate me.

Steven Spielberg

Amistad

In a sense, everybody has to kind of keep up with me, because I'm running all around the set finding shots and everybody's sort of running behind me and I don't often communicate when I'm in a kind of frenzy. The only person I really collaborate with when I get inspired is Janusz [Kaminski], the DP. And Janusz has to hear what my thoughts are, not just for this shot. I'm trying to set up for the next five or six shots, because Janusz has to know and make an informed decision artistically about how the whole sequence is going to look. And we'll have many discussions, and because we're close personal friends, we often discuss this off the set. So by the time they come on the set, even though I don't know my shots until I walk on the set that morning, we know how that scene is going to appear, how it's going to look. But in terms of shooting, I shoot very quickly. I shoot with one camera. I don't like multiple cameras. You never can get a true eye line [where the actor is looking] with a second camera—the eye line is false. So that the A camera is beautiful, the actor is talking personally to the actor off right. But the B camera—the actor is talking even three or four inches off the personal emotional connection with the other person he is speaking to. It's not personal. So I tend to use just one camera. On *Amistad*, I tried something I had never done before, because I had never shot nineteenth century, I had never shot anything out of the twentieth century, in terms of subject matter. I'm notorious for moving my camera around. I move it all the time. I've moved it all my career, and I thought, what if I didn't move my camera except four times in *Amistad*? And the four camera moves were only going to be at moments where I wanted a kind of epiphany. Because I really respect the old directors that don't even use close-ups until they require an epiphany to happen. I think that Howard Hawkes was one of the greatest directors in terms of saving the close-up, and John Ford as well. I found the shots ahead of time and I actually wrote them in the script. One where Cinque stood up and said, "Give us free."

The first thing I do is to try to find the theme of the scene. I try to determine for myself, "What am I trying to tell the audience?"—not about every single line the people are speaking, but, "Where am I trying to go with this scene? What is the idea that I'm trying to arrive at?" And the idea might be a plot point, but I feel if a scene doesn't engine a story forward, then that scene has no reason to be in the movie. If there is an indulgent moment where the photography is beautiful or there's a happy accident that happened with one of the children, and you kind of hate to lose it, but it really isn't going to help the next scene, then it really shouldn't be in the picture at all. I kind of make those determinations the night before or the week before.

When I get to the scene, I allow the actors to block themselves to begin with. I've found that left of their own devices, actors would prefer to stand in one place and do seven pages of dialogue and not go anywhere. There are actors who will say, "You know, it would be great if I came in here, and got up on this line, and moved on that breath." But for the most part it tends to be a static rehearsal, and that's when I've got to figure out where I want them to move and why. So there's a lot of blocking time. I take about and hour and a half to light, maybe two hours to block and light a master. But then once the master is lit, then pretty much the camera goes very quickly from setup to setup. I do a lot of reverses [shots in opposite direction], and I like to do a lot of reverse masters. I have four masters per scene. On *Amistad* there were at least four, sometimes five masters per scene. I camera cut my films. I play just what I know I'm gonna use in that master. Because, when I first began directing, I did nine pages of dialogue from twenty-five angles and got to the editing room and after about nine years of experience, I realized, "Look at all the waste I never put in my movies." And I've kind of learned as I've gotten more experienced to pretty much know where I want to use the values at the moment. And then I can do what they call "camera cut."

A lot of times, to get performance, it's sometimes important not to talk too much to the actor. Because I find that if you talk too much to the actor, the actor is simply a reflex of your own, and the actor isn't bringing any value or any ideas to the part. Each actor has a different way of communicating what he or she wants to say on film. And I often find that if an actor is having a great deal of difficulty with an emotion like crying or like bringing themselves to anger — and I've recently worked with an actress who couldn't cry and an actor who couldn't get angry — what I've done is, I've walked away. And I've allowed the actor to get so mad at themselves for my walking away and saying, "Well, we can try something else." The actor gets so furious with themself that once I see them working themselves up, I say, "Now we'll shoot! Come on back!" And they can usually deliver. But it's not really playing tricks on the actors, it's being able to recognize when the actor is not comfortable with a scene. And often what really helps an actor to get to a place where you're happy, the director is happy, is simply going off somewhere and talking about the whole movie, just a couple of sentences, what the movie means to me, and why this scene is important. And then you let the actor work it out, and I promise you, almost every time they work it out for themselves.

Djimon [Hounsou, who plays Cinque, the leader of the slave revolt] is such a gifted individual that I wish I could take credit for his performance. I didn't have to do anything with him. He was in character. His mood was right. He understood every breath he took and why he had to take that breath, and he made my job really easy.

When Anthony Hopkins began to do the scene and the camera was rolling, I forgot I was on a movie set—and when the take was over, I forgot I was the director, I forgot there was a camera in the room, and I thought that somebody had invited me to a theatre to watch a play. Anthony Hopkins really didn't like to go beyond three or four takes and I knew he had gotten it and he knew he had gotten it and often times it's frustrating for actors who pretty much know they've got it but the director is still sort of amorphously looking for something else that could be even better. And I think that the biggest challenge to be a director is when to walk away from something, when you are pretty certain you have it.

When I first met Peter [Firth, who plays the English captain] for this, the one thing we talked about was—in order to get the audience to believe him, that there really was slavery and he really was looking for slave ships and his job was to destroy slave colonies—that we had talked about stillness: that if he didn't move at all and everything was just the words, he didn't blink, he didn't move his head, he didn't gesture, that there would be such economy and such power and such focus from him that it would all come from his eyes and from his voice. So he didn't move.

Saving Private Ryan

I put myself in the role of a combat cameraman, which in a sense would be a lot better than putting myself in the role of an overseer, which most directors are. In most of my films, I'm an overseer—I try to give to all of you the most comprehensive angle that will tell you the most about what I'm trying to tell you. Whereas I was concerned about deconstructing this movie, and I was more concerned with putting you through the eyes of someone who couldn't see very well. Which is why my assistant director kept coming over to me and saying, "Why do you have a thousand actors on the beach if the camera's so low it only sees twenty-five people? I don't understand why you have all these poor Irish soldiers coming out every day and getting wet and getting hypothermia and standing in the water—you only see twenty-five people in the foreground." And I kept saying, "Well, if I stand up with the camera I'll get shot—I can't stand up." Let's really assume the point of view of John Huston when he made *The Battle of San Pietro*, that great documentary.

I shot the film in continuity. Which I hadn't done since *E.T.* And I only did it in *E.T.* because I wanted the children to understand where they were yesterday so they could figure out where they were today. And I started in the Higgins boats and I shot the movie in complete continuity, and I think more than anything else, the script evolved on location. Because the moments we were putting on film were telling us what the next moments needed to be. And in that sense it wasn't the formal process of a director and a writer in a room trying to find out who the dominant forces were and who the subordinate forces were and. . . . Tom Hanks was actually saying, "Don't make my character better." He had so many lines in the original screenplay and Tom just insisted, he said, "You know, I don't want to talk in this movie—there's too much to experience, I don't want to speak." So we wound up cutting out, I'd say, three-quarters of Tom's dialogue. And it was a choice that Tom made. Tom came to me and said, "Please cut out these lines. I wouldn't be lecturing my troops—I'd be leading them, not lecturing them."

When we were first starting the movie, we used the Irish army. I had between 750 and 1,000 actual soldiers from the Irish army, not including our own stunt people and our own actors. And we did not use the Irish navy. Because of that the Irish army was throwing up in the boats all day, and they were really sick, and that was the day that the general of the Irish army chose to come down and pay our location a visit. And because the seas were rough that day—and I wanted to get rough seas, because in fact when they made the crossing the seas were horrendous. It was the most inclement conditions you can imagine that all those soldiers had to cross the channel. And so what happened was we had bad seas, we sent the boats out, and there were big waves breaking over the Higgins boats, the flat-bottoms. And the general took one look at his boys out there, and he called us all in. And he sent the entire army back to their homes. And we were without the army. Then I was taken to task. I was sent in to the Irish colonel's tent the next morning and I had to do what they call formal dressing down. They read a proclamation that condemned my inhumanity to their troops, and my reaction to that dressing down was going to determine whether the Irish army came back and finished the movie or not. So I just took it. I just sat there and took it. And when it was all over, I had a piece of paper in my pocket, and I pulled it out, and I had a proclamation which I had written the night before, which was basically a proclamation that marveled and raved at the courage of the Irish army. So they condemned us, and we celebrated them, and we hugged and we kissed and we began to shoot the movie again. The whole movie took fifty-nine days to shoot, but disproportionate in that figure, it took twenty-four days to shoot just the landings on Omaha Beach.

I used a very unfortunate word which is often misunderstood. In an earlier response where I said I was like a "method" director. And people say, "Ooh, the 'method.' What a horrible Stanislavsky term that is." That simply means that you let the environment and you let the circumstances around you and you let the immediate moment inspire you. You look for the inspiration. You look for all the mojos. And in starting the movie in continuity, at least everyone knew we had to open the boats and the rangers had to come out of the boats, and they had to take some defilade behind those Belgian gates, those big steel crosses. So at least everyone was prepared the first day. They knew where we were shooting. And I had it laid out in blocks of two or three days. We would try to take the beach the same way the rangers took the beach. The first day we would try to just get from the Higgins boats to the Belgian gates. The third day of shooting we would simply try to get from the Belgian gates to the sea wall. That turned into five days of shooting just to get to the sea wall. But it was kind of like taking a beach on a relatively safe method. And that's all we had to do. My support crew — the special effects people especially, the stunt people — had to know what blocks we were shooting from day to day, because there were so many charges. You have to understand that they created a grid of squibs and explosions, and the actors were trained where not to be. And we beat it into them where they could not be, and where they had to be. And so there were so many safety meetings on this film. Most of the time was taken with repeated safety meetings. So accidentally one of my actors wouldn't wander into an area where we had taken the stakes out with the red tape that marked the danger zones. We didn't want anybody wandering into those areas. Those are only for the stunt men. And we had a tremendous contingent of stunt men on this picture. I was more concerned with people getting hurt than I was about getting the shot. So most of the time was spent, "OK, are you sure you know where you must not go? And if you get any sand in your eyes, will you please stop and not continue the shot? Don't anybody be a hero. Drop your gun or just go like this, and say, 'I'm out of the shot,' and we'll stop everything, we'll start over again." So much of it was like a football game. Huddling before each shot. And every shot I held my breath. There wasn't one shot in this movie where we didn't have some effect going off, because this wasn't a CGI movie, this wasn't a special effect film. This was a physical effect picture. There wasn't one moment where we weren't all just saying, "Oh, please, God, don't let anything go wrong here."

I found that it worked really well, especially when I was shooting over the German machine gun emplacements, to simply let the cameramen find their shots, and not tell them anything. And I pretty much left it up to them to get the shots. So in a sense, there were many little moments of individual directing efforts on the part of the camera operators. This was one moment where you could actually go to a camera operator and say, "For those two shots, you directed this picture, not me." And because I gave Mitch [Dubin], our main operator, a chance really to respond to being shot at. Because he was running behind the rangers, right up to the beach. And there was one shot that I'll never forget that he did. I don't know what brought him to do it, but I had put a number of soldiers on the ground who were really in agony, and as Mitch was running through the fields following Tom Hanks with explosions going off and the casement firing down at them, for some reason, he caught some guy out of the side of his eye, and he brought the camera down and just showed the face of a soldier who was screaming in pain, and then came back off of him again, and came back up again. I didn't tell him to do that. The environment was so intense, with such firepower seemingly coming down at Mitch that he just became intuitive with the camera, and made intuitive choices, as many of the operators made—as all the signal corps cameramen in the forties made when they were actually out there in the Pacific, in Europe, trying to document WWII. There were very few Steadicam shots. Probably no Steadicam shots at all anywhere on Omaha Beach. It was all handheld. And it was handheld with the shaker lens, and I would run behind with a monitor, with a small handheld monitor, so I at least had some idea what we were getting.

The scene where Giovanni Ribisi tells the story of his mother, pretending he's asleep. I had first of all shot his death. And his death was probably one of the most emotional things I'd ever been around as a director. And we shot it all day—it was torture for everybody. But it came off so well, when I first cut the film together, that I realized that Giovanni didn't have a story that prepared you to know him or care about him enough to care about his death. So I asked the writer to come back, and I asked him to write a scene, and I said let's go into a church, and let's do a scene with Giovanni talking about his mother. So that scene was written after the film was in first cut.

Everybody had ideas. Every actor came that morning with an idea of how they wanted to react to what they knew was going to be coming at them. I remember one day I went over to Tom Hanks, and we were shooting the capturing of what we called Steamboat Willie, the Wehrmacht soldier. And I had been feeling and empathizing with Tom the whole time, wondering when he was going to break, because I wanted him to break at some point. I didn't know when or how, and Tom was looking for a moment to break, but he didn't know when and how, either. And one day I walked over to him, I said, "You want to just try something? What if you just kind of walked over to the crater, and you sit down, you take out your map, you look at it, and you just start to lose it. And you just lose it." And Tom, he's an amazing person to work with. Instead of sitting with me and analyzing why he would lose it at that moment, and whether it was the right time, and whether he was really prepared for a crying scene, he went, "OK." So we set up two cameras. One on a slow dolly, and one with an 85 lens just on Tom's face, and Tom went, and he did that moment. And he broke down, and he cried.

And he cried as long as he needed to cry. And at the end of that, he was a wreck. He got up and he had to leave the set. He had to go behind some rubble. And he came back to me and he said, "Do you want to do it again?" I said, "No. Do you?" He said, "No." And that was it. That was the first take. It was in the movie.

We've all shot in rain before—we all had rain experiences, and rain's a very debilitating form of environment that you bring down on yourself and your company. But in this movie it really helped everybody feel miserable, because they were. And there was one little moment I remember in that scene with the French girl, where he was handing her off to a stranger. And the idea was that she would come back to her dad. And I thought that a natural thing would be—just personally, because I've got a lot of kids—that if I handed one of my kids off to a stranger, I would expect my kid to slap me across the face. So I told her, I said, "When you come back to your Dad, I want you to beat him. I want you to slap him as hard as you can across the face." And she just couldn't do it. She just couldn't hit anybody across the face. And this wonderful actor took her aside behind the scenes and said, "It won't hurt—I promise you it won't hurt." And she just tapped him like this, and he said, "No, hit me harder, harder." And he prepared her. When we went to do the scene, she really hauled off and slapped him. She really hit him a number of times. And then she came over to me after that and she said, "Can I do it again?"

— 5 —

Post-production

Editing

Barry Levinson

Bugsy

I've worked with the same editor [Stu Linder], for all the films I've done, so I only know from working with one person. And he only has one assistant. I always feel like we're sort of making a home movie. What's nice is when you've made movies and you've built up a group of people there's a shorthand, so you don't have to explain your sensibility. And he cuts very quickly. What I don't do is, see an assemblage of the whole film, because it may be like a nightmare. Unless the segments are sort of cut and rhythmically feel the way they were intended to be, there's no need to see the whole film. I feel all the scenes have to make sense on their own and be as tight as possible. Then you watch the whole film and then you begin to cut back on it. So there's a long period until I actually see it for the first time.

Oliver Stone

JFK

Because we had four months, I had four editor teams and four different rooms. I've always promoted from within. All my editors have come up from being assistants to the previous editors who all

170 Directors Close Up

left me at one point or another, they've had enough of me. I've burned them out. We had community meetings every day where we'd look at various stages of various cuts. They worked around the clock. I gave each one as much independence as I wanted them to feel as free as actors, to try anything. As long as they ultimately conform to a zeitgeist of the whole. And I tried to run this as a democracy. Generally it was five votes, four editors and me, and sometimes it would be one against four!

In month two if editor B was not working well with what he had, and wasn't flowing, then it would be given to editor C, who wanted to work on it. There were conflicting styles at points. And that was part of the director's job, to make sure that it blended. The four editors would choose things they felt closest to. Like with actors, there's a natural flow to editing as there's a natural flow to writing. We were playing with time—present, past, and future—so it was totally dissociative editing. We were not bound by any strictures at all of conventional editing. I felt totally free. It's a free association. We wanted to go with MTV. I love MTV. I said, "Let's go for consciousness, this is what it's about—put a splinter in the brain." In the first draft [of the screenplay] there were so many flashbacks on each page that it was an unreadable script. I took all the flashbacks out, of course, intending to put them back in—in the editing room. And we did it. If anything, we added more flashbacks. The scene with Ferri confessing in the motel room with Kevin [Costner] we must have cut fourteen times, with three different editor teams. It was the scene that was totally disassociative. It's all jump cut [where the editing, rather than appearing seamless and unnoticeable, "bounces" around].

John Madden
Shakespeare in Love

I've certainly worked on movies where I've turned the film upside down in post-production. I'm not necessarily disrespectful of the script, but you can make extraordinary discoveries. On this one, that was not the case. Because I had to commit so completely to the way it was going to be at the shooting stage that it was just a matter of hoping that it would go together right.

I worked on a movie with an editor who was cutting the movie and we were cutting a scene and I said, geez, look at that, that's the wrong chair in that scene. And he said, "What do you mean?" And I said "That's not the chair that was in the scene the last time we were in this room." And he said, "What, we've been in this room before?" He'd been working the whole movie and he never realized that it was the same location. And it's absolutely true.

Clint Eastwood

Unforgiven

I enjoy the shooting process, but I also enjoy being finished! I love being done! And the idea of going to a cutting room with two people or one person, or an assistant or two editors, is just heaven. You go in there and you stand there and you think, it's done, for better or for worse. So now the question . . . to put it . . . to glue it all together and see how it comes out.

I feel editing. I see the editing as I do it. I pre-edit in my mind. Once the film is all assembled, I'll go through it and I'll do a "cruel cut." What I call a "cruel cut" is I dump everything I think is unnecessary. And then I kind of think, well, this moment's missing, so I get it back to what I think plays and then I try to stay away from it for at least two weeks. Because, the more you look at it, the duller it plays, because you get brain dead.

Vittorio De Sica [the Italian director] had a rough cut the next day, after he finished shooting. But he only shot what he wanted to use. He just "camera cut" the film. But other people will take a lot of time. Three weeks to four weeks is about as long I can stay in there with any kind of sanity.

Once you've been on the set, you remember every frame of that film that's shot. There's no way it can ever escape you.

Neil Jordan

The Crying Game

Sometimes the editor can put two shots together that can change everything that you've designed. And it was interesting on this film.

There was an editor from Hong Kong, and I come into the editing room and he's done a really solid cut of the film. But half the way through I realize that his understanding of English is not what I thought it was. He's not fully hearing what the different actors are saying. And it was very interesting because he was responding to the most basic things, which was the emotion in the actors' faces. And there was a lot of dialogue in this film. And sometimes I would have to clear up the dialogue issue. But he was responding to the most basic thing, which is the picture in front of him.

Rob Reiner

A Few Good Men

A film editor has to understand the film because he's helping you shape the film and tell a story. So, if he doesn't get what story you're telling, it's gonna be painstaking because you're gonna have to deal with every single cut.

I don't conceptualize for the editing room, because most of the things I do, they're very character driven. If the performance is right or better in one take than another I may decide, "Well, I'm gonna stay with him a little longer," and that I can't determine until I actually put the stuff on film. I won't make a predetermination of how I'm gonna cut it beforehand.

I change performance tremendously in the editing room. I love doing this stuff. I will take the dialogue of one take, the dialogue of another take, marry that line and put it in the mouth of that third take, because I like the way the person looks on the certain take, but I don't like the way the dialogue's coming out. You can all of the sudden create another performance.

The digital stuff, I think there's obviously value to doing it. It's a lot shorter. I think you gain something, but you also give something up. You gain obviously speed, but there is a gestation period that you need, I think, to see a film come together and think about what you want with a film, and how you're shaping it. And I think you lose that. The instantaneousness of video editing, I think takes that.

Peter Weir
The Truman Show

The nightmare is, your structure isn't there. The nightmare is, you don't know where you're going. That's the way I've had it. Anyone with a long career has had it. But you know what you aim for, and hopefully have most of the time, is a solid skeleton for the film before you start. And you've got to go with it. You've got to learn off your dailies. But, in this case, it was incredibly much in detail. As it happened with the umpteen drafts of the script, so in the cuts. I've never had so many cuts. I think I got as high as seventeen full cuts.

If the tone wasn't right, the balance shifts. You were thrown out of the movie. I had to give you a movie experience. And it had to be about movies, rather than about television. So in fine tuning, I put this in pretty standard sort of changes. But you couldn't know until you tested them on the screen. The new editing systems are sensational in the possibilities they give us. Like you are cutting your picture as you go along. It's amazing, the speed with which you can assemble a cut. But on the other hand, you still have to get into the theatre. You can get into terrible dangers looking at the monitor, in terms of cutting too fast sometimes or missing details, going too close.

Andrew Davis
The Fugitive

Actually, dailies are probably one of the most enjoyable parts for me. Because you work so hard, you're nervous, and you're trying to put everything together, and you go to see dailies and you say, "My God, we really got something. There's a story here."

I like to tell the story with picture, and with collage. And then when you stop, and you listen to dialogue, it should be the real fine flavorings and seasonings of the characters. So there are a lot of sequences put together with music. I hear pieces of music and it's all there. It's dramatic, it's got everything in place, all you have to do is put pictures to it. I think you're constantly building with pictures and with sound effects and dialogue and music to create this whole kind of environment. We brought in some younger editors to help support what was going on. And we would literally change off sequences. Somebody would take a sequence, and then work on it, and then they'd say, "Well you try a shot at it."

There have been situations where people say, "Well, why do we need this? What is this all about?" And then they go to the screening, and people laugh or respond to it, and they go, "I think we need it." So that's nice. We dropped a lot of sequences, just for pace, and feeling that Harrison shouldn't have. There was a scene where Harrison stopped in a café and met a woman, and saw his face on television, and nervously got up and walked away. And we decided we didn't want to have him be warm and in the café. We wanted to keep the pressure on the story.

I'm not one of these directors who believes a lot in testing, and responding to the audience's needs. It's not that I'm arrogant, I'd just rather not have to deal with it. But luckily we got these incredible scores. It was like ninety-seven percent excellent and very good. It was like the highest scores Warner Brothers had ever gotten on any test screening. And we went to the screening the next day to show at the studio, and we had all these cards. So it went very easy. They basically said, "Don't touch it. Leave it alone." We made a thousand changes after that screening. But it was very supportive. And actually I remember Harrison saying he had never been to a meeting after a first screening that had been so smooth. So we were very, very lucky.

Robert Zemeckis

Forrest Gump

The editorial process—it's my favorite part of filmmaking, because all the madness and insanity and pressure of shooting is over. When you wrap [end of shoot], it just instantly funnels to just you, your editor, and your film—and you don't have to worry whether it's rainy out or if the sun is coming up. I call my editor "my second brain." He's the guy who you really have to rely on. I never seem to get enough time to edit, because it's always rushing into these release dates [when the picture is scheduled to be in the theatres]. But I'll look at what he's cutting when I'm shooting and we'll talk about it later. But I can't focus on it, so I put the distance there. He's roughing it in and making his cut and I don't really start working with him until we get into the cutting room.

Frank Darabont
The Shawshank Redemption

You always want to get the thing as tight as you can. A journalist once asked Abraham Lincoln how long a man's legs should be — long enough to reach the ground.

Roberto Benigni
Life Is Beautiful

Editing is really the moment where the movie takes the energy. It's there, it's the body. It's wonderful because you can watch the little sign of the face, first time. Everything is in tumult, of course, but it's stinging every organ of your body. You cannot judge exactly, but this moment for me is the most wonderful.

Mel Gibson
Braveheart

It was a real "the two of us" kind of process. I'd give him [the editor, Steven Rosenblum] what he needed and he was putting it together the way I wanted it and even better than I wanted it. And I was like, "Wow, this is even better than someone's final cut, this rough cut." [Rough cut is the earliest version of the edited film.] And everyday we'd go in and occasionally we'd start choking each other. You know how that is. You'd come to a difference of opinion. But we'd got around that problem, because I got, you know, those punching puppets — I got a nun and he got the fighting rabbi — so we'd be sitting there and we'd be punching the shit out of each other with these puppets until we'd start laughing and then we'd throw the puppets away and then get back to it. It would avoid direct confrontation.

What's on the floor was stuff that I'd labored too much to make a point, and I thought, "You get it already." And also, I'm not a big fan of testing it with audiences, but it's important because that's who it's for. If you're sitting in a theatre somewhere and fifteen or twenty-five women get up and go, "Oh my God!" and get up and run from the theatre screaming, you know you've got to lighten up somewhere.

Michael Radford
Il Postino

The editing process for me is the process I'm least good at, actually—I tend to try and put everything in the can. [The "can" refers to the film containers.] I did shoot a lot of cover. And it became instantly apparent that these long scenes between the two of them just held. So we made that the linchpin of the movie. And we cut this in a very old-fashioned way. Tom Priestly, who cut all my other pictures, was very much an old fashioned Hollywood editor, who liked to hunch himself over the Moviola [an editing machine] and not let you see what was going on. And to that extent you can keep a distance, you can come back and have a fresh eye. With Roberto [Perpignani, the editor], it was a total collaboration—he doesn't like to work on his own, he likes to really just sit there and talk it through and put it together while you're there and you have a look at it. And I loved that. It was like going back to film school. And like in shooting, you have to be alert. You shoot a scene, and then you throw away all the preconceptions as to why you shot that scene when you get into the cutting room. I mean, it's an absurd situation—you've shot a scene for a particular reason, and you use it for an entirely different reason.

We were two months in post-production, from the day we finished shooting to the day we had to deliver the print. I did actually recut it afterwards. I have to tell you about the mix [where the sounds are mixed together—dialogue, music, and sound effects] on this picture, because it was like nothing else. First, you have a lot of Italians—they dub pictures a lot ["dubbing" is replacing dialogue recorded while shooting with dialogue recorded in a studio, often with voices different from the original actors], so they have a dubbing director come in, and he starts to dub all the actors. You've got these performances out of people and he brings other people in and redoes the performances for you!

Into the final mix, we've got sixteen tracks up and I'd go to the dubbing mixer and we're sitting in the big studio right in the middle of Cinecitta [the Italian studio in Rome]. And I say, "Look, can I have a look at the dubbing charts, just to see where we are?" And he looks up at me and says, "Que? [Italian for "what"] What are dubbing charts?" He said, "No, here we put it up and let's see what happens." "Where did you learn that from?" he said, "The maestro, you know, Fellini." I said, "Fellini used to have six months — we've got eight days to dub this thing." We spent seven days dubbing two reels — he would forget, he would literally forget what was coming up. "Huh? Oh . . ." and this went on for seven days and wonderfully Italian, and we had one day to dub the rest of the picture. The composer came in the middle of the dub and he said, "What's going on here?" And the composer said, "I'm going to do the music." And the guy said, "Yeah, I could do with a spare pair of hands, this is getting difficult." And then we had a party.

Scott Hicks

Shine

The editor and I were in need of some therapy, I think, by the end.

For me the very central decisions that you make are the cinematographer, the designer and the editor. When all the pyrotechnics of shooting have stopped and you're confronted with the material out of which you're going to fashion the film, it's essential that first of all you share the same sense of humor that's going to get you through that very long and difficult process of fashioning the film.

Running through the rain is actually a really good example of the process of working with the editor. I had in my mind an image of a continuous thirty-second shot of David running through the rain where he's really at his lowest depth. But, of course, this is extremely difficult to do when you're shooting high speed with an actor who's running parallel with the camera in the rain at night. We really had slender resources in which to try and execute. So when we saw the rushes [the developed film projected on screen], it was a disappointment. There was no one take that was executed to the perfection that I wanted. And the editor said "Frankly, this is rubbish. You're going to have to forget about this scene completely and think of something else." So in the end, I said, "But look, that bit's good and look there's a good bit. Take them and jump cut them and use this piece of Rachmaninoff, and I'll come back on Thursday, and show me what you've done."

Anthony Minghella
The English Patient

The editor becomes the filmmaker with you, in what was for me, ten months of the process.

Mike Newell
Four Weddings and a Funeral

The editor shows me stuff as we go. But, then usually what happens is that he asks me to stay away. The great thing about most editors, I find, is that they show you not necessarily what's on the page, but what actually was in the head. And it's in the cutting room that the shit really happens, studio stuff, money stuff, disappointment, rage, "Why didn't we do this?" It doesn't work does it? And he must make up his mind where he's going to stand and usually a good one will stand with you. They are a right arm. They're people with great strength and great character. They are very accomplished and they're usually very clever people, very perceptive.

Quentin Tarantino
Pulp Fiction

If I wanted to make *Pulp Fiction* move like a bullet—the movie is two hours and 20 minutes—I guess I could've taken 20 minutes outta there. I didn't want to. I mean if I do a movie that's supposed to work like that, that's exactly how I'll do it, but that's not how I want to do it. And, that's not how I want to do this one. Like when you get to a scene like Jack Rabbit Slim's, part of the whole idea, is the whole thrust of that story was the date, the date, the date. When we got there, I didn't want to do, like, it normally is in a movie—ha, ha, ha, dance. Like everything's been condensed. I wanted us to be on a date, I wanted—the whole thing's been building up to that. I don't want to shorten it. I wanted them to be uncomfortable with each other. I didn't want all of the sudden they just start sparkling dialogue. They don't know what to say to each other. I wanted it to be uncomfortable. I shot it so it was that way. But, what you have going on is just the constant talks. If you were to lose this, this would move a lot quicker and we achieve the same thing, but much less painfully. But I think the pain is part of it. So it's the constant process of whittling it down and then saying, "Nope, I know we could lose this and no one would know it was lost," but I would know, and it's not just because I'm holding onto my baby—it's supposed to work that way.

Mike Leigh
Secrets & Lies

The film is made in the cutting room, and you really do have to have someone you click with. I've been blessed with John Gregory. And the thing about an editor like him—particularly with my kind of material, which grows as the film is being shot—he's just got an ability to take that material and put it together in a way that really makes sense.

James Cameron
Titanic

When I did *Strange Days* with Kathryn Bigelow, she asked me to get involved in the editing, and I wound up cutting a number of action sequence scenes and sort of mastered the AVID [an electronic digital editing machine] on that. So then I decided on *Titanic* that I'd cut the picture myself. Eventually I decided to bring in Richard Harris [the editor], who I'd worked with on two previous films, because I really believe that in the editing room you've got to have somebody to talk to and to put another perspective. I knew I was going to be living at the editing room, so I just cut to the chase and put the editing room at my house. The way I preferred to work on *Titanic* was, I would divide up the show—"You guys work on these scenes, you work on those, and I'm gonna work on these, because I sort of know what to do and I can do it faster than explaining it." And we'd all be working at the same time, and I'd look at their cuts and I'd ask them to come in and look at my cuts and comment. And then I'd say, "OK, why don't you go take this thing that I've been working on and go see if you can work with this idea, that idea, which aren't quite right, and give me that thing that you've been working on." So we just all would sort of play musical chairs, and I think that was a strengthening process, because it went through a number of sets of eyes and hands. I asked the studio for more time — which, by the way, I think is the great triumph of the film, is that we actually said, "You know what? We're gonna fuck this up if we go for this release date and I think we need another month in the editing room." And the studio said, "Yes," and that doesn't happen very often. They said, "You know what? We don't want to screw this up. First of all, we've got a lot of money in it; secondly, I think you've got a chance of doing something really pretty cool here." So, they gave us the extra time. So I wound up going back over nibbling out a few frames here and a few frames there, and it was kind of a marinating process, literally just sitting in that room by myself for about a month just running the sequences over and over. And suddenly something will pop. You've seen the thing 500 times — something will pop out that you've never thought of before. Or you'll remember a shot that was from another scene and you put it in and it just changes everything. And the very last thing I do — when we're really confident with the cut that we're almost there — is, I sit in the screening room and run the conformed picture with the image flopped in the gate. Because I find that as I've watched the scene over and over and over, my eye has learned where to go next in the next shot before that shot has come on the screen. So I wanted to short-circuit that pretrained response. It's a way of seeing the film for the first time — you only get to do it once, but you can learn a lot from it.

Curtis Hanson

L.A. Confidential

I let the editor do exactly what he wants while I'm shooting. That's their time to be creative. I watch dailies every day with the editor and then give any thoughts I have about specific takes that are, in my mind, the key takes. But beyond that, I let them do their cut. I will go in on the weekend, sometimes at night, into the editing room and look at a few scenes as they have them, just to give them my two cents to be helpful, but also to kind of recharge my own batteries. In the editing room, I'll give many notes, go away and let them execute them. And then as we keep refining, I'll end up being there more and more. And ultimately, I'm there all the time.

Steven Spielberg

Amistad

I've worked with my editor Michael Kahn for twenty-two years now, and Johnny Williams [the composer] for twenty-four years, so we've been a team for almost as long as I've been making feature films. My process editorially is, I like to cut on the set. I spend my lunch hours in the editing room and my evenings in the editing room with Michael. I do that for several reasons: Number one, I do a lot of reshooting, and I like to know that the set is still standing before we strike it [take it down]. I can see the entire scene assembled if I need another couple of shots. My process is, I don't know the movie before I make the movie. I only come to discover the movie as I'm making it. And editing, more than shooting, helps me discover the film and the story I'm trying to tell. And I don't believe in the AVID or Lightworks. [electronic editing]—I only work on the movie on the KEM [a flatbed film editing machine]. I'm old-fashioned. Even though the AVID is truly a more facile piece of technology, it doesn't give me more thinking time. It's very valuable when the assistants are pulling trims [individual strips of film that have been cut and categorized] to change a cut, or make a new cut, that I have ten minutes or twelve minutes to walk around and think about my movie. I think really fast on the set, but I don't think fast in the editing room.

Saving Private Ryan

The post-production on this particular film happened *during* the production of this particular film. There was no post-production. We were editing every single day we were shooting it. Mike Kahn, the

editor—he was a day behind the dailies, a day behind the production. So I was able to see whole sequences assembled before we left
the set. And that was very important, because I didn't quite know
what kind of a movie I was going to make. And I had most of Omaha
Beach cut together just before we left for England for the rest of our
picture. And that really helped me. It really helped me to go back
and fix things and correct mistakes I had made when the sets were
still standing. The biggest thing in post-production was sound, on
my film. Because we pretty much locked [the images in final cut]
Saving Private Ryan, I'd say, a month after we came back from
England. And most of the time took, with Gary Rydstrom and Gary
Summers, the sound designers, putting together the sound design—
which I just think is the most brilliant thing I've ever heard these
guys do before.

James L. Brooks
As Good as It Gets

My editor, Richie Marks, who I've done every picture with, and composer, Hans Zimmer, are like family members to me. Editing is
everything to me—it's where the performance is at. It's amazing
how much you change the performance. It's extraordinary. And it's
in the editing room also where filmmaking gets religious. I think just
the focus and attitude towards the film in the editing room is pure.

Music

Barry Levinson
Bugsy

If I'm using source music I'll lay the source music [as distinguished
from underscoring written by the composer] over a scene early on.
There's a dynamic—music is very influential on images and does
change things radically.

  [Ennio] Morricone, the composer, doesn't speak any English, so he
has a translator. When you watch the movie, the translator is speaking Italian, explaining the dialogue. It's quite an experience, but what

he's really talking about is in tones and textures and feelings and emotions. He wants to know what is the feeling—what does the character feel.

Morricone was explaining to me how he worked with Sergio Leone [Italian director of "spaghetti" westerns and *Once Upon a Time in America*]. Leone would explain the movie to him before he made it. He would tell him the story and Morricone would write the music. Then Leone would go off and shoot the film to the music.

Michael Radford

Il Postino

I have very great difficulty with music, always. It's a difficulty because it's the one area in which you can't meddle yourself. It's a great leap in the dark, and it's often a very expensive leap in the dark. You try to express in ordinary language something which is inexpressible. Because musicians think in different ways. The world is divided into musicians and people who can't do music. I started off this movie with Ennio Morricone. He would kind of sit around a grand piano in his apartment and thump out a theme. And he's one of the great composers, no doubt about it. I said to him one day, "I'd like the music to be discreet in this picture." And he looked at me and said, "I don't do discreet music." So he rang me up and said, "I'm off this picture." So I moved on to this guy who'd done the music for Fellini's *City of Women* [Luis Bacalov], who is the best collaborator for an ignoramus like me. He is an extraordinary musician, both as a player and as a composer. I'd said, "I want something that's popular, that'll catch people's attention, but is discreet." And he came up with the perfect thing and he improvised all that piano in the studio. It was just fantastic.

I think there's lots of different types of film music—there's film music that tells the interior state of the mind of the characters; there's music which "G's" up the action. I wanted a music that gave a flavor of an atmosphere to the entire film. But, of course, composers like to think logically and they want "Mario's theme or Neruda's theme." And I'd say, "Yeah, OK, if you want. We'll call it that." And here's a guy who really knows movies, so he knows very well that the moment you've got the stuff there, that somehow or another you're going to change it all around. It was written for one thing, and it's much better for something else.

Barbra Streisand
The Prince of Tides

When I was doing *Nuts*—I didn't feel the film required much music—that's why I could compose the 13-minute score. I believe this is such an alive process—I mean, just last week I was redoing the sound for videotape. I thought I made the music too loud in spots in the film, so now I've changed the music balance for video. So I don't think it's done till it's done. Usually my first instincts about levels are the best—then you start to overthink it.

Of course, film to me is like a symphony with slow adagio movements and fast staccato sections.

I had much less music at the beginning of previews. But then, I had a very "slow pace" score on my audience response cards. So every time I got a slow pace, I would add more music. And every time I added more music, the pace box went up. The music would keep it going.

I've also had a musician who plays all synthesized sounds come to the dubbing stage and play experimentally to the film—like in silent pictures.

Rob Reiner
A Few Good Men

Well, it's obvious music is critical. I mean, you can look at certain films without music and then with music and all of a sudden they become alive and they're lifted. I mean, they talk about *Chariots of Fire* as being one of those films that when it was screened without music they'd say, "What is this?" and then with music, lifted that film. I work very closely with the composer. I will sit with him, go through it, put a temp score together which gives you a jumping off point.

With the composer and with the music editor, the three of us will get together and we'll get some selections—put it up against the picture, you know — from other pictures, and then I'll actually sit with the composer, after he's done his initial pass, and he'll play me on his Synclavier [an electronic keyboard that can simulate sounds of a variety of other instruments] the things that he's got, and then you'll say, "Oooooh, I want to add some horns in there, or on that cue I want to go down." I know a little bit about music, so I can communicate a little bit with him as to what I want. That there's been a lot of music, but you don't know that there's music — that's what I tried to get, so that you don't hear the music, but it's there.

Robert Zemeckis

Forrest Gump

When you can have a relationship with your composer, that is like gold. Because you don't have any objectivity anymore. You say, "I don't know if this thing works. We're going to have to shore it up with music," and Al Silvestri, who I've collaborated with on the last six movies, says, "No." He says, "I wouldn't know what to write — I just don't hear any music there."

The hard part for *Forrest* was we had all these records that we put in the movie. And just wading through 30 years of music and trying to figure out how to work that into the film, that was what I think took most of our time in the editing room.

Oliver Stone

JFK

I called John Williams, who I'd worked with on *Born on the Fourth of July*. I thought it was a very emotional score and I was in accord with his aesthetic. I asked John, "Do you have any time? Can you give us thirty days?" I said, "Come to Dallas. Come to Dealy Plaza and experience it with us." He was there the first two weeks of shooting. He had a special feeling for John Kennedy. So in a sense he's written a requiem in his head already. And that was the main theme of the movie. And then in addition to that, he wrote our temp [temporary] score for us, before we edited. He gave us a conspirator theme for the Cubans; for Oswald he gave us a modification of that. He gave us a family theme for Jim [Garrison, the part played by Kevin Costner] and his wife and children. So there were three pieces and several miscellaneous pieces written by the time we were halfway through shooting. Essentially he'd written the score before the film was finished.

John Madden
Shakespeare in Love

As far as music is concerned, in every Peter Weir film I've ever seen, the music has kind of lived with me for years afterwards. And I work very, very much the same way as he does. There's a sort of atmosphere a film has for me. And Peter has always had an incredibly identifiable atmosphere. And the music is very, very crucial to me. I listen to music all the time in making a film. A certain kind of music which feels kind of right for me. And Stephen Warbeck, the composer, whom I obviously worked very closely with, is unbelievably low-tech. He's more low-tech than you could possibly imagine. He has one piano which has bits of old sandwiches clogging the keys up. But it's wonderful, because he's totally free. The way we usually work is, he throws out a few themes, or a few ideas, which then start to build into something else. Or they join up. Or we try them in different places, and we move them around. And we constantly draft, and redraft, and redraft the music. I end up living in his house, contributing to the sandwiches on the keyboard. And that, on this movie, was incredibly important. Because the patterns in the film are also musical patterns. In this case, we'd obviously committed to the music beforehand. Because of the dance music, it's part of the whole vocabulary of the film. So, more than any other one I've done, I think the music was kind of essential.

Steven Spielberg
Amistad

John Williams [the composer] always surprises me. There's never a score that he has written that I haven't been thoroughly moved by; and thoroughly surprised that he was capable of bringing a whole genre to something that he'd never knew how to do before.

James L. Brooks

As Good as it Gets

At the very end of the road, we had a picture that was getting laughs and was short of it's emotional life. And I was almost at the point of giving up and deploring this and he wouldn't let me. And part of what he [Hans Zimmer, the composer] kept on saying to me and part of what he was able to do with the music meant that the ambitions I'd always had for the picture at the beginning were the ambitions I still had at the end. I finished with the same ambitions, and I almost didn't. That was working closely with somebody.

Mel Gibson

Braveheart

I actually approached the making of the film from a very musical point of view. I found things that to me sounded primitive and Celtic and with lots of percussion, and I grew to love the sound of the pipes. And at rushes I had this whole collection of discs and I'd slip these things on for certain sequences at the dailies, and it really used to make it come to life. We finally sat there with the LSO [London Symphony Orchestra], a group of guys with strange little things, instruments—sort of like bamboo with bits of gaffer's tape rolled around it—and just blowing into hunks of bamboo and hitting themselves on the heads with things.

[In the battle sequence] I knew I didn't want any music once they clashed. The music was gone then. I just wanted it to be like a pretty raw experience for the audiences as much as it was for me. And just have it be as real and as ugly and crowded and crammed as possible.

James Cameron

Titanic

I'd worked with James Horner [the composer] on *Aliens*. I thought he'd done some spectacularly emotional scores in the last few years. He worked on the film for, I think, eight months. He said, "I'm gonna just do this movie. I'm not taking any other gig." Our very first meeting, he had seen a lot of the footage, he sat and looked at over a period of several days, I think thirty-two hours of daily selects, just to steep himself in the images. Nothing had been cut yet. He gave me some ideas he was thinking of. He was talking about Celtic instrumentations and kind of a traditional Irish sound, which I like, and the use of voice, which I thought was great. My only requests of him were, "Don't do a conventional period score. I don't want to hear a big violin section." And he said, "No violins?" And I said, "Find another way to be emotional." I said, "Just work on melody for the first two months. Just sit at your piano and when you've got one or two great themes, and you can play it on the piano, you're ninety percent of the way there." And the first time he played the three main melodies of the score for me, I literally cried at the first one and more so on the second one. And I knew I was there, and he hadn't really written a bit of the score proper yet.

Curtis Hanson

L.A. Confidential

There are many songs in the movie, and I, in fact, picked quite a few of them when we were writing the script. The advantage of having picked them in front, I found, was that I was actually able to play them on the set, when we were shooting, which was helpful. For instance, Kevin Spacey looking in the mirror—he was able to actually hear Dean Martin on the jukebox, which helped him feel what the thing would feel like in the movie: but it also helps me feel what the scene ultimately would feel like.

Jerry Goldsmith was my choice of composer, and he had a sort of odd job because all of these songs were already in the movie when I first showed it to him. He didn't have to worry about setting the period or even defining the characters, because you have the song already doing that. He had to weave it all together so that the songs and the score didn't feel like they were in different movies. And then use his score to underline the emotions. The idea that I'd had in terms of the songs was that, there would be this continuing motif of a trumpet. And then Jerry took that trumpet and put it into the score, which is actually a contemporary score, but it feels like it's wed to the songs.

Clint Eastwood
Unforgiven

I've had it happen in my early days — somebody comes back with a sweeping score that's just kind of overwhelming and you're going, "Uh, where's this go?" So you end up having to dump half of it. I usually have a fairly good concept of what I hear for the film. I've written a lot of music, and I've written music for three of the films that I've worked on, and I wrote the theme for *Unforgiven*. I just didn't want music to come in and overwhelm everything, I wanted it to be very supportive for the film, but not dominant.

Neil Jordan
The Crying Game

In *The Crying Game*, I tried to use a series of songs in an ironic way. In general I don't like the use of popular songs in movies, because I suppose I'm not a great fan of rock and roll. Someday I'd love to make a film without music, actually just with natural sounds.

Andrew Davis
The Fugitive

Aaron Copland is one of my favorite composers, and James Newton Howard gives you that kind of human, warm Americana quality. And he also is very rhythmic and hip. So he can give you the best of both worlds.

He was the first person who I showed a long, linear, forty-minute version of the opening, which was really sort of flaccid. And he looked at it, and his mouth fell open. He said, "You've got a hit movie here." I said, "What are you talking about? There's so much work to be done."

He was working on the score while we were still shooting. And actually was getting clips of sequences just thematically to think about: a chase theme, or a haunting theme. And actually we used James' music for the temp screening we had. We had some discussions about tone, and whether it was too funereal, or it needed to be more heroic. Just conceptual conversations. But it was very collaborative, and he was very open to all these discussions.

Quentin Tarantino
Pulp Fiction

Part of the way I find the music is, I figure out how the opening credit sequence is going to be. And I try to figure out what song I'm going to use for the opening credit sequence, because basically I feel if I'm playing a song, a piece of music over the opening credit sequence, this is the rhythm that movie is supposed to play at.

Frank Darabont
The Shawshank Redemption

You want the music to elicit some kind of emotional connection, and yet do it in such a way that is not obvious—it doesn't draw attention to itself in a way that I've seen other composers do, who will hit you over the head with four hundred violins at the key moment. Then comes the funny point where you've tempt [put in a temporary score] scored your movie with cues from *A River Runs through It* and *Scent of a Woman* and *Dances with Wolves* and you've mixed the movie and you've test screened it and you pretty much love your score and then comes the day, you have the new one, "Oh wait a minute—that doesn't sound right—why doesn't that sound right?" Well, well, idiot, because it's not *Dances with Wolves*!

— 6 —

The Best and the Worst

Barry Levinson

Bugsy

The shooting of it is what I love the most. Because there are so many things that are happening so quickly, and so many things that you have to fix, and so many surprises that take place, and so many interesting people that you work with. That explosion that's going on all the time creates an adrenaline rush in a way. It's almost euphoric at times.

Even part of the pain is the pleasure, because you're trying to get something on a scene and it's not working. It's just sort of laying there—it has no life. That's painful, but at the same time it's exciting to make it work. The area that I like the least is the aftermath—in terms of talking, in terms of the press—because somehow it begins to minimize it in some way. In the final analysis, when you look back, you're not sure how you got it all done. You don't know how it all came together. And it's all of those people and all of those moments that make up a film. And it's magic. And you can't explain it.

Neil Jordan

The Crying Game

The trouble with making a film is, it's the most pleasurable thing in the world. Because your whole day is filled. You wake up in the morning, you tumble out of bed, there's a car there, it takes you to the set, and it's great. What more stimulating thing can you do than, the first thing, talk to two actors or begin to worry about the paint on a bit of scenery? I find it actually, at it's best, it's the most pleasurable form of spending a day you can imagine. You're busy, and then you go out to dinner at night. If you are off on an artistic bent, everything you possibly could want to do in some states you get to do, if you direct a film.

The worst part for me is the plane flights, because I live in Ireland. And for better or for worse, this strange place [Los Angeles] is the center of the world film industry, so I keep having to make the ten-hour flight back and forwards and back and forwards—and I'm terrified of flying, so that for me is the worst!

Andrew Davis
The Fugitive

The pleasure is collaborating. It's sort of being a part of the circus. Being able to walk in, and do anything you want to do. Being taken seriously when they shouldn't take you seriously. That's the greatest fun for me. It's also tremendous to have people enjoy your movie.

The hardest part, I guess, is being second-guessed. When you have a kind of vision of things, and you want to pursue it, and you want to try to experiment. And there may be people around saying, "What is that about? Why do you want to try that?" I know that it can be very lonely out there, even though you're the director, and you're supposed to be the captain of the ship and there's a lot of responsibility and a lot of burden on your shoulders. And it's a question of finding a support mechanism and a team of people to share that with.

John Madden
Shakespeare in Love

For me having the ability to say, "No, I want it to be this way" is absolutely wonderful. And there are times when you want somebody else to be asked all the questions. I go through the best and the worst every single day. You go to bed at night, thinking this is an absolutely fantastic job. And you get up in the morning wanting to go anywhere but where you're going.

Barbra Streisand
The Prince of Tides

I get very obsessed till I get the script right. I can't sleep, I can't think straight. Then it's worrisome during pre-production. I mean, getting all the casting right. You go through the angst of that.

But, there are really so many pleasures on a day-to-day basis. I love the discipline of: we have *this* amount of time, we have *this* amount of money, we have *this* amount of energy. There is such an aliveness, such a spontaneity to every day, every moment, every problem, trying to capture the truth of the moment, trying to create an atmosphere where the actor is free to bare his soul—to reveal his truth.

Quentin Tarantino
Pulp Fiction

The single worst part of directing—and it's one of the things that when I think about it, I try not to think too early in the process, because it almost makes me wanna not do it—it's not the big fights; it's all the little nitpicky questions about this or that or the other, that when you're editing the movie and you're putting it under this microscope, that no movie should be looked at under a microscope. When the producers are watching it, they're making their little notes.

I think the best part is, like, when you've done a good day, when you've, like, you *did it*—you've fuckin' nailed it. And they're better than you could've ever imagined, and everyone knows that you're doing good work—you just go home and you just feel so good. And then, when you watch your film with an audience and you've got 'em. You feel the laughter and they're in. Like in my stuff, it's like laugh, laugh, laugh, and then—BOOM—I'm going to stop you from laughing. And then it stops. And then I get you laughing again, and it's like, that's great.

Mel Gibson
Braveheart

The hardest part—hmmm—staying a step ahead of everybody else.

I just love the experience—I mean, you can get in critical moments of self-doubt, where you think, "Should I go hang myself now?" which are pretty depressing. But I just don't see the down side. I think I'm incredibly fortunate to be able to do it.

Peter Weir
The Truman Show

I would say that it becomes an addiction. It's hard to imagine giving it up. I remember meeting Fred Zinnemann the latter years of his life in London, and he was like a small bird with a cane, having a cup of tea in his office, and he said, "You know, I don't think I will ever make another film." And I thought he was joking. The man was in his eighties. And I luckily didn't laugh. I said, "Well, who knows." But I realized that, of course, he was a young man. Creatively, of course, you don't age in the same way. And I found it very touching.

Frank Darabont
The Shawshank Redemption

Wasn't it Milos Forman who said shooting a movie was a necessary evil to get into the editing room? That's really my favorite place to be. That's where you can actually concentrate your focus on making the film.

I think my least favorite aspect of the process is the sheer mental and physical stamina required to get you through the shoot. I found that to be an extraordinary drain, to the point where it actually colors your enthusiasm for what you're doing, which I think is a danger.

Robert Zemeckis

Forrest Gump

The best part is showing your movie to an audience for the first time. And I also feel it's the worst part!

Mike Newell

Four Weddings and a Funeral

The worst is the "focus group," where this indistinct, randomly chosen group of thirty people will sit in the first two rows of the theatre and you have to then, with the studio, sit one row behind them, as you then have to hear them saying, "I don't really get this."

I always used to like when they had black-and-white dubs in the dubbing theatre [used while mixing the sounds]—when they put the color up for the run-through of the reel [after the mix] and you would see it with all the sound, suddenly with all the sound and the color as well and how it was going to be—I used to love that.

Cameron Crowe

Jerry Maguire

The worst part is dealing with the casting process.

The best part is when something simple and unexpected becomes the real soul of your movie.

Scott Hicks

Shine

The worst part is turning up on any given day when suddenly you don't have an idea in your head and you hope when those forty faces turn to you—and you try not to show the panic and you work your way through it.

The best part are those days when everything lays out in front of you and you see things so clearly. You find exactly where to put the camera. You're in tune with what you're doing.

James Cameron

Titanic

Best is when it's done and it's a big hit! But honestly, in terms of the actual process itself, for me it's the moment of discovery on the set with an actor, when an actor creates something that you didn't expect, and it's wonderful, and you're happy to have it in your film.

The worst part for me, I guess, is probably the moment when the lights are going down at the first preview, because that's the moment of truth.

Roberto Benigni

Life Is Beautiful

The best — it's wonderful to tell a story. And to draw it like it is. This is a kind of a gift. Wonderful! For me this is so fascinating, I am completely captured by this idea. And the worst is when I cannot tell a story, because it's very very painful. The sorrow, making a movie, is very very deep. I have pleasure, but there is a side that is so painful making a movie. But this is life.

Gus Van Sant

Good Will Hunting

The worst is probably shooting. It's the toughest period. It's just something that's a necessary evil! But also it's probably the best, too, because it's the part that you always talk about, when you're talking about filmmaking — it's the most exciting. I remember Dennis Hopper I heard say once: "The only thing worse than making a film is not making a film." Or waiting to make one.

Curtis Hanson

L.A. Confidential

The best part is being able to do it. I mean to me, to be able to direct a movie is a dream come true. It doesn't even have to be going well. If it's going OK, I just feel so lucky to be able to be there doing it.

The worst part, of course, is when it's not going OK, and you feel that your dream is turning into shit and there's nothing you can do about it!

James L. Brooks
As Good as It Gets

Exhaustion. And I guess maybe worst and best is maybe the loss of yourself.

Michael Radford
Il Postino

Well, I always used to say that the very best part of being a director is having the idea and imagining yourself nominated for an Oscar — all the rest is a pain.

Clint Eastwood
Unforgiven

The best is having the opportunity to interpret an artful piece of writing that you admire, and the ability to interpret that and to watch it evolve is great fun. It has some great satisfying moments, and it has some terrifying moments along the way. And there's that final terrifying moment when you let go of it and put it out for the public and say, "Is anybody going to see this?" I think there's a point in every film, that's about three-fourths of the way through, you are going, "Does anybody really want to see this?"

Rob Reiner
A Few Good Men

The best part is having directed. It's expressing yourself, your thoughts and your feelings.

The worst part is the hours. They're just brutal, and you gain too much weight!!

Steven Spielberg

Amistad

The worst part of directing a movie for me is getting up early in the morning. I hate that! I just hate getting up before the birds and driving to work in the dark and then watching the sunrise as you pull into the main gate of the studio—that's tough. And the other worst thing about making a movie is having a thousand people ask you a thousand questions every day, every hour. And having to answer everyone's questions and having to be so attentive and so responsible and there to be everyone's friend and psychoanalyst. And that's draining.

One of the greatest things about directing is, you gain yourself. You sort of are reborn every time you make a new movie. And you see yourself differently, every time you make a movie. I think our films tend to inform us. We grew up with them, and we also sadly watch our films, watch our children, grow up, graduate, and within the space of a year, they belong to somebody else and they go away.

Saving Private Ryan

I think the best thing about directing is when you've had a thought that somehow is better than the thought you had. And that's a nice feeling. The worst thing about directing I think is something that we all have to go through, and that's that moment where you are judged. I think the judgment is the worst part about being a director. Starting with whoever you show the picture to first, whether it's your wife, or your partner, your best friend, the studio, and then eventually the critics, and then eventually the public. That for me is where I go into hiding if I can.

Mike Leigh

Secrets & Lies

The worst part is that moment when you don't know what you are doing. The best bit is, you make a film.

Oliver Stone

JFK

I think the pleasure is in the dreaming of it. And the pain is in the destruction of the dream.

Anthony Minghella

The English Patient

Every day is filled with pleasure and pain. The best and worst are often holding hands.

— 7 —

Biographies

Biographies 1999*

Roberto Benigni— Life Is Beautiful

Roberto Benigni is a first-time DGA Feature Film Directorial Award nominee for his film *Life Is Beautiful*. He is one of the world's most acclaimed comic filmmakers and entertainers. In the United States, Roberto is best known for his many memorable comic performances in such films as Jim Jarmusch's *Down by Law* and *Night on Earth*, as well as for his role as the infamous Inspector Clouseau's son in Blake Edwards' *Son of the Pink Panther*. Recently he has appeared in Wim Wender's *Far Away, So Close!* Around the world, Roberto is known as a filmmaker with his own unique style. Among the films he has written, directed, and starred in are *The Little Devil* with Walter

---

* Images of Roberto Benigni, John Madden, Steven Spielberg, and Peter Weir adapted from the video of the "Meet the Nominees" Symposium 1999 © Directors Guild of America. All rights reserved.

201

Matthau, *The Monster*, and *Johnny Stecchino*, which became the most successful film in the history of Italian cinema. Roberto will next appear in the long-awaited screen version of the popular European comic book *Asterix* with Gerard Depardieu.

John Madden— Shakespeare in Love

John Madden was born in Portsmouth and educated at Clifton College and Cambridge. He began his career as Artistic Director of the Oxford and Cambridge Shakespeare Company, moving later to the BBC to work in television and radio drama.

He moved to America in 1975 to develop radio drama with *Earplay*, the National Public Radio drama project. Winning the Prix Italia with Arthur Kopit's *Wings*, he subsequently directed the play for the stage at Yale.

Further stage work included the premieres of Jules Feiffer's *Grown Ups*, Christopher Durang's *Beyond Therapy*, and Arnold Wesker's *Caritas*. During the time he taught in the acting and playwriting programs at the Yale School of Drama.

In 1984 he began to work extensively in film, directing for the BBC and for commercial television. His films included *Poppyland*, *After the War*, a series of films by Frederic Raphael, *The Widowmaker*, and several films in the *Inspector Morse* series.

He returned to America in 1990 to make his first feature film, *Ethan Frome*, adapted by Richard Nelson from Edith Wharton's novella, starring Liam Neeson and Patricia Arquette, followed by *Golden Gate*, a story of cultural collision in Chinatown, San Francisco, in the 1950s and 1960s. The film was written by David Hwang and stars Matt Dillon and Joan Chen. *Prime Suspect—The Lost Child* received a BAFTA nomination for Best Series, and his BBC film *Truth or Dare*, starring John Hannah and Helen Baxendale, won the Scottish BAFTA for Best Single Drama.

His film *Mrs. Brown* (screenplay by Jeremy Brock, starring Dame Judi Dench and Billy Connolly) received two Oscar and eight BAFTA nominations, including Best Film.

His latest film, *Shakespeare in Love*, with screenplay by Tom Stoppard and Marc Norman, stars Joseph Fiennes and Gwyneth Paltrow. It received three Golden Globe Awards, including Best Picture, and has received seven Academy Awards, including Best Picture.

John Madden is married and lives in London with his wife and two children.

Steven Spielberg—Saving Private Ryan and Amistad

Steven Spielberg is a nine-time DGA Award nominee, having won previously for *The Color Purple* and *Schindler's List*, which also garnered Oscars for Best Picture and Best Director. His other DGA Award nominated films are *E.T.: The Extra-Terrestrial*, *Raiders of the Lost Ark*, *Close Encounters of the Third Kind*, *Empire of the Sun*, *Jaws*, and *Amistad*. Steven has directed, produced, or executive-produced seven of the top-grossing films of all-time. He is the recipient of the Lifetime Achievement Award from the American Film Institute and the prestigious Irving G. Thalberg Award from the Academy of Motion Picture Arts and Sciences.

Spielberg's 1998 film *Saving Private Ryan* was nominated for eleven Academy Awards and won five, including Best Director. *Saving Private Ryan*, to date, has also won two Golden Globe Awards for Best Picture and Best Director, in addition to the Best Picture Award from the New York Film Critics Circle, and Best Picture and Best Director Awards from the Los Angeles Film Critics Association and the Broadcast Film Critics.

Peter Weir— The Truman Show

Peter Weir briefly attended Sydney University, dropped out to join his father's real estate business, and with money saved, he left for Europe on a working holiday in 1965. Returning to Sydney in 1966, he took a job as a stagehand at a TV station. Peter then began working on a variety of short films as writer, director, and performer. In 1969 he signed on with the Commonwealth Film Unit (now "FILM AUSTRALIA") as a production assistant, which lead to opportunities to direct a number of short films and eventually features. He remained with the "Unit" until 1973 when he left to make his first feature length film.

Weir's contribution to the Australian film renaissance of the late 1970s lay in his ability to portray the imminent disruption of the rational world by irrational forces hovering just beyond our mundane lives. His reputation as the most stylish of the new Australian directors was built on his charting of that country's landscape and cultural oddities with a sense of wonder.

Peter is renowned for such films as *Gallipoli, Picnic at Hanging Rock, The Mosquito Coast,* and *The Year of Living Dangerously,* for which Linda Hunt won the Oscar for Best Supporting Actress. He received an Oscar nomination in 1991 for the screenplay of his romantic comedy *Green Card,* starring Gerard Depardieu and Andie MacDowell. In 1985, he directed Harrison Ford in *Witness,* which garnered eight

Oscar nominations, including Best Picture and Best Director. *The Mosquito Coast* (1985) and 1990s *Dead Poets Society* also earned him an Oscar nomination for Best Director, as well as the BAFTA Award for Best Picture and Italy's Donatello Award for Best Direction.

The Truman Show (1998) starred Jim Carrey and was nominated for three Academy Awards, including Best Director, as well as a nomination of Outstanding Directorial Achievement in Theatrical Direction from the Directors Guild of America.

Biographies 1998*

James L. Brooks— *As Good as It Gets*

James L. Brooks is the recipient of multiple Academy and Emmy Awards, and a three-time DGA Award nominee. He is responsible for some of film and television's most memorable contributions to contemporary culture. Mr. Brooks has written and created such television classics as *Taxi*, *The Mary Tyler Moore Show*, *Rhoda*, *Lou Grant*, *Room 222*, *The Tracey Ullman Show*, and *The Simpsons*. He wrote/produced/directed *Terms of Endearment*, which won the DGA Award for Outstanding Directorial Achievement and garnered three Academy Awards, including Best Picture and Best Director. Mr. Brooks' other film credits include the Oscar-nominated *Broadcast News*, *War of the Roses*, *Big*, *Say Anything*, *I'll Do Anything*, and *Jerry Maguire*. His

---

* Images of James L. Brooks, James Cameron, Curtis Hanson, and Gus Van Sant adapted from the video of the "Meet the Nominees" Symposium 1998 © Directors Guild of America. All rights reserved.

film *As Good As It Gets* (1997) received many Oscar nominations, including a win for Best Picture.

James Cameron—*Titanic*

James Cameron was born in Kapuskasing, Ontario, Canada. In 1971, he moved to California and studied physics at Fullerton College, while working as a machinist and a truck driver. In 1978, Mr. Cameron set his sights on a career in movies and raised money from a consortium of dentists to produce a short film in 35mm. In 1982, he wrote a low-budget, high-impact vehicle called *The Terminator*, which went on to receive international acclaim, and made over $80 million worldwide. Mr. Cameron has subsequently written/produced/directed some of the film world's most successful, highest-grossing action and visual effects adventures, including *The Abyss, Terminator 2: Judgment Day, Aliens, Rambo II, True Lies*, and *Titanic*.

Titanic literally stormed the globe, setting records in every country in which it was released and ultimately grossing more than $600 million at the domestic box office and over $1.2 billion abroad. Titanic's worldwide global box office total of $1.8 billion doubled the tally of the previous record holder.

In addition to toppling every established performance record, Titanic was recognized and honored by numerous organizations, receiving fourteen Academy Award nominations and winning a record-tying eleven Oscars that included Best Picture, Director, Visual Effects, Music, Song, Cinematography, Sound, and Costume, as well as additional nominations and awards from the Directors Guild of America, Screen Actors Guild, Writers Guild of America,

Producers Guild of America, People's Choice Awards, BAFTA, and many others.

Post *Titanic*, Cameron has begun exploring several new entertainment avenues. In 1998, Cameron formed a television development and production venture with Charles Eglee, and together they are readying their maiden effort, a one-hour dramatic series for Twentieth Century Fox Television and FBC titled *Dark Angel*. Cameron has also immersed himself in the study of man's potential next great step in the exploration of space: Mars. Through his own research, and working closely with experts at NASA and throughout the private sector, Cameron has developed a wholly feasible near-term mission architecture, which could put humans on the red planet within the next fifteen years. These central plans provide the spine of two related entertainment projects that Cameron is currently writing and producing: a five-hour miniseries and a 3D IMAX film (the latter of which Cameron will co-direct), both focusing on the first manned mission to Mars. In addition to these extraordinary undertakings, Cameron has numerous feature film projects in various stages of development, although he has yet to announce what his next "traditional" feature film directorial effort will be.

Curtis Hanson—
L.A. Confidential

Curtis Hanson is a writer, director, and producer. He edited and did the photography for *Cinema* magazine before turning to screenwriting and directing. In 1978 Hanson wrote the multiple-award-winning Canadian feature *The Silent Partner*. In 1982, he co-wrote with director Samuel Fuller the screenplay for *White Dog*, and one year later co-wrote the screenplay for Carroll Ballard's *Never Cry Wolf*. His directing credits include the 1987 thriller *The Bedroom Window* (which he also wrote), starring Steve Guttenberg, Elizabeth McGovern, and Isabelle Huppert; *Bad Influence* (1990), starring Rob Lowe and James Spader; *The Hand That Rocks the Cradle* (1992), starring Rebecca De Mornay and Annabella Sciorra; and *The River Wild* (1994), starring Meryl Streep, Kevin Bacon, and David Strathairn. Hanson also directed, produced, and co-wrote (with Brian Helgeland) the screenplay for *L.A. Confidential*. In addition to winning 1997 Academy Awards for Best Adapted Screenplay and Best Supporting Actress (Kim Basinger), the film won the Best Adapted Screenplay award from the Writers Guild of America and was the first picture ever to win Best Picture and Best Director from every major critics' organization. Hanson is currently in post-production on *Wonder Boys*, which stars Michael Douglas, Tobey Maguire, Frances McDormand, Katie Holmes, and Robert Downey, Jr.

Gus Van Sant—
Good Will Hunting

Gus Van Sant has been winning over critics and audiences alike since bursting on the scene with his widely acclaimed feature *Mala Noche*, which won the Los Angeles Film Critics Award for Best Independent/Experimental Feature of 1987. He has also directed other award-winning features, including *Drugstore Cowboy*, *My Own Private Idaho*, *To Die For*, and *Even Cowgirls Get the Blues*. Mr. Van Sant's direction of Nicole Kidman in the black comedy *To Die For* won a Golden Globe Award, and the film was screened at the 1995 Cannes and Toronto Film Festivals.

Throughout his career Mr. Van Sant has continued to make evocative short films that have been winning awards in film festivals around the world. In 1996 Van Sant directed Allen Ginsberg reading his poem *Ballad of the Skeletons* to the music of Paul McCartney and Philip Glass, which premiered at the 1997 Sundance Film Festival. A longtime musician, he has also directed music videos for such artists as David Bowie, Elton John, Tracy Chapman, The Red Hot Chili Peppers, and Hanson.

Van Sant was nominated for an Academy Award for Best Director in 1998 for *Good Will Hunting*, which received a total of nine Academy Award Nominations and went on to gross 250 million dollars worldwide. Van Sant's highly controversial remake of the Alfred Hitchcock classic *Psycho* was the first shot-for-shot recreation of a classic film.

Van Sant is currently directing a short film titled *Easter* that was scripted by Harmony Korine (author of *Kids* and director of *Gummo*). He is also developing a film with Robin Williams about the cartoonist John Callahan.

Biographies 1997*

Anthony Minghella— *The English Patient*

Anthony Minghella made an auspicious feature film debut in 1991 with *Truly, Madly, Deeply*, which he wrote as well as directed after a decade of writing for theatre and television. The film won numerous accolades, including awards for Minghella from the British Film and

---

* Images of Anthony Minghella, Mike Leigh, Scott Hicks, and Cameron Crowe adapted from the video of the "Meet the Nominees" Symposium 1997 © Directors Guild of America. All rights reserved.

Television Academy (BAFTA) and the Writer's Guild of Great Britain. In 1993, Minghella directed his second film, *Mr. Wonderful,* starring Matt Dillon and Mary Louise Parker. Born of Italian parents in 1954 on the Isle of Wight, Minghella lectured at the University of Hull until 1981, when he began his playwriting career. In 1984 he was named the most promising playwright of the year by the London Theatre Critics for three plays, *A Little Like Drawing, Love Bites,* and *Two Planks and a Passion.* Two years later the London critics honored *Made in Bangkok* as Best Play of the Year. Minghella's radio play *Hang Up* won the Prix D'Italia in 1988. Another radio play, *Cigarettes and Chocolate,* was a finalist for the Prix D'Italia in 1989 and won several other honors. Anthony Minghella wrote the pilot script and regularly contributed to British television's award-winning series *Inspector Morse,* and his television trilogy, *What If It's Raining?,* was highly acclaimed throughout Europe. Minghella wrote all nine of the short television films in the Emmy Award-winning *Storyteller* series for Jim Henson and NBC. He also wrote another film for the same team, *Living with Dinosaurs,* which won an international Emmy in 1990. *The English Patient,* starring Ralph Fiennes, Kristin Scott Thomas, and Juliette Binoche, won nine Academy Awards, including Best Director and Best Picture, as well as an award for Outstanding Directorial Achievement from the Directors Guild of America. Minghella's most recent project is *The Talented Mr. Ripley* and stars Matt Damon and Gwyneth Paltrow.

Mike Leigh—*Secrets & Lies*

Mike Leigh, writer and film director, was born in 1943 in Salford, Lancashire. He trained at the Royal Academy of Dramatic Art, at Camberwell and Central Art Schools, and at the London Film School.

His style, in which the commonplace is often tinged with the extraordinary, has been dubbed "social surrealism," or as Leigh prefers to call it, "heightened realism." A creative force in London's experimental fringe theatre since the 1960s, Leigh has written and directed more than twenty stage plays.

His first feature film was *Bleak Moments* (1971), which won the Grande Prix at Chicago and Locarno Film Festivals. This was followed by the full-length television films, *Hard Labor* (1973), *Nuts in May* (1975), *The Kiss of Death* (1976), *Who's Who* (1978), *Grown-Ups* (1980) *Home Sweet Home* (1982), *Meantime* (1983), and *Four Days in July* (1984), which was shot entirely on location in Belfast.

His later feature films, *High Hopes* (1988), *Life Is Sweet* (1990), and *Naked* (1992), were highly successful internationally, all winning numerous prestigious awards, including Best Director for *Naked* at the 1993 Cannes Film Festival.

In 1995 he made the film *Secrets & Lies*, which in May 1996 won the Palme d'Or. The film went on to receive international acclaim, winning, among many other awards, the L.A. Critics awards for Best Film and Director, BAFTA awards for Best Original Screenplay, and the Alexander Korda award for Best British Film. The film also received five Oscar nominations, as well as a nomination from the Directors Guild of America for Outstanding Directorial Achievement for Theatrical Direction. *Career Girls* was made in 1996 and released in 1997. His latest film, *Topsy-Turvy*, was first shown at the 1999 Venice Film Festival and will open in the United States in December 1999.

Mike Leigh formed Thin Man Films with producer Simon Channing-Williams in 1988.

Scott Hicks—*Shine*

Scott Hicks was born and raised in East Africa and is an Emmy Award–winning director whose work encompasses films, television

drama, and documentaries, as well as commercials and music videos. Hicks' film *Sebastian and the Sparrow*, which he also wrote and produced, is a story of a rich boy and a street kid who team up to find the latter's mother. The film was a winner in three international film festival competitions, including Frankfurt, where it was awarded the Lucas Prize as Best Film (1990). Following a successful cinema season and television release in Australia, the film was invited to participate in numerous other international festivals. Hicks also directed and co-wrote the acclaimed documentary series the *Great Wall of Iron*, an in-depth portrait of the People's Liberation of China, and the four-hour series *Submarines: Sharks of Steel*. Both were recognized as award winners in various groups and became two of the highest-rated programs to air on America's The Discovery Channel. Hick's directed a telefilm, *Call Me Mr. Brown*, in 1985 and the Australian miniseries *Finders Keepers* in 1991. Hicks wrote and directed *The Space Shuttle* in 1994 and *The Ultimate Athlete*, a documentary project, in 1996.

He is best known for his internationally acclaimed film *Shine*, which received seven Oscar nominations in 1997, including two for Hicks personally, in the Best Director and Best Original Screenplay categories, as well as a nomination from the Directors Guild of America for Outstanding Directorial Achievement in Theatrical Direction in 1997. He also received a Golden Globe nomination and nominations from the Writers Guild of America and BAFTA.

His next film, *Snow Falling on Cedars*, produced by Kathleen Kennedy and Frank Marshall, was released by Universal Pictures in December 1999.

Scott lives in with his wife Kerry Heysen (who served as Creative Consultant on *Shine* and Associate Producer on *Snow*

Falling on Cedars) and their two sons in Adelaide, South
Australia.

Cameron Crowe—
Jerry Maguire

Cameron Crowe was born in Palm
Springs, California, and raised in San
Diego. He began a career in journalism
at the age of fifteen, writing for such
publications as *Penthouse*, *Playboy*,
Creem, and the *Los Angeles Times*. At
sixteen, he joined the staff of *Rolling Stone*, where he was a contributing editor and later an associate editor. Crowe profiled such
influential music world figures as Bob Dylan, David Bowie, Neil
Young, Eric Clapton, and the members of Led Zeppelin. In 1979,
Crowe (then 22) returned to high school to research a book on teen
life. *Fast Times at Ridgemont High* became a best-seller, and Universal
Pictures, which had optioned the book while it was still in galley
form, signed Crowe to write the screenplay. Released in the spring
of 1982 and directed by Amy Heckerling, *Fast Times at Ridgemont
High* became one of the year's biggest hits and launched the careers
of such stars as Sean Penn, Jennifer Jason Leigh, Judge Reinhold,
Forest Whitaker, Nicolas Cage, and Eric Stoltz. Crowe's screenplay
was nominated for a Writers Guild of America Award for Best
Screen Adaptation. In 1989, Crowe made his feature film directorial
debut with his original screenplay *Say Anything*. The critically
acclaimed film starred John Cusack and Ione Skye. He followed
with *Singles* in 1992. Matt Dillon, Bridget Fonda, Kyra Sedgwick,
and Campbell Scott starred in this highly praised romantic comedy.
In 1996 Cameron directed *Jerry Maguire*, starring Tom Cruise, Rene
Zellweger, and Cuba Gooding, Jr. In 1997 Crowe received a

nomination from the Directors Guild of America for Outstanding Directorial Achievement for a Feature, as well as Academy Award nominations for Best Screenplay Written Directly for the Screen and Best Picture. Cameron Crowe is currently in production on a Dreamworks film due out in 2000. In November of 1999, Knopf published Crowe's *Conversations with WILDER*, a rare series of interviews conducted with the legendary writer/director Billy Wilder.

Biographies 1996*

Michael Radford— *Il Postino*

Michael Radford was born on February 24, 1946, in New Delhi, India, to an English father and an Austrian mother. He grew up mainly in the Middle East, where his father served in the British Army. He was educated at Bedford School and at Worcester College, Oxford. At the age of twenty-five, having been a teacher for a number of years in Edinburgh, he went to the National Film School and was one of the first twenty-five students in its inaugural year.

Upon graduating from the National Film School in 1974, he embarked on a series of documentaries, mainly for the BBC, including *The Madonna and the Volcano* (Grand Prix Nyon 1976) and the *Last Stronghold of the Pure Gospel*. In 1980, he wrote and directed his first feature film for BBC Scotland, entitled *The White Bird Passes*, adapted from the novel by Jessie Kesson. It was the success of this collaboration that led to the writing and making of *Another Time, Another*

---

* Images of Michael Radford and Mel Gibson adapted from the video of the "Meet the Nominees" Symposium 1996 © Directors Guild of America. All rights reserved.

Place, one of the first films commissioned by Channel Four for the cinema, selected for the Quinzaine des Realisateurs at Cannes in 1983 and winner of fifteen major prizes at festivals around the world. The critical success of this film launched his career in feature films. Radford's second film, the following year (1984), was the cinematic adaptation of George Orwells's *1984* starring Richard Burton and John Hurt. The film won the British Film Award for best film and best actor, as well as numerous other international prizes.

White Mischief, starring Greta Scacchi and Joss Ackland, followed this in 1987. Although the film has now become somewhat of a cult film in the United States, it was a commercial failure and Radford did not make another film for more than six years.

During this period he left England and went to live first in France and later in Italy, writing screenplays and directing commercials. It was his longstanding friendship with the Italian actor Massimo Troisi that led to the writing and making of *Il Postino*, the first Italian film ever made by an Englishman. The film has become the highest-grossing foreign language film in the history of cinema, as well as being nominated for five Academy Awards, including best director and best screenplay, and being the winner of more than thirty-five international awards, including BAFTA for best director and best foreign film. It was a film made under the most tragic of circumstances, as the star of the film was dying during the making of it and was not to live to enjoy its success.

Since *Il Postino*, Radford has co-written and directed *B Monkey*, his first film in Britain for eight years, and is about to embark upon *The Swedish Cavalier*, to be produced in France by Jean-Louis Livi and Philippe Carcassonne. Radford speaks four languages, is divorced, and has an eight-year-old son, Felix.

Mel Gibson—*Braveheart*

Mel Gibson was born in upstate New York and moved with his family to Australia when he was twelve years old. Gibson attended the National Institute of Dramatic Arts at the University of South Wales in Sydney. His stage appearances include *Death of a Salesman*. Gibson

was eventually brought to the attention of director George Miller who cast him in *Mad Max*, the film that first brought him worldwide recognition. This was followed by the title role in *Tim*. Gibson's portrayal of a handicapped young man won him an Australian Film Institute Best Actor Award. He was further established as an international star by the two hit sequels to *Mad Max* — *The Road Warrior* and *Mad Max Beyond Thunderdome*— along with Peter Weir's *Gallipoli*, which brought Gibson a second Australian Best Actor Award. A few years later, Weir and Gibson again collaborated on *The Year of Living Dangerously*. Gibson made his American film debut in *The River*. He stared in another popular trilogy with the high-grossing *Lethal Weapon* Series. Gibson's other films include *The Bounty, Mrs. Soffel, Tequila Sunrise, Bird on a Wire, Air America*, and *Hamlet*. When Gibson starred in *Hamlet*, directed by Franco Zeffirelli, the film was the first to be produced by Gibson's production company Icon Pictures. The role brought him the William Shakespeare Award from the Folger Theatre in Washington, D.C. Icon also produced with Mel Gibson starring in *Forever Young* and *Maverick*. Gibson made his directorial debut and starred in *The Man without a Face*, another Icon production. In 1995 Gibson produced, directed, and starred in the critical and box office success *Braveheart*, which received ten Academy Award nominations, including Best Picture and Best Director, as well as receiving a Golden Globe Award for Best Director. Also, he received a Special Achievement in Filmmaking Award given by the National Board of Review and was honored as the 1996 NATO/ShoWest Director of the Year, as well as being the recipient of the Best Director Award given by the Broadcast Film Critics Association. In 1996, Gibson starred in *Ransom*, directed by Ron Howard, for Disney's Touchstone pictures. This film is a remake of the 1956 MGM film telling the story of a New York millionaire who must employ daring tactics to retrieve his kidnapped son. He received a Golden Globe nomination for Best Actor in a Motion Picture (Drama), as well as winning the People's Choice Award for Favorite Motion Picture Actor, and the Blockbuster Entertainment Award for Favorite Male (suspense).

In 1997, Gibson starred in the romantic-thriller *Conspiracy Theory*, co-starring Julia Roberts and directed by Richard Donner, for Warner Brothers. In 1998, Gibson starred in *Lethal Weapon 4*, grossing close to $300 million worldwide. In 1999, he starred in *Payback*, an Icon production marking the directorial debut of Brian Helgeland, who wrote the screenplay for this hard-edged thriller that is based on Donald F. Westlake's (writing as Richard Stark) novel *The Hunter*.

Biographies 1995*

Robert Zemeckis— Forrest Gump

Robert Zemeckis was born and raised on the south side of Chicago, and began making films with an 8mm camera while in high school. He attended Northern Illinois University before transferring to the University of Southern California School of Cinema. After winning a Student Academy award for his film *Field of Honor*, Robert showed the film to directors Steven Spielberg and John Milius. Later the filmmakers made it possible for Robert and his USC writing partner Bob Gale to get a development deal for their original screenplay *1941*, which Spielberg chose to direct. Robert made his directorial debut in 1978

---

with a screenplay he co-wrote with Bob Gale, *I Wanna Hold Your Hand*. The two teamed again to write *Used Cars*, which Robert also directed. He has also directed several projects for small screen, including an episode of Steven Spielberg's *Amazing Stories*, and an episode for HBO's *Tales From the Crypt*, on which he also serves as an executive producer. He executively produced and directed a pilot episode of the CBS series *Johnny Bago*, a series he helped create. Robert's third feature film was *Romancing the Stone*, followed by *Back to The Future, Who Framed Roger Rabbit?* (for which he received a DGA award nomination), *Back to the Future Part II, Back to the Future Part III, Death Becomes Her,* and the sci-fi drama *Contact*, which achieved worldwide grosses in excess of $2 billion.

Forrest Gump (1994) won the DGA award for Outstanding Directorial Achievement, as well as garnering the Academy Awards for Best Picture and Best Actor, and NATO ShowWest "Director of the Year." The film earned in excess of $600 million worldwide. Zemeckis utilized the latest technological wizardry, as he had done with his earlier films, to tell the story of the amiable Forrest Gump as his life crisscrosses in and out of some of the nation's most significant events and he interacts with some of the most significant people.

Zemeckis took a turn directing for the small screen again, when he executive-produced and directed *The Pursuit Of Happiness*, a feature-length documentary on the influence and effect of drugs and alcohol on society in the twentieth century, for Showtime.

An obvious proponent of using technology to enhance the creative aspects of films, Zemeckis is also extremely concerned with how the current development of new technologies will affect artists in the coming years. Because of this concern, Zemeckis is an avid supporter of the Artists Rights Foundation.

Quentin Tarantino—*Pulp Fiction*

Hollywood history has it's share of artistic rebels and writer/director Quentin Tarantino has already established himself as one of the most unique and talented filmmakers of his generation. Not bad for this former video store rental clerk whose biggest professional cred-

it a couple of years ago was an appearance as an Elvis impersonator on *The
Golden Girls*.

Tarantino wrote, directed, and
starred in *Pulp Fiction*, which won the
prestigious Palm D'Or at the 1994
Cannes Film Festival, numerous critics
awards, a Golden Globe for Best
Screenplay, was nominated for seven
Academy Awards, including Best
Picture and Best Director, and received
an Academy Award for Best
Screenplay. A trilogy of interrelated stories about seedy criminals in
contemporary Hollywood, the film stars John Travolta, Bruce Willis,
Uma Thurman, Samuel L. Jackson, Eric Stoltz, Harvey Keitel, Tim
Roth, Maria de Medeiros, Amanda Plummer, and Christopher
Walken. The film has also made over $100 million in the U.S. box
office alone.

While still working at a Southern California video store, Tarantino
passed his time writing screenplays. Tarantino's first produced project was *Reservoir Dogs*. Made on a shoestring budget with a cadre of
impressive talent (including Harvey Keitel, Tim Roth, and Michael
Madsen), Tarantino's twisted tale of cops and robbers made an
immediate impact on audiences and critics all over the world.
Released by Miramax, the film continues to draw audiences in
Europe and midnight screenings in the United States nearly three
years after it first hit the festival circuit.

Hollywood was obviously enamored of Tarantino's harrowing
vision of contemporary life, where torture, violence, and humiliation
are turned on their head as Tarantino's memorably malevolent characters take a walk on the seedier side of life. Clamoring for more
Tarantino material, Hollywood bought up some of the properties
Tarantino had written as an unknown. *True Romance* was made into
a critically successful film by Tony Scott, and starred Christian Slater,
Patricia Arquette, and featured a host of cameos from actors like
Brad Pitt and Gary Oldman. Oliver Stone turned Tarantino's *Natural*

Born Killers into a feature starring Woody Harrelson and Juliette Lewis as serial killers on the run.

With his production partner Lawrence Bender (through their company A Band Apart Productions), he served as executive producer on October Films' *Killing Zoe*, directed by Roger Avary, and starring Jean-Hugues Anglade, Julie Delpy, and Eric Stoltz.

His acting roles include *Destiny Turns On the Radio*, in which he plays Johnny Destiny, directed by Jack Baran, and a role in *Desperado*, which was Robert Rodriguez's follow-up to *El Mariachi*.

In 1995 Tarantino also completed the omnibus feature *Four Rooms*, produced by Lawrence Bender, in which he wrote, directed, and starred in a segment, as well as executive producing. Set in a Hollywood hotel on New Year's Eve night, the film follows the adventures of a bell-boy as he witnesses the goings on in four different hotel rooms, directed by Allison, Robert Rodriguez, Alexandre Rockwell, and Tarantino and released in 1995 by Miramax.

Not content to stay idle, Tarantino turned his attention toward the small screen with a cameo on an episode of Margaret Cho's *All American Girl* entitled "Pulp Sitcom." This was followed by his television directorial debut with an episode of the hit drama *ER* entitled "Motherhood." Renowned for his gritty, realistic style of writing, he also performed a dialogue polish on the hit film *Crimson Tide*.

Tarantino executive produced and starred in *From Dusk till Dawn* from his own script, featuring George Clooney, Harvey Keitel, and Juliette Lewis. Directed by Robert Rodriguez, *From Dusk till Dawn* was released by Miramax in 1996. He also executive produced *Curdled* featuring Billy Baldwin and Angela Jones for Miramax. Their confidence in Tarantino led to the formation of his own independent distribution arm, Rolling Thunder. Created to provide a showcase for unique films that would not otherwise receive distribution, twenty-five percent of all profits from Rolling Thunder will be donated towards film preservation. Rolling Thunder's first release was Wong Kar-Wai's *Chungking Express*. This was followed by a re-release of Jack Hill's cult classic *Switchblade Sisters*.

In his latest film move, Tarantino wrote, directed, and produced *Jackie Brown*, a comic crime caper loosely based on Elmore

Leonard's novel *Rum Punch*, starring black action goddess Pam Grier, veteran actor Robert Forster, Samuel L. Jackson, Robert De Niro, Bridget Fonda, and Michael Keaton, and was released by Miramax in December of 1997.

Most recently, Tarantino took a turn for the theatre, taking a lead role in the dramatic thriller *Wait Until Dark*, starring against Marisa Tomei in his Broadway debut.

Frank Darabont—*The Shawshank Redemption*

Frank Darabont's parents fled Hungary during the 1956 uprising. Frank was born three years later in 1959 in Monterbeliard, France, and was brought to America when he was still a baby. He attended Hollywood High School, suffered through the disco era, and began his career in film in 1980 as a production assistant on a low-budget film called *Hell Night*. Frank then spent the next six years working in a set construction and as a set dresser, while struggling to be a screenwriter. During this time he also wrote and directed *The Woman in the Room*, a thirty-minute film based on the short story by Stephen King. In 1986, people finally started paying him to write, which he has been gratefully doing ever since. Some of his writing credits include feature films *Nightmare on Elm Street 3: Dream Warriors* (1987), *The Blob* (1988), and *The Fly II* (1989). For television, he has written eight episodes of *The Young Indiana Jones Chronicles* and two episodes of the HBO series *Tales From the Crypt*, one of which (*The Ventriloquist's Dummy*) was nominated for a Writers Guild Award in 1990. In the same year, Frank directed *Buried Alive*, a cable network movie for USA Network. In 1994 he had his feature film directorial debut with *The Shawshank Redemption*, for which he also wrote the screenplay.

The Shawshank Redemption was nominated for a DGA Award for Outstanding Directorial Achievement in Theatrical Direction as well as several Academy Awards, including Best Picture. Also, in 1994, Frank co-wrote the screenplay for the feature film *Mary Shelley's Frankenstein*. Darabont's current project is *The Green Mile*, starring Tom Hanks, released in December 1999.

Mike Newell— *Four Weddings and a Funeral*

Mike Newell joined Granada Television as a production trainee in 1963 after graduating in English from Cambridge University. While at Granada he directed numerous television plays, including *Them Down There, Ready When You Are Mr. McGill, Destiny,* and *The Melancholy Hussar,* before moving into the world of films. His feature credits include *The Man in the Iron Mask* (1976), *The Awakening* (1977), *Bad Blood* (1980), *Dance with a Stranger* (1984), which was awarded the Prix Italia, *Amazing Grace and Chuck* (1986), *Soursweet* (1987), *Enchanted April* (1991), which received three Oscar nominations, and *Into the West* (1992). His 1994 release *Four Weddings and a Funeral* was nominated for a DGA Award, an Academy Award for Best Picture, and a BAFTA Award for Best Film and Achievement in Direction. The film won British Film of the Year, British Director of the Year, and a Cesar Award for Best Foreign Language Film. In 1995, Mike released *An Awfully Big Adventure*, which like *Four Weddings* screened at the Sundance Film Festival. In 1997, Newell directed *Donnie Brasco*, starring Al Pacino and Johnny Depp, which tells the story of an FBI agent who infiltrates the mob and then finds he identifies more with the Mafia life then his own life. In 1999 he directed *Pushing Tin*, starring John

Cusack, Billy Bob Thornton, Cate Blanchett, and Angelina Jolie. Newell also executive produced the film *Best Laid Plans* in 1999.

Biography 1994*

Andrew Davis—
The Fugitive

Andrew Davis is the son of parents who met in the repertory theatre. Davis received a degree in journalism from the University of Illinois. He began his work in motion pictures as assistant cameraman to Haskell Wexler on the 1969 classic *Medium Cool*. Wexler's ultra-realistic approach was to have a great influence on Davis, who then became director of photography on numerous award-winning television commercials and documentaries, as well as on fifteen studio and independent features. In 1976, joined by fellow cine-matographers, Andy challenged IATSE's restrictive studio roster system in a landmark class-action suit that forced the industry to open its doors to young technicians in all crafts.

Davis' directorial debut, *Stony Island* (1979), was a critically acclaimed semi-autobiographical independent musical that he co-wrote and produced. It was followed by the thriller *The Final Terror* (1981), which starred newcomers Daryl Hannah, Joe Pantoliano, Rachel Ward, and Adrian Zmed. Davis then co-wrote the screenplay for Harry Belafonte's rap musical *Beat Street* before moving into the director's chair full-time with *Code of Silence* (1985), starring Chuck Norris. Davis directed, co-produced, and co-wrote *Above The Law*

---

* Image of Andrew Davis adapted from the video of the "Meet the Nominees" Symposium 1994 © Directors Guild of America. All rights reserved.

(1988), which was Steven Seagal's feature debut. Davis then directed *The Package* (1989), starring Gene Hackman and Tommy Lee Jones. In *Under Siege* Davis teamed Steven Seagal with Tommy Lee Jones and Gary Busey, resulting in Fall 1992's top-grossing picture.

Davis has an established and enviable reputation for helming intelligent action thrillers, most notably the Academy Award-nominated *The Fugitive* (1992), the fourth-highest-grossing picture in Warner Brothers' history. Starring Harrison Ford and Tommy Lee Jones, the film earned Jones an Academy Award and garnered seven Academy Award nominations, including Best Picture. Additionally, *The Fugitive* was nominated for a 1993 Golden Globe and the Directors Guild of America Outstanding Directorial Achievement Award in Theatrical Direction.

Davis' feature *Steal Big, Steal Little* (1995) starred Andy Garcia as rival twin brothers. The 1996 feature *Chain Reaction,* starring Keanu Reeves and Morgan Freeman, brought Davis back to his home town of Chicago. In addition to directing, Davis produced the project with Richard Zanuck and Arne Schmidt. Davis' latest project was *A Perfect Murder* (1998), a thriller starring Michael Douglas and Gwyneth Paltrow.

Currently Andrew Davis and Mike Madevoy's Phoenix Pictures have acquired the motion picture rights to the book *Holes* written by Louis Sachar, a renowned author from Austin, Texas. Davis will direct and produce the film through his production company, Chicago Pacific Entertainment, which is based in Santa Barbara, California.

Biographies 1993[*]

Rob Reiner—A Few Good Men

A Few Good Men's producer/director Rob Reiner has established himself as one of Hollywood's top directors, creating films that win

---

[*] Images of Rob Reiner, Neil Jordan, and Clint Eastwood adapted from the video of the "Meet the Nominees" Symposium 1993 © Directors Guild of America. All rights reserved.

both audience enthusiasm and critical acclaim. His first film, 1984's *This Is Spinal Tap*, a "rockumentary" on the ups and downs of a fictitious British rock band, received wide acclaim and established Reiner's reputation as a filmmaker of unique vision and sparkling satiric wit. His other credits include *The Sure Thing* (1985), a hate-turned-to-love story about two colle-gians, and *Stand By Me* (1986), which depicted four boys coming of age in

the 1950s and received an Academy award nomination for Best Adapted Screenplay, while Reiner garnered Best Director nomina-tions from the Directors Guild of America and the Hollywood Foreign Press Association. Following was the much-loved fantasy *The Princess Bride* (1987) and 1989's *When Harry Met Sally . . .* , the hit romantic comedy that received an Oscar nomination for Best Original Screenplay, five Golden Globe Awards, and a Directors Guild Nomination. In 1990 came his film *Misery*, for which Kathy Bates garnered an Oscar for her portrayal of deranged fan Annie Wilkes. The year 1992 brought the mega box-office hit *A Few Good Men*, starring Tom Cruise, Jack Nicholson, and Demi Moore, which garnered another DGA Best Director nomination as well as four Academy Award nominations, including that for Best Picture. *North* was released in 1994 and starred Elijah Wood, Bruce Willis, Jon Lovitz, Jason Alexander, and Julia Louis-Dreyfus. Reiner directed the hit comedy *The American President* in 1995, which starred Michael Douglas and Annette Bening. *Ghosts of Mississippi* followed in 1996 and was the true story of the re-prosecution of Byron De La Beckwith, the racist murderer of civil rights leader Medgar Evers, starring Alex Baldwin, Whoopi Goldberg, and James Woods. Recently completed is *The Story of Us*, starring Bruce Willis and Michelle Pfeiffer, a romantic comedy exploring the question, "Can a marriage survive fifteen years of marriage?"

Prior to his directorial debut, Reiner, son of comedian Carl Reiner, acted in many television and feature films and wrote for the *Smothers Brothers Comedy Hour*. It was, however, his award winning portrayal of Michael Stivic, Archie Bunker's son-in-law in the phenomenal hit series *All In The Family*, that made him a household name.

In 1997 Rob Reiner and his wife joined forces on a national public awareness and engagement campaign to communicate the importance of the prenatal period through the first three years of life. As a result of Reiner's work with the National Governor's Association, in February of that year a ten-governor, bipartisan task force was assigned to develop state policies for very young children. Then in April, a White House summit on early brain development, hosted by President Clinton and the First Lady, was the launch point for the "I Am Your Child" campaign. An hour-long prime-time special followed on ABC-TV, which Reiner co-produced, co-wrote, and directed. The "I Am Your Child" campaign has made parenting information available on the Internet through the www.imyourchild.org Web site.

Rob Reiner is a principal and cofounder of Castle Rock Entertainment. In addition to directing feature films, he is involved in all phases of Castle Rock's creative activities. Rob Reiner is married to Michele Singer Reiner, a professional photographer, and they have three children.

Neil Jordan— *The Crying Game*

Born in Sligo, in northwest Ireland, Jordan began his career as a novelist. In 1974 he founded the Irish Writers Cooperative, and in 1979, his collection of stories, *Night in Tunisia*, won *The Guardian* newspaper's fiction prize. He has also published two novels, *The Past* and *The Dream of the Beast*. Jordan began his film career as a creative consultant on *Excalibur*, directed by John Boorman, in 1981. *Angel* (aka *Danny Boy*), Jordan's debut film, which he wrote and directed, won the *London Evening Standard*'s Most Promising Newcomer Award in 1982. His next film, *The Company of Wolves* (1984), adapted from a story by Angela Carter, starred Angela Lansbury and was honored with Best Film and Best Director Awards by the London Critics' Circle, and a Golden Scroll for Outstanding Achievement from the Academy of Science Fiction and Horror Films. Jordan's third film, *Mona Lisa* (1986), starred Bob Hoskins, Michael Caine, and Cathy Tyson and was selected for competition at the Cannes Film Festival. The Cannes jury subsequently awarded Hoskins Best Actor. He also received a Best Actor Award from the National Society of film Critics and an Academy Award nomination. *Mona Lisa* won a Golden Globe Award, a Los Angeles Film Critics Award, and a Best Screenplay nomination from the Writers Guild of America. It was also nominated in the categories Best Film, Best Achievement in Direction, and Best Original Screenplay at the 1986 BAFTA Awards. In 1988, Jordan directed the comedy *High Spirits*, starring Peter O'Toole, Daryl Hannah, and Steve Guttenberg, followed by the next year's *We're No Angels*, which starred Robert De Niro and Sean Penn and was Jordan's first entirely American production. *The Miracle* (1990), the second film that Jordan shot in his native Ireland and the first made in his hometown of Bray, starred Beverly D'Angelo and Donal McCann and won the *London Evening Standard*'s Best Screenplay Award in 1991. *The Crying Game*, written and directed by Neil Jordan, was his seventh film and his fifth collaboration with Stephen Wooley and Palace Pictures. Part love story, part confrontation of one's own destiny, according to the director, the film deals with real life-or-death issues, with people at the most extreme edges of a political situation. *The Crying Game* (1992) earned six Oscar nominations and included a win for Best Screenplay by Jordan, as well as a nomination for Outstanding Directorial Achievement in Theatrical Direction from the Directors Guild of America in 1993. In 1993 Jordan landed the plum, if daunting, assignment of adapting Anne Rice's tricky bestseller *Interview with the Vampire* to the screen. In 1996, Jordan returned to Ireland to shoot his next film, *Michael Collins*, a cherished project for which he had spent more than a decade developing the script. This biopic of the still-controversial Irish hero told a story that had taken nearly four decades to get to the screen. In 1999 Jordan directed the psychological thriller *In Dreams*, starring Annette Bening.

Clint Eastwood— Unforgiven

Unforgiven is Clint Eastwood's sixteenth feature film as a director and his thirty-sixth in a starring role. Although he has taken on a variety of roles throughout his career, the origins of Eastwood's appeal remain the Western, within which he has created his own subgenre—that of the loner who sees too much and is driven by a hard-edged knowledge of himself. Eastwood began his career as a contract actor in a string of minor films for Universal Pictures. The "spaghetti western" directed by Sergio Leone, *A Fistful of Dollars* (1967), changed his career forever, illuminating a star on the rise and beginning a sequence of unprecedented hits. *Hang 'Em High* in 1968 brought Universal Pictures its quickest payoff in history. That same year, Eastwood formed his Malpaso Company, allowing him the options of producing and directing, as well as starring in his own projects. Malpaso has continued to provide filmmakers with the independent base from which all its projects evolve. Eastwood's debut as a director was the chilling *Play Misty for Me* (1971), in which he starred with Jessica Walter and Donna Mills. *Dirty Harry* followed the same year and launched several sequels. It was directed by Don Siegel and marked Eastwood's initial association with Warner Brothers as a distributing company. Among his many acting assignments, also adding to Eastwood's diverse list of popular and critical successes, were his directorial projects, which include *High Plains Drifter* (1972), *Breezy* (1973), *The Eiger Sanction* (1974), *The Outlaw Josey Wales* (1976), and *The Gauntlet* (1977), as well as *Bronco Billy* (1980), *Firefox* and *Honkytonk Man* (both 1982), *Sudden Impact* (1983), *Pale River* and *Vanessa in the Garden*—an episode for television's *Amazing Stories* series—(both 1985), *Heartbreak Ridge* (1986), and *The Bird* (1988). *Bird*, a tribute to jazz saxophonist Charlie Parker, was released to international acclaim and earned Eastwood the Hollywood Foreign Press Association's best Director Golden Globe award, as well as numerous national and international awards for stars Forest Whitaker and Diane Verona. Eastwood continued directing films such as *White Hunter, Black Heart, The Rookie, Unforgiven, The Bridges of Madison County, Absolute Power, Midnight In the Garden of Good and Evil, True Crime,* and most recently, *Space Cowboys,* which in addition to directing, he also produced.

Eastwood's diverse abilities have brought him international stature, box office success, and numerous awards. His revisionist Western *Unforgiven,* released in August 1992, generated $100 million at the box office and has been named on more than 200 "Ten Best" lists by critics. *Unforgiven* received numerous awards and nominations, including an award for Outstanding Directorial Achievement for Theatrical Direction from the Directors Guild of America, and four Oscars for Best Director, Best Picture, Best Supporting Actor, and Best Sound. This also marked the first time in his career that Eastwood received an Oscar nomination for Best Actor.

In 1995 Eastwood was given one of the most highly regarded awards in the motion picture industry, the Irving G. Thalberg Memorial Award, for his accomplishments in film as an actor, director, and producer.

Biographies 1992*

Barbra Streisand—*The Prince of Tides*

The Prince of Tides, which Barbra Streisand directed, produced, and starred in, earned her a nomination for Best Director by the Directors Guild of America and was yet another latest bold mark in a career highlighted by a series of "firsts." For her very first Broadway

* Images of Barbra Streisand, Barry Levinson, and Oliver Stone adapted from the video of the "Meet the Nominees" Symposium 1992 © Directors Guild of America. All rights reserved.

appearance in *I Can Get It for You Wholesale*, she won the New York Drama Critics Circle Award and received a Tony nomination. For her very first record album, *The Barbra Streisand Album*, she won two 1963 Grammy Awards, the youngest person, age 22, to win for Best Female Vocal Performance and Album of the Year. She was honored with an Emmy Award for her first television special, *My Name is Barbra*, in 1965. For her motion picture debut, in *Funny Girl*, she won the 1968 Academy Award as Best Actress. She is the first female composer ever to win an Academy Award for her song "Evergreen," the love theme from her hit film *A Star Is Born*. Forty-two of her albums have become gold (Elvis Presley is the only artist that exceeds that), twenty-five have reached platinum status, and thirteen have gone multi-platinum, the most for any female artist in all categories. She has been honored with eight Grammy Awards and is the only performer who has had #1 albums in four decades. The Recording Industry Association of America recently designated Barbra Streisand as Female Artist of the Century. She has received 10 Golden Globes, the most for any artist.

Undertaking the challenge of making the motion picture *Yentl*, Streisand is recorded as the first woman ever to produce, direct, write, and star in a major film.

The filmmaker entertainer was born April 24 in Brooklyn to Diana and Emanuel Streisand. Her father, who passed away when Barbra was fifteen months old, was a teacher and a scholar. An honor student at Erasmus Hall High School in Brooklyn, the teenage Streisand plunged, unassisted and without encouragement, into show business by winning a singing contest at a small Manhattan club. Soon she was attracting music industry attention at such spots as the Bon Soir and the Blue Angel. Streisand signed a contract with Columbia Records in 1962, and her debut album quickly became the nation's top-selling record by a female vocalist. She was then signed to play the great comedienne Fanny Brice in the Broadway production of *Funny Girl*, and her distinctly original musical-comedy performance won her a second Tony nomination. When she signed a ten-year contract with CBS Television to produce and star in TV specials, the contract gave her complete artistic control, an unheard-of concession to an artist so young and inexperienced. The first special, *My Name is Barbra*, earned five Emmy Awards, and the following four shows, including the memorable *Color Me Barbra*, earned the highest critical praise and audience ratings. Few movie debuts have been as auspicious as Streisand's in *Funny Girl*. In addition to winning the 1968 Academy Award, she won the Golden Globe and was named Star of the Year by the National Association of Theatre Owners. After appearing in the films *Hello Dolly!*, *On a Clear Day You Can See Forever*, *The Owl and the Pussycat*, and *What's Up, Doc?*, in 1972 she starred in *Up the Sandbox*, one of the first American films to deal with the growing women's movement. It was the premiere picture for her own production company, Barwood Films. In 1973, *The Way We Were* brought her an Academy Award nomination as best actress. *A Star Is Born*, released in 1976, was the first movie to benefit from her energy and insight as a producer. When Streisand completed her first movie, she had read a short story titled "Yentl, the Yeshiva Boy" and hoped to make it her second film. However, it took fourteen years of development before the dream came true. *Yentl*, a romantic drama with music, is a movie that celebrates women trying to be all that they can be. Streisand's directorial debut received four 1984 Academy Award nominations (including a Best Supporting Actress nomination for Amy Irving), and she received Golden Globe Awards as both best director (becoming the first woman to win that honor) and producer of the best picture (musical or comedy) of 1984. The awards represent two of the eleven Golden Globes she received throughout her career. She was accorded the Hollywood Foreign Press Association's Year 2000 Cecil B. DeMille Award for Lifetime Achievement. Through her Barwood Films, she also produced and starred in *Nuts*, the unusual story of a smart woman shaped into an angry, antisocial character by peculiar circumstances, a difficult role judged to be one of her finest performances. She also wrote the music for the powerful drama released in 1987.

Streisand's *The Prince of Tides*, based on Pat Conroy's best-selling novel, is an emotional masterpiece, and the performances of Nick

Nolte, Blythe Danner, and Kate Nelligan are powerful and profound-
ly poignant. *The Prince of Tides* was the first motion picture directed
by its star ever to receive a nomination from the Directors Guild of
America for Outstanding Directorial Achievement in Theatrical
Direction, as well as seven Academy Award nominations, including
a Best Actor nomination for Nick Nolte. Barbra Streisand produced
the heralded drama in addition to directing and starring in it.

After working with her for two weeks, the book's author, Pat
Conroy, gave Streisand a copy of his novel with the inscription: "To
Barbra Streisand: The Queen of Tides . . . you are many things,
Barbra, but you're also a great teacher . . . one of the greatest to come
into my life. I honor the great teachers and they live in my work and
they dance invisibly in the margins of my prose. You've honored me
by taking care of it with such great seriousness and love. Great
thanks, and I'll never forget that you gave *The Prince of Tides* back to
me as a gift. Pat Conroy."

Recipient in 1995 of an Honorary Doctorate in Arts from Brandeis
University, Barbra Streisand is perhaps the only artist to earn Oscar,
Tony, Emmy, Grammy, Golden Globe, Cable Ace and Peabody
Awards. Her most recent motion picture directorial effort, the TriStar
Pictures' *The Mirror Has Two Faces*, continued the tradition of each
Streisand-directed film being accorded Academy Award nomina-
tions, including her second best song nomination for co-writing the
music to, "I Finally Found Someone." The romantic comedy, her third
triple effort as director/producer/star, received two Oscar nomina-
tions in 1997 and led, as well, to Lauren Bacall's winning the Golden
Globe's Best Supporting Actress and earning an Academy Award
nomination. It is noteworthy that each of the films directed by Ms.
Streisand resulted in an acting Academy Award nomination.

Barbra Streisand's Barwood Films has placed great emphasis on
bringing to television dramatic explorations of pressing social, historic, and political issues, which would not otherwise be addressed
in more widely viewed television movies. *The Rescuers*, a series of six
dramas to be broadcast on Showtime, pays tribute to non-Jews who
heroically saved Jews from the Holocaust. Through Barwood, Ms.
Streisand helped bring to millions of television viewers a drama
investigating military harassment of and repression of the civil
rights of gays. It was acknowledged that the critically praised

Serving in Silence: The Margarethe Cammermeyer Story, would never have been realized on network television had not Barbra Streisand put her executive producing talents and considerable artistic and social-issue influence behind it. It had great impact in conveying its urgent civil rights issue and it earned three Emmys, six Emmy nominations, and the Peabody Award in the process. Barwood's CBS Movie of the Week, *The Long Island Incident: The Carolyn McCarthy Story*, inspired a national debate on gun control with its true story of a wife and mother who surmounted tragedy to win a seat in Congress after initiating a crusade to achieve sensible controls on guns. Similarly, Barwood is currently preparing for Showtime a film supporting the Middle East peace process. *Two Hands That Shook the World* will parallel the lives of Yitzhak Rabin and Yasser Arafat up to their historic handshake at the White House.

And like the true Renaissance woman she is, her life and her art are dedicated to the humanities as reflected by the Streisand Foundation, which is committed to gaining women's equality, the protection of both human rights and civil rights and liberties, the needs of children at risk in society, and the preservation of the environment. Through the Streisand Foundation, she directed the United States Environmental Defense Fund's research for and participation in the recent Global Warming world summit conference in Kyoto. Her environmental dedication is reflected, also in her donation to the Santa Monica Mountains Conservancy of the five-home, twenty-four-acre Malibu estate on which her One Voice concert had been performed. The site has been dedicated as a center for ecological studies. Ms. Streisand is a leading spokesperson and fund-raiser for social causes close to her heart, including AIDS. During the twenty-seven years that preceded her limited 1994 tour and the Las Vegas New Year's appearances, she had devoted her live concert performances exclusively to the benefit of those causes she supports. Her concern with social issues is reflected not only in the dedications of her personal life, but in the subject matter of the films she has initiated, each of which has addressed some social consideration.

Recent honors reflecting the range of her involvement in charitable and social causes include the 1992 Commitment to Life Award from AIDS Project Los Angeles for her dedication to help people living with that disease, and the ACLU Bill of Rights Award for her ongoing defense of constitutional rights. Ms. Streisand's feelings about the rights and obligations of artists to participate in the political process were brought into sharp focus by her early 1995 speech at Harvard University under the sponsorship of the John F. Kennedy School of Government. The address won unprecedented reportage and reproduction in such print media as the *New York Times* and the *Washington Post*. It was carried a record number of times on C-Span. Her speech at Harvard's Kennedy School of Government on "The Artist as Citizen," was reprinted in Senator Robert Torricelli's book *In Our Own Words*, a collection of the greatest speeches of the twentieth century.

Prior to the 1986 elections, she performed her first full-length concert in 20 years, raising money for the Hollywood Women's Political Committee to disburse to liberal candidates. The money raised that night helped elect five Democratic Senators, which restored a Democratic majority in the Senate. To date, more than $10 million, including $7 million in profits from "Barbra Streisand: One Voice," has been channeled to charities through the Streisand Foundation, which continues to occupy much of the star's energy and resources. Her passionate political activism continues.

On July 1, 1998, Barbra married actor/director James Brolin.

Barry Levinson—*Bugsy*

Academy Award-winning director–screenwriter–producer Barry Levinson has crafted an enviable reputation in the film industry as a director who blends literate and intelligent visions into films.

Levinson was awarded the 1988 Best Director Oscar for the multiple award-winning *Rain Man,* starring

Dustin Hoffman and Tom Cruise. In 1987, he directed Robin Williams in the comedy *Good Morning, Vietnam,* which went on to become one of the year's most acclaimed and popular movies. In 1991 *Bugsy,* which was directed and produced by Barry Levinson, was nominated for ten Academy Awards, including Best Picture and Best Director.

Born and raised in Baltimore, Levinson has used his hometown as the setting for three widely praised features: *Diner,* the semi-autobiographical comedy–drama that marked his directorial debut; *Tin Men,* starring Danny DeVito and Richard Dreyfuss as warring aluminum siding salesmen; and *Avalon,* in which his native city takes center stage through the recollections of an immigrant family.

After attending American University in Washington, D.C., Levinson moved to Los Angeles, where he began acting as well as writing and performing comedy routines. He then went on to write for several television variety shows, including *The Marty Feldman Comedy Machine,* which originated in England, *The Lohman and Barkley Show, The Tim Conway Show,* and *The Carol Burnett Show.* A meeting with Mel Brooks led Levinson to collaborate with the veteran comedian on the features *Silent Movie* and *High Anxiety,* the latter additionally notable for his film acting debut.

As a screenwriter, Levinson has received three Academy Award nominations, for . . . *And Justice for All, Diner,* and *Avalon.* Levinson's other directorial credits include *The Natural, Young Sherlock Holmes, Toys, Jimmy Hollywood, Disclosure, Sleepers, Sphere,* and *Wag the Dog.*

Barry returned to Baltimore to film the *Homicide: Life on the Street* television series. His work on this critically acclaimed drama earned him an Emmy for Best Individual Director of a Drama Series. The series has also received three Peabody Awards, two Writers Guild Awards, and an Excellence in Quality Television Founders Award for the 1994 and 1995 seasons. In 1996 the series won the Nancy Susan Reynolds Award for outstanding portrayal of sexual responsibility in a dramatic series as well as a PRISM Commendation. In 1998 the series garnered a TCA Award for the program of the year and drama of the year.

Barry's feature *Sleepers* (1996), a film based on the best-selling book by Lorenzo Carcaterra, starring Robert De Niro, Brad Pitt, Jason Patric, Kevin Bacon, and Dustin Hoffman, garnered critical acclaim and box office success. The close of 1997 saw Barry at his most prolific, releasing two films nearly back to back, *Wag the Dog* and *Sphere*. *Wag the Dog*, a political satire written by Hilary Henkin and David Mamet, was nominated for two Academy Awards. *Sphere* (1998) is a science-fiction film adapted from the Michael Crichton novel, stars Sharon Stone and Samuel L. Jackson, and marks the fourth collaboration with Dustin Hoffman (*Rain Man, Sleepers, Wag the Dog*).

Until 1998 Levinson produced films through his production company Baltimore Pictures, Inc. Critically acclaimed releases include *Quiz Show, Donnie Brasco*, and *The Second Civil War* (HBO). At the beginning of 1998 Barry Levinson partnered with Paula Weinstein, forming Baltimore/Spring Creek Pictures. Together they produced *Analyze This* (1999), a comedy starring Robert De Niro and Billy Crystal, which opened to instant box office success. Barry became one of *Variety*'s "Billion Dollar Directors" as well as ShoWest's "Director of the Year" in 1998.

Barry was honored in February 1999 with a Creative Achievement Award by the 13th Annual American Comedy Awards. In May 1999, American University of Washington, D.C., conferred upon Barry the degree of Doctor of Fine Arts, *honoris causa*, for his distinguished work in the field of communications and his defining impact on the motion picture and television industry. Barry was honored for his commitment to the craft of filmmaking, his dedication to telling insightful stories, his exquisite sensitivity to the details of life as we live it, and his gifts and accomplishments as a director. Barry and Baltimore Pictures received the 1999 Humanitas award for *Homicide: Life on the Street*'s "Shades of Grey" episode.

Barry's fourth Baltimore feature, *Liberty Heights*, was released in November 1999 to wide critical acclaim. Critics praised this film as possibly the best of his Baltimore series. This humorous, touching drama captures the spirit of change in Baltimore circa 1954, addressing issues of race, class, and religion.

Oliver Stone—JFK

Director–writer Oliver Stone was born in New York City in 1946. He served in Vietnam from 1967 to 1968 and also worked as a teacher and merchant seaman in Southeast Asia from 1965 to 1966. He graduated from the New York University Film School in 1971.

Oliver Stone explores perhaps America's most important and controversial event of this century with *JFK*, a look at the conspiracy behind the assassination of President Kennedy. Stone's *JFK* (1991), starring Kevin Costner, Tommy Lee Jones, and Gary Oldman, chronicles New Orleans District Attorney Jim Garrison's investigation into the assassination of President Kennedy. The film takes a fresh look at all the credible assassination theories in a gripping thriller that raises the nation's persistent questions, doubts, and suspicions. Filmed on location in Dallas, New Orleans, and Washington D.C., *JFK* also features an extensive gallery of appearances by acclaimed actors, including Edward Asner, Walter Matthau, Jack Lemmon, and Donald Sutherland. The film received three Academy Award nominations in 1992 for Best Picture, Best Director, and Best Writing, Screenplay Based on Material from Another Medium, as well as a nomination from the Directors Guild of America for Outstanding Directorial Achievement in Theatrical Direction.

Stone, a three-time Academy Award winner, directed and co-wrote *The Doors*, which starred Val Kilmer as Jim Morrison and chronicled the rise and fall of one of the great rock bands of the 1960s. In 1990, Stone received an Academy Award for his direction of *Born on the Fourth of July*, which received a total of seven nominations. Additionally, Stone received the Directors Guild of America Award and was nominated for his screenplay (with Rob Kovic) by the Writers of America. In 1986, Stone directed and wrote *Platoon*, which was nominated for eight Academy Awards, winning four, including Best Picture and Best Director. Stone also received the Directors Guild of America Award and a British Academy award for his direction as well as a nomination for his screenplay from the Writers Guild of America. In 1987, Stone co-wrote (with

Stanley Weiser) and directed *Wall Street*, which earned Michael Douglas an Academy Award for Best Actor. In 1988, Stone directed and co-wrote (with Eric Bogosian) *Talk Radio*. Stone also wrote and directed *The Hand* (1981) and *The Seizure* (1973) and wrote screenplays for several motion pictures, including *Conan the Barbarian*, *Scarface*, *Year of the Dragon* (with Michael Cimino), and *Midnight Express*, for which he received an Academy Award and the Writers Guild of America Award. He also produced the upcoming *Zebrahead* and *South Central*, and, with Ed Pressman, co-produced *Blue Steel* and *Reversal of Fortune*.

Additional directing credits include *Heaven and Earth* (1993); *Natural Born Killers* (1994); and *Nixon* (1995), which Stone also co-wrote and which was nominated for an Academy Award for Best Writing, Screenplay Written Directly for the Screen in 1996. Following in 1997 was *U-Turn*, and in 1999 he co-wrote and directed *Any Given Sunday* starring Al Pacino, Dennis Quaid, James Woods, and Ed Burns.

Jeremy Kagan— Moderator*

Jeremy Kagan works as a director, writer, and producer in feature films and television. After graduate film school at NYU, he joined the first group of fellows at the American Film Institute and then started his professional career directing series, which led to many television movies (his favorite being one he wrote as well—*Katherine: A Portrait of An American Revolutionary*, starring Sissy Spacek). His first theatrical

---

movie was the box office hit *Heroes*. Among some of his other features as a director are *The Big Fix, The Chosen* (Grand Prix at the Montreal World Film Festival and Christopher Award in 1982), *By the Sword*, and *The Journey of Natty Gann* (the first American film to win a Gold Prize at the Moscow Film Festival in 1987). He has produced and directed and written a number of cable movies, including *Conspiracy: The Trial of the Chicago 8* (HBO, 1988 ACE Awards for Best Special Dramatic Special), *Descending Angel, Courage,* and *Roswell: The UFO Cover-Up* (nominated for a 1994 Golden Globe). Mr. Kagan won the 1996 Emmy for Outstanding Direction of a Drama Series. His recent works include the Showtime movie *Color of Justice* and *The Hired Heart* for Lifetime, and a movie for CBS, *The Ballad of Lucy Whipple*. He has also worked in animation, documentaries, music videos, and multimedia. He teaches master classes at USC's graduate film school, is on the National Board of the Directors Guild of America, and has been the Artistic Director at Robert Redford's Sundance Institute. Jeremy has served as the moderator for all of the Directors Guild of America's "Meet the Nominee Feature Film Symposiums," upon which this book was based.

Appendix[*]

Elia Kazan:
On What Makes a Director

Some of you may have heard of the auteur theory. That concept is partly a critic's plaything. Something for them to spat over and use to fill a column. But it has its point, and that point is simply that the director is the true author of the film. The director *tells* the film, using a vocabulary the lesser part of which is an arrangement of words.

A screenplay's worth has to be measured less by its language than by its architecture and how that dramatizes the theme. A screenplay, we directors soon enough learn, is not a piece of writing as much as it is a construction. We learn to feel for the skeleton under the skin of words.

Meyerhold, the great Russian stage director, said that words were the decoration on the skirts of action. He was talking about theatre, but I've always thought his observations applied more aptly to film.

It occurred to me when I was considering what to say here that since you all don't see directors — it's unique for Wesleyan to have a filmmaker standing where I am after a showing of work, while you have novelists, historians, poets and writers of various kinds of studies living among you — that it might be fun if I were to try to list for you and for my own sport what a film director needs to

---

[*] An address to the students of Wesleyan College, Middletown, CT in 1973, following a two-week retrospective of Elia Kazan's films.

know as what personal characteristics and attributes he might advantageously possess.

How must he educate himself?

Of what skills is his craft made?

What kind of a man must he be?

Of course, I'm talking about a book-length subject. Stay easy, I'm not going to read a book to you tonight. I will merely try to list the fields of knowledge necessary to him, and later those personal qualities he might happily possess, give them to you as one might give chapter headings, section leads, first sentences of paragraphs, without elaboration.

Here we go.

Literature. Of course. All periods, all languages, all forms. Naturally a film director is better equipped if he's well read. Jack Ford, who introduced himself with the words, "I make Westerns," was an extremely well and widely read man.

The Literature of the Theatre. For one thing, so the film director will appreciate the difference from film. He should also study the classic theatre literature for construction, for exposition of theme, for the means of characterization, for dramatic poetry, for the elements of unity, especially that unity created by pointing to climax and then for climax as the essential and final embodiment of the theme.

The Craft of Screen Dramaturgy. Every director, even in those rare instances when he doesn't work with a writer or two — Fellini works with a squadron — must take responsibility for the screenplay. He has not only to guide rewriting but to eliminate what's unnecessary, cover faults, appreciate nonverbal possibilities, ensure correct structure, have a sense of screen time, how much will elapse, in what places, for what purposes. Robert Frost's "Tell Everything a Little Faster" applies to all expositional parts. In the climaxes, time is unrealistically extended, "stretched," usually by close-ups.

The film director knows that beneath the surface of his screenplay there is a subtext, a calendar of intentions and feelings and inner events. What appears to be happening, he soon learns, is rarely what is happening. This subtext is one of the film director's most valuable tools. It is what he directs. You will rarely see a veteran director holding a script as he works—or even looking at it. Beginners, yes.

Most directors' goal today is to write their own scripts. But that is our oldest tradition. Chaplin would hear that Griffith Park had been flooded by a heavy rainfall. Packing his crew, his stand-by actors and his equipment in a few cars, he would rush there, making up the story of the two reel comedy en route, the details on the spot.

The director of films should know comedy as well as drama. Jack Ford used to call most parts "comics." He meant, I suppose, a way of looking at people without false sentiment, through an objectivity that deflated false heroics and undercut self-favoring and finally revealed a saving humor in the most tense moments. The Human Comedy, another Frenchman called it. The fact that Billy Wilder is always amusing doesn't make his films less serious.

Quite simply, the screen director must know either by training or by instinct how to feed a joke and how to score with it, how to anticipate and protect laughs. He might well study Chaplin and the other great two reel comedy-makers for what are called sight gags, non-verbal laughs, amusement derived from "business," stunts and moves, and simply from funny faces and odd bodies. This vulgar foundation—the banana peel and the custard pie—are basic to our craft and part of its health. Wyler and Stevens began by making two reel comedies, and I seem to remember Capra did, too.

American film directors would do well to know our vaudeville traditions. Just as Fellini adored the clowns, music hall performers, and the circuses of his country and paid them homage again and again in his work, our filmmaker would do well to study magic. I believe some of the wonderful cuts in *Citizen Kane* came from the fact that Welles was a practicing magician and so understood the drama of sudden unexpected appearances and the startling change. Think, too, of Bergman, how often he uses magicians and sleight of hand.

The director should know opera, its effects and its absurdities, a subject in which Bernardo Bertolucci is schooled. He should know the American musical stage and its tradition, but even more important, the great American musical films. He must not look down on these; we love them for very good reasons.

Our man should know acrobatics, the art of juggling and tumbling, the techniques of the wry comic song. The techniques of the commedia dell'arte are used, it seems to me, in a film called *Oh Lucky Man!* Lindsay Anderson's master, Bertolt Brecht, adored the Berlin satirical cabaret of his time and adapted their techniques.

Let's move faster because it's endless.

Painting and Sculpture; their history, their revolutions and counter revolutions. The painters of the Italian Renaissance used their mistresses as models for the Madonna, so who can blame a film director for using his girlfriend in a leading role—unless she does a bad job.

Many painters have worked in the theatre. Bakst, Picasso, Aronson, and Matisse come to mind. More will. Here, we are still with Disney.

Which brings us to Dance. In my opinion, it's a considerable asset if the director's knowledge here is not only theoretical but practical and personal. Dance is an essential part of a screen director's education. It's a great advantage for him if he can "move." It will help him not only to move actors but move the camera. The film director, ideally, should be as able as a choreographer, quite literally so. I don't mean the tango in Bertolucci's *Last* or the high school gym dance in *American Graffiti* as much as I do the battle scenes in D.W. Griffith's *Birth of a Nation*, which are pure choreography and very beautiful. Look at Ford's cavalry charges that way. Or Jim Cagney's dance of death on the long steps in *The Roaring Twenties*.

The film director must know music, classic, so called—too much of an umbrella word, that! Let us say of all periods. And as with sculpture and painting, he must know what social situations and currents the music came out of.

Of course, he must be particularly *into* the music of his own day—acid rock; Latin rock; blues and jazz; pop; Tin Pan Alley; barbershop; corn; country; Chicago; New Orleans; Nashville.

The film director should know the history of stage scenery, its development from background to environment and so to the settings *inside which* films are played out. Notice I stress *inside which* as opposed to *in front of*. The construction of scenery for filmmaking was traditionally the work of architects. The film director must study from life, from newspaper clippings and from his own photographs, dramatic environments and particularly how they affect behavior.

I recommend to every young director that he start his own collection of clippings and photographs and, if he's able, his own sketches.

The film director must know costuming, its history through all periods, its techniques and what it can be as expression. Again, life is a prime source. We learn to study, as we enter each place, each room, how the people there have chosen to present themselves. "How he comes on," we say.

Costuming in films is so expressive a means that it is inevitably the basic choice of the director. Visconti is brilliant here. So is Bergman in a more modest vein. The best way to study this again is to notice how people dress as an expression of what they wish to gain from any occasion, what their intention is. Study your husband, study your wife, how their attire is an expression of each day's mood and hope, their good days, their days of low confidence, their time of stress and how it shows in clothing.

Lighting. Of course. The various natural effects, the cross light of morning, the heavy flat top light of midday—avoid it except for an effect—the magic hour, so called by cameramen, dusk. How do they affect mood? Obvious. We know it in life. How do they affect behavior? Study that. Five o'clock is a low time, let's have a drink! Directors choose the time of day for certain scenes with these expressive values in mind. The master here is Jack Ford who used to plan his shots within a sequence to best use certain natural effects that he could not create but could very advantageously wait for.

Colors? Their psychological effect. So obvious I will not expand. Favorite colors. Faded colors. The living grays. In *Baby Doll* you saw a master cameraman—Boris Kaufman—making great use of white on white, to help describe the washed out Southern whites.

And, of course, there are the instruments which catch all and should dramatize all; the tools the director speaks through, the *camera* and the *tape recorder*. The film director obviously must know the camera and its lenses, which lens creates which effect, which one lies, which one tells the cruel truth. Which filters bring out the clouds. The director must know the various speeds at which the camera can roll and especially the effects of small variations in speed. He must also know the various camera mountings, the cranes and the dollies and the possible moves he can make, the configurations in space through which he can pass this instrument. He must know the zoom well enough so he won't use it or almost never.

He should be intimately acquainted with the tape recorder. Andy Warhol carries one everywhere he goes. Practice "bugging" yourself and your friends. Notice how often speech overlaps.

The film director must understand the weather, how it's made and where, how it moves, its warning signs, its crises, the kind of clouds and what they mean. Remember the clouds in *Shane*. He must know weather as dramatic expression, be on the alert to capitalize on changes in weather as one of his means. He must study how heat and cold, rain and snow, a soft breeze, a driving wind affect people and whether it's true that there are more expressions of group rage during a long hot summer and why.

The film director should know the City, ancient and modern, but particularly his city, the one he loves like De Sica loves Naples, Fellini—Rimini, Bergman—his island, Ray—Calcutta, Renoir— the French countryside, Clair—the city of Paris. His city, its features, its operation, its substructure, its scenes behind the scenes, its functionaries, its police, firefighters, garbage collectors, post office workers, commuters and what they ride, its cathedrals and its whorehouses.

The film directors must know the country—no, that's too general a term. He must know the mountains and the plains, the deserts of our great Southwest, the heavy oily-bottom-soil of the Delta, the hills of New England. He must know the water off Marblehead and Old Orchard Beach, too cold for lingering and the water off the Florida Keys which invites dawdling. Again, these are means of expression that he has and among them he must make his choices. He must know how a breeze from a fan can animate a dead-looking set by stirring a curtain.

He must know the sea, first-hand, chance a ship wreck so he'll appreciate its power. He must know under the surface of the sea; it may occur to him, if he does to play a scene there. He must have crossed our rivers and know the strength of their currents. He must have swum in our lakes and caught fish in our streams. You think I'm exaggerating. Why did old man Flaherty and his Mrs. spend at least a year in an environment before they exposed a foot of negative? While you're young, you aspiring directors, hitchhike our country!

And topography, the various trees, flowers, ground cover, grasses. And the subsurface, shale, sand, gravel, New England ledge, six feet of old river bottom? What kind of man works each and how does it affect him?

Animals, too. How they resemble human beings. How to direct a chicken to enter a room on cue. I had that problem once and I'm ashamed to tell you how I did it. What a cat might mean to a love scene. The symbolism of horses. The family life of the lion, how tender! The patience of a cow.

Of course, the film director should know acting, its history and its techniques. The more he knows about acting, the more at ease he will be with actors. At one period of his growth, he should force himself on stage or before the camera so he knows this experientially, too. Some directors, and very famous ones, still fear actors instead of embracing them as comrades in a task. But, by contrast, there is the great Jean Renoir, see him in *Rules of the Game*. And his follower and lover Truffaut in *The Wild Child*, now in *Day for Night*.

The director must know how to stimulate, even inspire the actor. Needless to say, he must also know how to make an actor seem *not* to act. How to put him or her at their ease, bring them to that state of relaxation where their creative faculties are released.

The film director must understand the instrument known as the *voice*. He must also know *speech*. And that they are not the same, as different as resonance and phrasing. He should also know the various regional accents of his country and what they tell about character.

All in all he must know enough in all these areas so his actors trust him completely. This is often achieved by giving the impression that any task he asks of them, he can perform, perhaps even better than they can. This may not be true, but it's not a bad impression to create.

The film director, of course, must be up on the psychology of behavior, "normal" and abnormal. He must know that they are linked, that one is often the extension or intensification of the other and that under certain stresses which the director will create within a scene as it's acted out, one kind of behavior can be seen becoming the other. And that is drama.

The film director must be prepared by knowledge and training to handle neurotics. Why? Because most actors are. Perhaps all. What makes it doubly interesting is that the film director often is. Stanley Kubrick won't get on a plane—well, maybe that isn't so neurotic. But we are all delicately balanced—isn't that a nice way to put it? Answer this: how many interesting people have you met who are not—a little?

Of course, we work with the psychology of the audience. We know it differs from that of its individual members. In cutting films great comedy directors like Hawks and Preston Sturges allow for the group reactions they expect from the audience, they play on these. Hitchcock has made this his art.

The film director must be learned in the erotic arts. The best way here is through personal experience. But there is a history here, an artistic technique. Pornography is not looked down upon. The film director will admit to a natural interest in how other people do it. Boredom, cruelty, banality are the only sins. Our man, for instance, might study the Chinese erotic prints and those scenes on Greek vases of the Golden Age which museum curators hide.

Of course, the film director must be an authority, even an expert on the various attitudes of lovemaking, the postures and intertwining of the parts of the body, the expressive parts and those generally considered less expressive. He may well have, like Buñuel with feet, special fetishes. He is not concerned to hide these, rather he will probably express his inclinations with relish.

The director, here, may come to believe that suggestion is more erotic than show. Then study how to go about it.

Then there is war. Its weapons, its techniques, its machinery, its tactics, its history—oh my—

Where is the time to learn all this?

Do not think, as you were brought up to think, that education starts at six and stops at twenty-one, that we learn only from teachers, books, and classes. For us that is the least of it. The life of a film director is a totality and he learns as he lives. Everything is pertinent, there is nothing irrelevant or trivial. O Lucky Man, to have such a profession! Every experience leaves its residue of knowledge behind. Every book we read applies to us. Everything we see and hear, if we like it, we steal it. Nothing is irrelevant. It all belongs to us.

So history becomes a living subject, full of dramatic characters, not a bore about treaties and battles. Religion is fascinating as a kind of poetry expressing fear and loneliness and hope. The film director reads *The Golden Bough* because sympathetic magic and superstition interest him, these beliefs of the ancients and the savages parallel those of his own time's people. He studies ritual because ritual as a source of stage and screen mise-en-scène is an increasingly important source.

Economics a bore? Not to us. Consider the demoralization of people in a labor pool, the panic in currency, the reliance of a nation on imports and the leverage this gives the country supplying the needed imports. All these affect or can affect the characters and milieus with which our film is concerned. Consider the facts behind the drama of *On the Waterfront*. Wonder how we could have shown more of them.

The film director doesn't just eat. He studies food. He knows the meals of all nations and how they're served, how consumed, what the variations of taste are, the effect of the food, food as a soporific, food as an aphrodisiac, as a means of expression of character. Remember the scene in *Tom Jones*? *La Grande Bouffe*?

And, of course, the film director tries to keep up with the flow of life around him, the contemporary issues, who's pressuring whom, who's winning, who's losing, how pressure shows in the politician's body and face and gestures. Inevitably, the director will be a visitor at night court. And he will not duck jury duty. He studies advertising and goes to "product meetings" and spies on those who make the ads that influence people. He watches talk shows and marvels how Jackie Susann peddles it. He keeps up on the moves, as near as he can read them, of the secret underground societies. And skyjacking, what's the solution? He talks to pilots. It's the perfect drama—that situation—no exit.

Travel. Yes. As much as he can. Let's not get into that.

Sports? The best directed shows on TV today are the professional football games. Why? Study them. You are shown not only the game from far and middle distance and close-up, you are shown the bench, the way the two coaches sweat it out, the rejected sub, Craig Morton, waiting for Staubach to be hurt and Woodall, does he really like Namath? Johnson, Snead? Watch the spectators, too. Think how you might direct certain scenes playing with a ball, or swimming or sailing—even though that is nowhere indicated in the script. Or watch a ball game like Hepburn and Tracy in George Steven's film *Woman of the Year*!

I've undoubtedly left out a great number of things and what I've left out is significant, no doubt, and describes some of my own short-comings.

Oh! Of course, I've left out the most important thing. The subject the film director must know most about, know best of all, see in the greatest detail and in the most pitiless light with the greatest appreciation of the ambivalences at play is—what?

Right. Himself.

There is something of himself, after all, in every character he properly creates. He understands people truly through understanding himself truly.

The silent confessions he makes to himself are the greatest source of wisdom he has. And of tolerance for others. And for love, even that. There is the admission of hatred to awareness and its relief through understanding and a kind of resolution in brotherhood.

What kind of person must a film director train himself to be?

What qualities does he need? Here are a few. Those of—

A white hunter leading a safari into dangerous and unknown country;

A construction gang foreman, who knows his physical problems and their solutions and is ready, therefore, to insist on these solutions;

A psychoanalyst who keeps a patient functioning despite intolerable tensions and stresses, both professional and personal;

A hypnotist, who works with the unconscious to achieve his ends;

A poet, a poet of the camera, able both to capture the decisive moment of Cartier Bresson or to wait all day like Paul Strand for a single shot which he makes with a bulky camera fixed on a tripod;

An outfielder for his legs. The director stands much of the day, dares not get tired, so he has strong legs. Think back and remember how the old time directors dramatized themselves. By puttees, right.

The cunning of a trader in a Baghdad bazaar.

The firmness of an animal trainer. Obvious. Tigers!

A great host. At a sign from him fine food and heartwarming drink appear.

The kindness of an old-fashioned mother who forgives all.

The authority and sternness of her husband, the father, who forgives nothing, expects obedience without question, brooks no nonsense.

These alternatively.

The illusiveness of a jewel thief—no explanation, take my word for this one.

The blarney of a PR man, especially useful when the director is out in a strange and hostile location as I have many times been.

A very thick skin.

A very sensitive soul.

Simultaneously.

The patience, the persistence, the fortitude of a saint, the appreciation of pain, a taste for self-sacrifice, everything for the cause.

Cheeriness, jokes, playfulness, alternating with sternness, unwavering firmness. Pure doggedness.

An unwavering refusal to take less than he thinks right out of a scene, a performer, a coworker, a member of his staff, himself.

Direction, finally, is the exertion of your will over other people, disguise it, gentle it, but that is the hard fact.

Above all—*courage*. Courage, said Winston Churchill, is the greatest virtue; it makes all the others possible.

One final thing. The ability to say "I am wrong," or "I was wrong." Not as easy as it sounds. But in many situations, these three words, honestly spoken, will save the day. They are the words, very often, that the actors struggling to give the director what he wants most need to hear from him. Those words, "I was wrong, let's try it another way," the ability to say them can be a life-saver.

The director must accept the blame for everything. If the script stinks, he should have worked harder with the writers or himself before shooting. If the actor fails, the director failed him! Or made a mistake in choosing him. If the camera work is uninspired, whose idea was it to engage that cameraman? Or choose those setups? Even a costume after all—the director passed on it. The settings. The music, even the goddamn ads, why didn't he yell louder if he didn't like them? The director was there, wasn't he? Yes, he was there! He's always there!

That's why he gets all that money, to stand there, on that mound, unprotected, letting everybody shoot at him and deflecting the mortal fire from all the others who work with him.

The other people who work on a film can hide.

They have the director to hide behind.

And people deny the auteur theory!

After listening to me so patiently you have a perfect right now to ask, "Oh, come on, aren't you exaggerating to make some kind of point?"

Of course I'm exaggerating and it is to make a point.

But only a little exaggerating.

The fact is that a director from the moment a phone call gets him out of bed in the morning ("Rain today. What scene do you want to shoot?") until he escapes into the dark at the end of shooting to face, alone, the next day's problems, is called upon to answer an unrelenting string of questions, to make decision after decision in one after another of the fields I've listed. That's what a director is, the man with the answers.

Watch Truffaut playing Truffaut in *Day for Night*, watch him as he patiently, carefully, sometimes thoughtfully, other times very quickly, answers questions. You will see better than I can tell you how these answers keep his film going. Truffaut has caught our life on the set perfectly.

Do things get easier and simpler as you get older and have accumulated some or all of this savvy?

Not at all. The opposite. The more a director knows, the more he's aware how many different ways there are to do every film, every scene.

And the more he has to face that final awful limitation, not of knowledge but of character. Which is what? The final limitation and the most terrible one is the limitations of his own talent. You find, for instance, that you truly do have the faults of your virtues. And that limitation, you can't do much about. Even if you have the time.

One last postscript. The director, that miserable son of a bitch, as often as not these days has to get out and promote the dollars and the pounds, scrounge for the liras, francs and marks, hock his family's home, his wife's jewels, and his own future so he can make his film. This process of raising the wherewithal inevitably takes ten to a hundred times longer than making the film itself. But the director does it because he has to, who else will? Who else loves the film that much?

So, my friends, you've seen how much you have to know and what kind of a bastard you have to be. How hard you have to train yourself and in how many different ways. All of which I did. I've never stopped trying to educate myself and to improve myself.